INSTRUCTOR-LED TRAINING

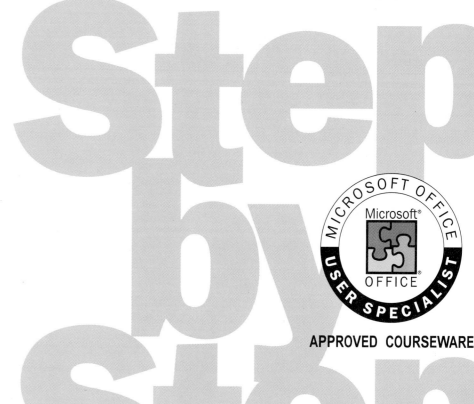

APPROVED COURSEWARE

Microsoft®
Word 2000
Microsoft Office Application

Expert Skills Student Guide

ActiveEducation™

PUBLISHED BY
Microsoft Press
A Division of Microsoft Corporation
One Microsoft Way
Redmond, Washington 98052-6399

Library of Congress Cataloging-in-Publication Data
Microsoft Word 2000 Step by Step Courseware Expert Skills Student Guide / ActiveEducation.
      p. cm.
   Includes index.
   ISBN 0-7356-0721-4 (4 color) -- ISBN 0-7356-0984-5 (1 color)
   1. Microsoft Word.   2. Word processing. I. ActiveEducation (Firm)
Z52.5.M52 M497   2000
652.5'5369--dc21   99-044097

Printed and bound in the United States of America.

1 2 3 4 5 6 7 8 9   WCWC   5 4 3 2 1 0

Distributed in Canada by Penguin Books Canada Limited.

A CIP catalogue record for this book is available from the British Library.

Microsoft Press books are available through booksellers and distributors worldwide. For further information about international editions, contact your local Microsoft Corporation office or contact Microsoft Press International directly at fax (425)
936-7329. Visit our Web site at mspress.microsoft.com.

For ActiveEducation:
Managing Editor: Ron Pronk
Series Editor: Kate Dawson
Project Editor: Carrice L. Cudworth
Writers: Ron Pronk, Holly Freeman,
  Jennifer Mears
Production/Layout: Nicole C. French, Craig K. Wise,
  Linda Savell, Tracey Varnell, Lawrance Coles
Technical Editor: Jennifer Jordan
Proofreader: Nicole C. French
Indexer: Lisa Probasco

For Microsoft Press:
Project Editors: Jenny Moss Benson,
  Kristen Weatherby
Acquisitions Editor: Susanne M. Forderer

Contents

Course Overview

Welcome to the *Step by Step Courseware* series for Microsoft Office 2000 and Microsoft Windows 2000 Professional. This series facilitates classroom learning, letting you develop competence and confidence in using an Office application or operating system software. In completing courses taught with *Step by Step Courseware*, you learn to use the software productively and discover how to make the software work for you. This series addresses core-level and expert-level skills in Microsoft Word 2000, Microsoft Excel 2000, Microsoft Access 2000, Microsoft Outlook 2000, Microsoft FrontPage 2000, and Microsoft Windows 2000 Professional.

The *Step by Step Courseware* series provides:

- A time-tested, integrated approach to learning.
- Task-based, results-oriented learning strategies.
- Exercises based on business scenarios.
- Complete preparation for Microsoft Office User Specialist (MOUS) certification.
- Attractive student guides with full-featured lessons.
- Lessons with accurate, logical, and sequential instructions.
- Comprehensive coverage of skills from the basic to the expert level.
- Review of core-level skills provided in expert-level guides.
- A CD-ROM with practice files.

A Task-Based Approach Using Business Scenarios

The *Step by Step Courseware* series builds on the strengths of the time-tested approach that Microsoft developed and refined for its Step by Step series. Even though the Step by Step series was created for self-paced training, instructors have long used it in the classroom. For the first time, this popular series has been adapted specifically for the classroom environment. By studying with a task-based approach, you learn more than just the features of the software. You learn how to accomplish real-world tasks so that you can immediately increase your productivity using the software application.

The lessons are based on tasks that you might encounter in the everyday work world. This approach allows you to quickly see the relevance of the training. The task-based focus is woven throughout the series, including lesson organization within each unit, lesson titles, and scenarios chosen for practice files.

An Integrated Approach to Training

The *Step by Step Courseware* series distinguishes itself from other series on the market with its consistent delivery and completely integrated approach to learning across a variety of print and online training media. With the addition of the *Step by Step Courseware* series, which supports classroom instruction, the *Step by Step* training suite now provides a flexible and unified training solution.

Print-Based Self-Training in the Step by Step Training Suite

The proven print-based series of stand-alone *Step by Step* books has consistently been the resource that customers choose for developing software skills on their own.

Online Training in the Step by Step Training Suite

For those who prefer online training, the *Step by Step Interactive* products offer highly interactive online training in a simulated work environment, complete with graphics, sound, video, and animation delivered to a single station (self-contained installation), local area network (LAN), or intranet. *Step by Step Interactive* has a network administration module that allows a training manager to track the progress and quiz results for students using the training. For more information, see *mspress.microsoft.com*.

Preparation for Microsoft Office User Specialist (MOUS) Certification

This series has been certified as approved courseware for the Microsoft Office User Specialist certification program. Students who have completed this training are prepared to take the related MOUS exam. By passing the exam for a particular Office application, students demonstrate proficiency in that application to their employers or prospective employers. Exams are offered at participating test centers. For more information, see *www.mous.net*.

A Sound Instructional Foundation

All products in the *Step by Step Courseware* series apply the same instructional strategies, closely adhering to adult instructional techniques and reliable adult learning principles. Lessons in the *Step by Step Courseware* series are presented in a logical, easy-to-follow format, helping you find information quickly and learn as efficiently as possible. To facilitate the learning process, each lesson follows a consistent structure.

Designed for Optimal Learning

The following "Lesson Features" section shows how the colorful and highly visual series design makes it easy for you to see what to read and what to do when practicing new skills.

Lessons break training into easily assimilated sessions. Each lesson is self-contained, and lessons can be completed in sequences other than the one presented in the table of contents. Sample files for the lessons don't depend on completion of other lessons. Sample files within a lesson assume only that you are working sequentially through a complete lesson.

The *Step by Step Courseware* series features:

- **Lesson objectives.** Objectives clearly state the instructional goals for each lesson so that you understand what skills you will master. Each lesson objective is covered in its own section, and each section or topic in the lesson is covered in a consistent way. Lesson objectives preview the lesson structure, helping you grasp key information and prepare for learning skills.

- **Informational text for each topic.** For each objective, the lesson provides easy-to-read, technique-focused information.

- **Hands-on practice.** Numbered steps give detailed, step-by-step instructions to help you learn skills. The steps also show results and screen images to match what you should see on your computer screen. The accompanying CD contains sample files used for each lesson.

- **Full-color illustrations in color student guides.** Illustrated screen images give visual feedback as you work through exercises. The images reinforce key concepts, provide visual clues about the steps, and give you something to check your progress against.

- **MOUS icon.** Each section or sidebar that covers a MOUS certification objective has a MOUS icon in the margin at the beginning of the section. The number of the certification objective is also listed.

- **Tips.** Helpful hints and alternate ways to accomplish tasks are located throughout the lesson text.

- **Important.** If there is something to watch out for or something to avoid, this information is added to the lesson and indicated with this heading.

- **Sidebars.** Sidebars contain parenthetical topics or additional information that you might find interesting.

- **Margin notes.** Margin notes provide additional related or background information that adds value to the lesson.

- **Button images in the margin.** When the text instructs you to click a particular button, an image of the button and its label appear in the margin.

- **Lesson Glossary.** Terms with which you might not be familiar are defined in the glossary. Terms in the glossary appear in boldface type within the lesson and are defined upon their first use within lessons.

- **Quick Quiz.** You can use the short-answer Quick Quiz questions to test or reinforce your understanding of key topics within the lesson.

Lesson Features

Lesson objectives clearly state the instructional goals for each lesson so that you understand what skills you will master.

Lesson introductions list the practice files for the lesson and explain any necessary file preparation.

Each topic begins with explanatory information that teaches concepts and techniques.

Important notes state warnings or cautions.

The Microsoft Office User Specialist (MOUS) logo indicates that the section covers a task that will be tested on the certification exam.

Tips provide helpful hints and alternative ways to complete tasks.

Numbered steps provide detailed instructions to guide you through practicing new skills.

Illustrations give you visual feedback as you work through the lesson.

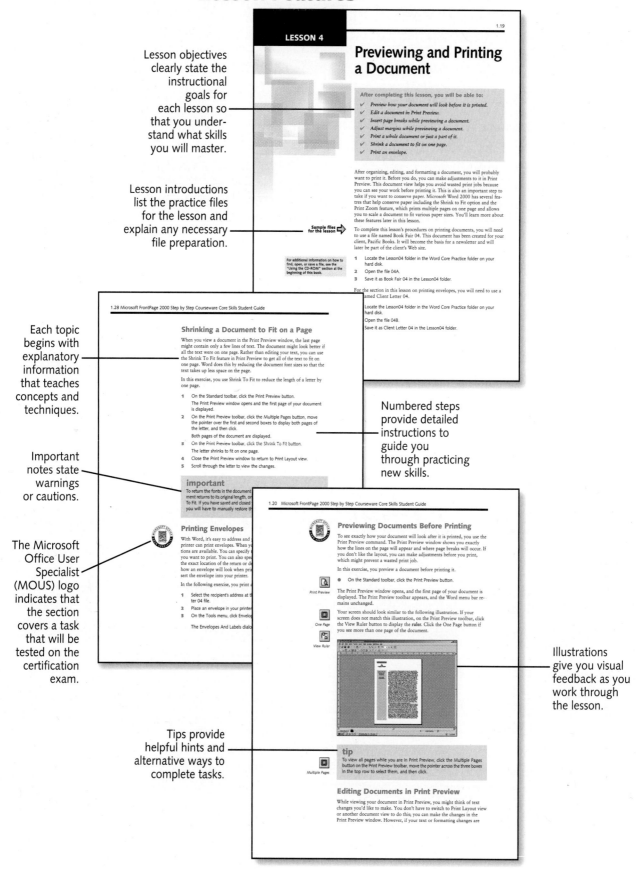

Margin notes provide additional information.

Lesson Glossary defines key terms shown in boldface within the lesson.

Lesson Wrap-Up covers remaining file admin-istration details to end the lesson.

Quick Quiz short-answer questions quiz you on the lesson concepts.

Putting It All Together exercises challenge you to apply what you've learned and require you to apply skills in a new way.

Quick Reference summarizes skills learned in the lesson.

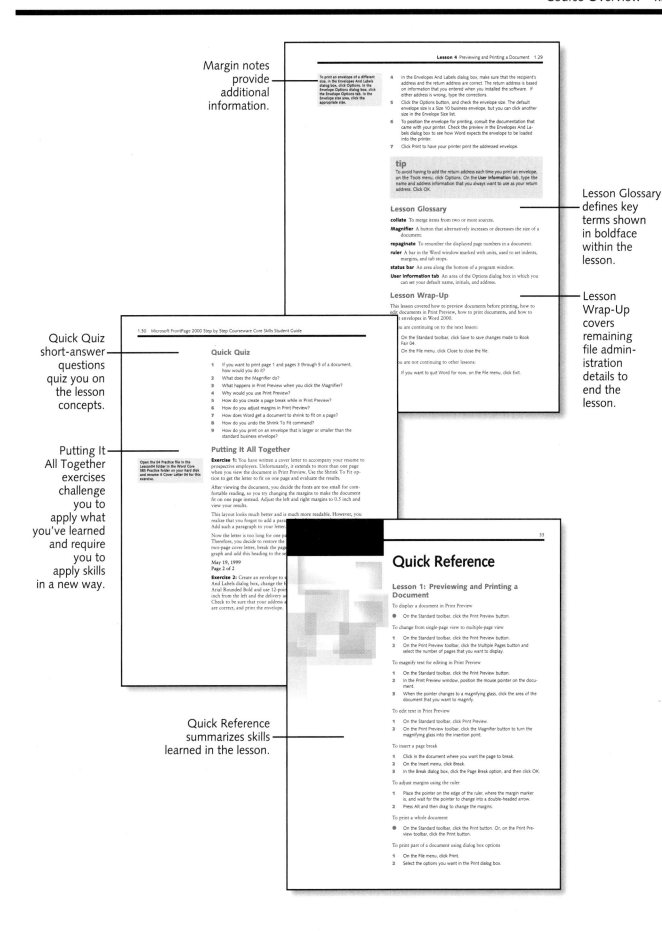

Lesson 4 Previewing and Printing a Document   1.29

To print an envelope of a different size, in the Envelopes And Labels dialog box, click Options. In the Envelope Options dialog box, click the Envelope Options tab. In the Envelope size area, click the appropriate size.

4   In the Envelopes And Labels dialog box, make sure that the recipient's address and the return address are correct. The return address is based on information that you entered when you installed the software. If either address is wrong, type the corrections.

5   Click the Options button, and check the envelope size. The default envelope size is a Size 10 business envelope, but you can click another size in the Envelope Size list.

6   To position the envelope for printing, consult the documentation that came with your printer. Check the preview in the Envelopes And La-bels dialog box to see how Word expects the envelope to be loaded into the printer.

7   Click Print to have your printer print the addressed envelope.

tip
To avoid having to add the return address each time you print an envelope, on the Tools menu, click Options. On the **User Information** tab, type the name and address information that you always want to use as your return address. Click OK.

Lesson Glossary

collate   To merge items from two or more sources.

Magnifier   A button that alternatively increases or decreases the size of a document.

repaginate   To renumber the displayed page numbers in a document.

ruler   A bar in the Word window marked with units, used to set indents, margins, and tab stops.

status bar   An area along the bottom of a program window.

User information tab   An area of the Options dialog box in which you can set your default name, initials, and address.

Lesson Wrap-Up

This lesson covered how to preview documents before printing, how to edit documents in Print Preview, how to print documents, and how to [prin]t envelopes in Word 2000.

[If y]ou are continuing on to the next lesson:

On the Standard toolbar, click Save to save changes made to Book Fair 04.
On the File menu, click Close to close the file.

[If y]ou are not continuing to other lessons:

If you want to quit Word for now, on the File menu, click Exit.

1.30   Microsoft FrontPage 2000 Step by Step Courseware Core Skills Student Guide

Quick Quiz

1   If you want to print page 1 and pages 3 through 5 of a document, how would you do it?
2   What does the Magnifier do?
3   What happens in Print Preview when you click the Magnifier?
4   Why would you use Print Preview?
5   How do you create a page break while in Print Preview?
6   How do you adjust margins in Print Preview?
7   How does Word get a document to shrink to fit on a page?
8   How do you undo the Shrink To Fit command?
9   How do you print on an envelope that is larger or smaller than the standard business envelope?

Putting It All Together

Open the 04 Practice file in the Lesson04 folder in the Word Core SBS Practice folder on your hard disk and rename it Cover Letter 04 for this exercise.

Exercise 1: You have written a cover letter to accompany your resume to prospective employers. Unfortunately, it extends to more than one page when you view the document in Print Preview. Use the Shrink To Fit op-tion to get the letter to fit on one page and evaluate the results.

After viewing the document, you decide the fonts are too small for com-fortable reading, so you try changing the margins to make the document fit on one page instead. Adjust the left and right margins to 0.5 inch and view your results.

This layout looks much better and is much more readable. However, you realize that you forgot to add a para[graph] Add such a paragraph to your letter.

Now the letter is too long for one pa[ge] Therefore, you decide to restore the [original] two-page cover letter, break the page [before the last para]graph and add this heading to the se[cond page]

May 19, 1999
Page 2 of 2

Exercise 2: Create an envelope to [accompany the letter. In the Envelopes] And Labels dialog box, change the f[ont of the return address to] Arial Rounded Bold and use 12-poi[nt type. Position the return address 1] inch from the left and the delivery a[ddress 3 inches from the left.] Check to be sure that your address a[nd the recipient's address] are correct, and print the envelope.

33

Quick Reference

Lesson 1: Previewing and Printing a Document

To display a document in Print Preview

●   On the Standard toolbar, click the Print Preview button.

To change from single-page view to multiple-page view

1   On the Standard toolbar, click the Print Preview button.
2   On the Print Preview toolbar, click the Multiple Pages button and select the number of pages that you want to display.

To magnify text for editing in Print Preview

1   On the Standard toolbar, click the Print Preview button.
2   In the Print Preview window, position the mouse pointer on the docu-ment.
3   When the pointer changes to a magnifying glass, click the area of the document that you want to magnify.

To edit text in Print Preview

1   On the Standard toolbar, click Print Preview.
2   On the Print Preview toolbar, click the Magnifier button to turn the magnifying glass into the insertion point.

To insert a page break

1   Click in the document where you want the page to break.
2   On the Insert menu, click Break.
3   In the Break dialog box, click the Page Break option, and then click OK.

To adjust margins using the ruler

1   Place the pointer on the edge of the ruler, where the margin marker is, and wait for the pointer to change into a double-headed arrow.
2   Press Alt and then drag to change the margins.

To print a whole document

●   On the Standard toolbar, click the Print button. Or, on the Print Pre-view toolbar, click the Print button.

To print part of a document using dialog box options

1   On the File menu, click Print.
2   Select the options you want in the Print dialog box.

■ **Putting It All Together exercises.** These exercises give you another opportunity to practice skills that you learned in the lesson. Completing these exercises helps you to verify whether you understand the lesson, to reinforce your learning, and to retain what you have learned by applying what you have learned in a different way.

■ **Quick Reference.** A complete summary of steps for tasks taught in each lesson is available in the back of the guide. This is often the feature that people find most useful when they return to their workplaces. The expert-level guides include the references from the core-level guides so that you can review or refresh basic and advanced skills on your own whenever necessary.

■ **Index.** Student guides are completely indexed. All glossary terms and application features appear in the index.

Suggestions for Improvements

Microsoft welcomes your feedback on the *Step by Step Courseware* series. Your comments and suggestions will help us to improve future versions of this product. Please send your feedback to SBSCfdbk@microsoft.com.

Support requests for Microsoft products should not be directed to this alias. Please see "Using the CD-ROM" for information on support contacts.

Conventions and Features Used in This Book

This book uses special fonts, symbols, and heading conventions to highlight important information or to call your attention to special steps. For more information about the features available in each lesson, refer to the "Course Overview" section on page vii.

Convention	Meaning
Sample files for the lesson	This icon identifies the section that lists the files that the lesson will use and explains any file preparation that you need to take care of before starting the lesson.
If your hard disk uses a letter other than C, substitute the appropriate drive letter in place of C.	Notes in the margin area are pointers to information provided elsewhere in the workbook or provide brief notes related to the text or procedures.
2000 New!	This icon indicates a new or greatly improved feature in this version of the software product and includes a short description of what is new.
MICROSOFT OFFICE USER SPECIALIST W2000E.3.4	This icon indicates that the section where this icon appears covers a Microsoft Office User Specialist (MOUS) exam objective. The number below the icon is the MOUS objective number. For a complete list of the MOUS objectives, see the "MOUS Objectives" section on page xix.
tip	Tips provide helpful hints or alternative procedures related to particular tasks.
important	Importants provide warnings or cautions that are critical to exercises.
Save	When a toolbar button is referenced in the lesson, the button's picture and label are shown in the margin.
Alt+Tab	A plus sign (+) between two key names means that you must press those keys at the same time. For example, "Press Alt+Tab" means that you hold down the Alt key while you press Tab.
Boldface type	This formatting indicates text that you need to type Or It indicates a glossary entry that is defined at the end of the lesson.

Using the CD-ROM

The CD-ROM included with this student guide contains the practice files that you'll use as you perform the exercises in the book. By using the practice files, you won't waste time creating the samples used in the lessons, and you can concentrate on learning how to use advanced features of Microsoft Word 2000. With the files and the step-by-step instructions in the lessons, you'll also learn by doing, which is an easy and effective way to acquire and remember new skills.

The CD-ROM also includes a Microsoft Word file called Testbank.doc, which provides multiple-choice and true/false questions that you can use to test your knowledge following the completion of each lesson or the completion of the *Microsoft Word 2000 Step by Step Courseware Expert Skills* course.

System Requirements

Your computer system must meet the following minimum requirements for you to install the practice files from the CD-ROM and to run Microsoft Word 2000.

important

The Word 2000 software is not provided on the companion CD-ROM at the back of this book. This course assumes that you have already purchased and installed Word 2000.

- A personal computer running Microsoft Word 2000 on a Pentium 75-megahertz (MHz) or higher processor with the Microsoft Windows 95 or later operating system with 24 MB of RAM, or the Microsoft Windows NT Workstation version 4.0 operating system with Service Pack 3 and 40 MB of RAM.

- At least 6 MB of available disk space (after installing Word 2000 or Microsoft Office 2000).

- A CD-ROM drive.

- A monitor with VGA or higher resolution (Super VGA recommended; 15-inch monitor or larger recommended).

- A Microsoft mouse, a Microsoft IntelliMouse, or other compatible pointing device.

If You Need to Install
or Uninstall the Practice Files

Your instructor might already have installed the practice files before you arrive in class. However, your instructor might ask you to install the practice files on your own at the start of class. Also, if you want to work through any of the exercises in this book on your own at home or at your place of business after class, you will need to first install the practice files.

To install the practice files:

1   Insert the CD-ROM in the CD-ROM drive of your computer.

A menu screen appears.

important

If the menu screen does not appear, start Windows Explorer. In the left pane, locate the icon for your CD-ROM, and click this icon. In the right pane, double-click the file StartCD.

2   Click Install Practice Files, and follow the instructions on the screen.

The recommended options are preselected for you.

3   After the files have been installed, click Exit.

A folder called Word Expert Practice has been created on your hard disk, the practice files have been placed in that folder, and a shortcut to the Microsoft Press Web site has been added to your desktop.

4   Remove the CD-ROM from the CD-ROM drive.

Use the following steps when you want to delete the lesson practice files from your hard disk. Your instructor might ask you to perform these steps at the end of class. Also, you should perform these steps if you have worked through the exercises at home or at your place of business and want to work through the exercises again. Deleting the practice files and then reinstalling them ensures that all files and folders are in their original condition if you decide to work through the exercises again.

To uninstall the practice files:

1   On the Windows taskbar, click the Start button, point to Settings, and then click Control Panel.

2   Double-click the Add/Remove icon.

3   Click Word Expert Practice in the list, and click Add/Remove. (If your computer has Windows 2000 Professional installed, click the Remove or the Change/Remove button.)

4   Click Yes when the confirmation dialog box appears.

Using the Practice Files

Each lesson in this book explains when and how to use any practice files for that lesson. The lessons are built around scenarios that simulate a real work environment, so you can easily apply the skills you learn to your own work. The scenarios in the lessons use the context of the fictitious Lakewood Mountains Resort, a hotel and convention center located in the mountains of California.

On the first page of each lesson, look for the margin icon *Sample files for the lesson*. This icon points to the paragraph that explains which files you will need to work through the lesson exercises.

By default, Word 2000 places the Standard and Formatting toolbars on the same row below the menu bar to save space. To match the lessons and exercises in this book, the Standard and Formatting toolbars should be separated onto two rows before the start of this course. To separate the Standard and Formatting toolbars:

● Position the mouse pointer over the move handle (the vertical bar), at the left end of the Formatting toolbar until it turns into the move pointer (a four-headed arrow), and drag the toolbar down and to the left until it appears on its own row under the Standard toolbar.

The following is a list of all files and folders used in the lessons. All the files for the lessons appear within the Word Expert Practice folder.

File Name	Description
Lesson01	Folder used in Lesson 1
August Flyer 01	File used in Lesson 1
Hiking 01	File used in Lesson 1
LMR Wait Staff Test 01	File used in Putting It All Together
LMR Weekly Agenda 01	File used in Lesson 1
Lesson02	Folder used in Lesson 2
Cleaning Staff Manual 02	File used in Putting It All Together
Leaf 02	Graphic used in Lesson 2
LMR Employee Handbook 02	File used in Lesson 2
LMR Weekly 02	File used in Lesson 2
Promotion Memo 02	File used in Lesson 2
Welcome Pamphlet 02	File used in Lesson 2
Lesson03	Folder used in Lesson 3
LMR 3rd Quarter Revene.xls 03	File used in Lesson 3
LMR Revenue 03	File used in Lesson 3
LMR Weekly 03	File used in Lesson 3
Lesson04	Folder used in Lesson 4
LMR Revenue_Spring 04	File used in Lesson 4
LMR Revenue_Summer 04	File used in Lesson 4
LMR Revenue_Summer.xls 04	File used in Lesson 4
Lesson05	Folder used in Lesson 5
Tailspin Ad 05	File used in Lesson 5
Lesson06	Folder used in Lesson 6
LMR Letter 06	File used in Lesson 6
LMR Teacher Database 06.xls	File used in Lesson 6

(continued)

continued

File Name	Description
Lesson07	Folder used in Lesson 7
LMR Letter 07	File used in Putting It All Together
LMR Promotion Memo 07	File used in Lesson 7
LMR Teacher Database 07.xls	File used in Putting It All Together
Lesson08	Folder used in Lesson 8
LMR Survey 08	File used in Lesson 8
SkillCheck 08	File used in Putting It All Together
Lesson09	Folder used in Lesson 9
LMR Sales Brochure 09	File used in Lesson 9
LMR Welcome Pamphlet 09	File used in Lesson 9
Lesson10	Folder used in Lesson 10
LMR Pamphlet 10	File used in Lesson 10
LMR Visitor Pamphlet 10	File used in Putting It All Together
Lesson11	Folder used in Lesson 11
Adult Learners 11	File used in Putting It All Together
Instructional Principles 11	File used in Lesson 11
Section I	File used in Lesson 11

Replying to Install Messages

When you work through some lessons, you might see a message indicating that the feature that you are trying to use is not installed. If you see this message, insert the Microsoft Word 2000 CD or Microsoft Office 2000 CD 1 in your CD-ROM drive, and click Yes to install the feature.

If You Need Help with the Practice Files

If you have any problems regarding the use of this book's CD-ROM, you should first consult your instructor. If you are using the CD-ROM at home or at your place of business and need additional help with the practice files, see the Microsoft Press Support Web site at *mspress.microsoft.com/support.*

important

Please note that support for the Word 2000 software product itself is not offered through the above Web site. For help using Word 2000, rather than this Microsoft Press book, you can visit *support.microsoft.com/directory* or call Word 2000 Technical Support at (425) 635-7070 on weekdays between 6 A.M. and 6 P.M. Pacific Standard Time. Microsoft Product Support does not provide support for this course.

MOUS Objectives

Core Skills

Objective	Activity
W2000.1.1	Use the Undo, Redo, and Repeat command
W2000.1.2	Apply font formats (Bold, Italic, and Underline)
W2000.1.3	Use the Spelling feature
W2000.1.4	Use the Thesaurus feature
W2000.1.5	Use the Grammar feature
W2000.1.6	Insert page breaks
W2000.1.7	Highlight text in document
W2000.1.8	Insert and move text
W2000.1.9	Cut, Copy, Paste, and Paste Special using the Office Clipboard
W2000.1.10	Copy formats using the Format Painter
W2000.1.11	Select and change font and font size
W2000.1.12	Find and replace text
W2000.1.13	Apply character effects (superscript, subscript, strikethrough, small caps, and outline)
W2000.1.14	Insert date and time
W2000.1.15	Insert symbols
W2000.1.16	Create and apply frequently used text with AutoCorrect
W2000.2.1	Align text in paragraphs (Center, Left, Right, and Justified)
W2000.2.2	Add bullets and numbering
W2000.2.3	Set character, line, and paragraph spacing options
W2000.2.4	Apply borders and shading to paragraphs
W2000.2.5	Use indentation options (Left, Right, First Line, and Hanging Indent)
W2000.2.6	Use the Tabs command (Center, Decimal, Left, and Right)
W2000.2.7	Create an outline style numbered list
W2000.2.8	Set tabs with leaders
W2000.3.1	Print a document
W2000.3.2	Use print preview
W2000.3.3	Use Web Page Preview
W2000.3.4	Navigate through a document
W2000.3.5	Insert page numbers
W2000.3.6	Set page orientation

Objective	Activity
W2000.3.7	Set margins
W2000.3.8	Use GoTo to locate specific elements in a document
W2000.3.9	Create and modify page numbers
W2000.3.10	Create and modify headers and footers
W2000.3.11	Align text vertically
W2000.3.12	Create and use newspaper columns
W2000.3.13	Revise column structure
W2000.3.14	Prepare and print envelopes and labels
W2000.3.15	Apply styles
W2000.3.16	Create sections with formatting that differs from other sections
W2000.3.17	Use Click & Type
W2000.4.1	Use Save
W2000.4.2	Locate and open an existing document
W2000.4.3	Use Save As (different name, location, or format)
W2000.4.4	Create a folder
W2000.4.5	Create a new document using a Wizard
W2000.4.6	Save as Web Page
W2000.4.7	Use templates to create a new document
W2000.4.8	Create hyperlinks
W2000.4.9	Use the Office Assistant
W2000.4.10	Send a Word document via e-mail
W2000.5.1	Create and format tables
W2000.5.2	Add borders and shading to tables
W2000.5.3	Revise tables (insert and delete rows and columns, change cell formats)
W2000.5.4	Modify table structure (merge cells, change height and width)
W2000.5.5	Rotate text in a table
W2000.6.1	Use the drawing toolbar
W2000.6.2	Insert graphics into a document (WordArt, ClipArt, and Images)

Expert Skills

Objective	Activity	Page
W2000E.1.1	Apply paragraph and section shading	1.6
W2000E.1.2	Use text flow options (Windows/Orphans options and keeping lines together)	1.1
W2000E.1.3	Sort lists, paragraphs, tables	3.9, 3.10
W2000E.2.1	Create and modify page borders	2.12
W2000E.2.2	Format first page differently than subsequent pages	2.17
W2000E.2.3	Use bookmarks	11.14
W2000E.2.4	Create and edit styles	2.3
W2000E.2.5	Create watermarks	2.19
W2000E.2.6	Use find and replace with formats, special characters, and non-printing elements	2.12, 2.14. 2.16
W2000E.2.7	Balance column length (using column breaks appropriately)	2.19
W2000E.2.8	Create or revise footnotes and endnotes	11.3
W2000E.2.9	Work with master documents and sub-documents	11.16
W2000E.2.10	Create and modify a table of contents	10.3, 10.5
W2000E.2.11	Create a cross-reference	10.9
W2000E.2.12	Create and modify an index	10.7, 10.10
W2000E.3.1	Embed worksheets in a table	3.2
W2000E.3.2	Perform calculations in a table	3.5
W2000E.3.3	Link Excel data as a table	3.6
W2000E.3.4	Modify worksheets in a table	3.2
W2000E.4.1	Add bitmapped graphics	2.17
W2000E.4.2	Delete and position graphics	1.5
W2000E.4.3	Create and modify charts	4.2, 4.6
W2000E.4.4	Import data into charts	4.10
W2000E.5.1	Create a main document	6.3
W2000E.5.2	Create a data source	6.5
W2000E.5.3	Sort records to be merged	6.10
W2000E.5.4	Merge main document and data source	6.8
W2000E.5.5	Generate labels	6.16
W2000E.5.6	Merge a document using alternate data sources	6.14
W2000E.6.1	Insert a field	1.4
W2000E.6.2	Create, apply, and edit macros	7.2, 7.9, 7.10
W2000E.6.3	Copy, rename, and delete macros	7.12, 7.14, 7.17
W2000E.6.4	Create and modify forms	8.2
W2000E.6.5	Create and modify a form control (e.g., add an item to a drop-down list)	8.5, 8.7
W2000E.6.6	Use advanced text alignment features with graphics	1.8

Objective	Activity	Page
W2000E.6.7	Customize toolbars	5.2
W2000E.7.1	Insert comments	9.6
W2000E.7.2	Protect documents	9.10
W2000E.7.3	Create multiple versions of a document	9.14
W2000E.7.4	Track changes to a document	9.2
W2000E.7.5	Set default file location for workgroup templates	9.13
W2000E.7.6	Round Trip documents from HTML	9.18

Taking a Microsoft Office User Specialist Certification Test

The Microsoft Office User Specialist (MOUS) program is the only Microsoft-approved certification program designed to measure and validate your skills with the Microsoft Office suite of desktop productivity applications: Microsoft Word, Microsoft Excel, Microsoft PowerPoint, Microsoft Access, and Microsoft Outlook.

By becoming certified, you demonstrate to employers that you have achieved a predictable level of skills in the use of a particular Office application. Certification is often required by employers either as a condition of employment or as a condition of advancement within the company or other organization. The certification examinations are sponsored by Microsoft but administered through Nivo International.

For each Microsoft Office 2000 application, two levels of MOUS tests are currently or will soon be available: core and expert. For a core-level test, you demonstrate your ability to use an application knowledgeably and without assistance in a day-to-day work environment. For an expert-level test, you demonstrate that you have a thorough knowledge of the application and can effectively apply all or most of the features of the application to solve problems and complete tasks found in business.

Preparing to Take an Exam

Unless you're a very experienced user, you'll need to use a test preparation course to prepare to complete the test correctly and within the time allowed. The *Step by Step Courseware* training program is designed to prepare you for either core-level or expert-level knowledge of a particular Microsoft Office application. By the end of this course, you should have a strong knowledge of all exam topics, and with some additional review and practice on your own, you should feel confident in your ability to pass the appropriate exam.

After you decide which exam to take, review the list of objectives for the exam. This list can be found in the "MOUS Objectives" section at the front of the appropriate *Step by Step Courseware* student guide; the list of MOUS objectives for this book begins on page xix0. You can also easily identify tasks that are included in the objective list by locating the MOUS logo in the margin of the lessons in this book.

For an expert-level test, you'll need to be able to demonstrate any of the skills from the core-level objective list, too. Expect some of these core-level tasks to appear on the expert-level test. In the *Step by Step Courseware Expert Skills Student Guide*, you'll find the core skills included in the "Quick Reference" section at the back of the book.

You can also familiarize yourself with a live MOUS certification test by downloading and installing a practice MOUS certification test from *www.mous.net*.

To take the MOUS test, first see *www.mous.net* to locate your nearest testing center. Then call the testing center directly to schedule your test. The amount of advance notice you should provide will vary for different testing centers, and it typically depends on the number of computers available at the testing center, the number of other testers who have already been scheduled for the day on which you want to take the test, and the number of times per week that the testing center offers MOUS testing. In general, you should call to schedule your test at least two weeks prior to the date on which you want to take the test.

When you arrive at the testing center, you might be asked for proof of identity. A driver's license or passport is an acceptable form of identification. If you do not have either of these items of documentation, call your testing center and ask what alternative forms of identification will be accepted. If you are retaking a test, bring your MOUS identification number, which will have been given to you when you previously took the test. If you have not prepaid or if your organization has not already arranged to make payment for you, you will need to pay the test-taking fee when you arrive. The current test-taking fee is $50 (U.S.).

Test Format

All MOUS certification tests are live, performance-based tests. There are no multiple-choice, true/false, or short answer questions. Instructions are general: you are told the basic tasks to perform on the computer, but you aren't given any help in figuring out how to perform them. You are not permitted to use reference material other than the application's Help system.

As you complete the tasks stated in a particular test question, the testing software monitors your actions. An example question might be:

> Open the file LMR Guests, and turn on change tracking. Delete the first paragraph, and insert the text *Welcome!* At the end of the second paragraph, add the comment *I liked the original wording better.*, and then delete the comment.

The sample tests available from *www.mous.net* give you a clear idea of the type of questions that you will be asked on the actual test.

When the test administrator seats you at a computer, you'll see an online form that you use to enter information about yourself (name, address, and other information required to process your exam results). While you complete the form, the software will generate the test from a master test bank and then prompt you to continue. The first test question will appear in a window. Read the question carefully, and then perform all the tasks stated in the test question. When you have finished completing all tasks for a question, click the Next Question button.

You have 45 to 60 minutes to complete all questions, depending on the test that you are taking. The testing software assesses your results as soon as you complete the test, and the results of the test can be printed by the test administrator so that you will have a record of any tasks that you performed incorrectly. A passing grade is 75 percent or higher. If you pass, you will receive a certificate in the mail within two to four weeks. If you do not pass, you can study and practice the skills that you missed and then schedule to retake the test at a later date.

Tips for Successfully Completing the Test

The following tips and suggestions are the result of feedback received by many individuals who have taken one or more MOUS tests:

- Make sure that you are thoroughly prepared. If you have extensively used the application for which you are being tested, you might feel confident that you are prepared for the test. However, the test might include questions that involve tasks that you rarely or never perform when you use the application at your place of business, at school, or at home. You must be knowledgeable in *all* the MOUS objectives for the test that you will take.

- Read each exam question carefully. An exam question might include several tasks that you are to perform. A partially correct response to a test question is counted as an incorrect response. In the example question on the previous page, you might turn on change tracking, delete the first paragraph, and insert the text and the comment, but neglect to delete the comment. This would count as an incorrect response and would result in a lower test score.

- You are allowed to use the application's Help system, but relying on the Help system too much will slow you down and possibly prevent you from completing the test within the allotted time. Use the Help system only when necessary.

- Keep track of your time. The test does not display the amount of time that you have left, so you need to keep track of the time yourself by monitoring your start time and the required end time on your watch or a clock in the testing center (if there is one). The test program displays the number of items that you have completed along with the total number of test items (for example, "35 of 40 items have been completed"). Use this information to gauge your pace.

- If you skip a question, you cannot return to it later. You should skip a question only if you are certain that you cannot complete the tasks correctly.

- Don't worry if the testing software crashes while you are taking the exam. The test software is set up to handle this situation. Find your test administrator and tell him or her what happened. The administrator will work through the steps required to restart the test. When the test restarts, it will allow you to continue where you left off. You will have the same amount of time remaining to complete the test as you did when the software crashed.

- As soon as you are finished reading a question and you click in the application window, a condensed version of the instruction is displayed in a corner of the screen. If you are unsure whether you have completed all tasks stated in the test question, click the Instructions button on the test information bar at the bottom of the screen and then reread the question. Close the instruction window when you are finished. Do this as often as necessary to ensure you have read the question correctly and that you have completed all the tasks stated in the question.

If You Do Not Pass the Test

If you do not pass, you can use the assessment printout as a guide to practice the items that you missed. There is no limit to the number of times that you can retake a test; however, you must pay the fee each time that you take the test. When you retake the test, expect to see some of the same test items on the subsequent test; the test software randomly generates the test items from a master test bank before you begin the test. Also expect to see several questions that did not appear on the previous test.

LESSON 1

Using Advanced Paragraph and Picture Formatting

After completing this lesson, you will be able to:

✔ *Control text flow options.*

✔ *Insert fields.*

✔ *Move, size, and delete pictures.*

✔ *Control text wrapping.*

So you've created a Microsoft Word 2000 document that contains text and pictures. The document communicates your ideas; however, it still needs a little finessing. Maybe the text breaks awkwardly on a couple of pages or the pictures could be displayed in a more attractive way. Perhaps you would like to have the current date appear on the document every time you open it. Word lets you take your documents to the next level. You can manipulate text and pictures in many ways. You can control the way lines in a paragraph break across a page and insert a code that Word uses to put the current date on a document every time you open or print it. You can also move a picture into a block of text and control how the text wraps around it.

In this lesson, you will learn how to control paragraph breaks; insert the data and time; move, size, and delete pictures; and control the way text wraps around a picture.

Sample files for the lesson

To complete the procedures in this lesson, you will need to use the practice files August Flyer 01, LMR Weekly Agenda 01, and Hiking 01 in the Lesson01 folder in the Word Expert Practice folder located on your hard disk.

W2000E.1.2

Controlling Text Flow Options

As you create a document, text moves from one page to the next. Occasionally, a sentence that you started on one page might end on the next page, thus making the reader have to turn the page in the middle of a sentence. In the publishing industry, when a sentence is broken in this way, it is considered to be a *bad break* and is fixed. Word has an option that lets you automatically fix two kinds of bad breaks called widows and orphans.

A **widow** is a word or broken sentence that appears on its own line at the top of a page. An **orphan** is a word or a broken sentence that appears on its own line at the bottom of a page.

Fixed Widow

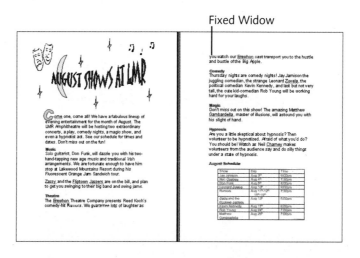

Orphan

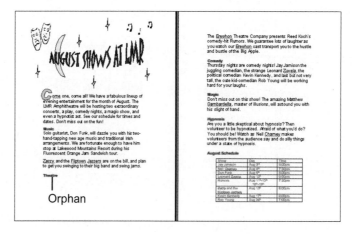

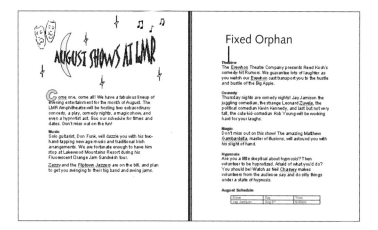

In the following exercises, the Standard and Formatting toolbars have been separated. For additional information on how to separate the toolbars, see the "Using the CD-ROM" section at the beginning of this book.

Word automatically controls widows and orphans; however, you can turn the widow and orphan control option on and off to view how text is affected.

In this exercise, you turn off widow and orphan control, create a widow by typing text, and then activate widow and orphan control to view how Word removes the widow.

Open

1   On the Standard toolbar, click the Open button. Navigate to the Lesson01 folder in the Word Expert Practice folder, and double-click the file August Flyer 01.

2   Scroll to the last paragraph on the first page.

3   Click after the sentence that ends with the text *Big Apple*.

4   On the Format menu, click Paragraph.

The Paragraph dialog box is displayed.

5   Click the Line And Page Breaks tab.

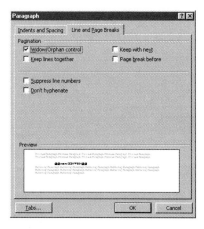

6   If necessary, clear the Widow/Orphan Control check box, and click OK.

7   Press the Spacebar once.

8   Type **For your convenience, this hilarious play will run for two weekends**.

Part of the new text appears at the bottom of the first page, and part of it shows up at the top of the second page, creating a widow.

9   On the Format menu, click Paragraph.

The Paragraph dialog box appears.

10   Select the Widow/Orphan Control check box, and click OK.

The entire sentence is now located at the top of the second page, eliminating the widow.

11   Save the document as **August Flyer 01 Edited**, and close the file.

Word saves and closes the file.

Inserting Fields

W2000E.6.1

Later in this book, you'll insert fields into a form letter that personalize the letter after it has been integrated with a database of names and addresses (see Lesson 6, "Merging Documents for Mailing").

Later in this book, you'll insert a list field, a check box field, and text fields into a form, which will enable users to select and type responses in the form (see Lesson 8, "Creating Forms").

In Lesson 10, "Working with Tables of Contents and Indexes," you'll insert fields that generate a table of contents and index.

You can automatically update information in a document by inserting a **field**. Depending on the type of field that you insert, Word will insert a hidden **field code** that will perform a function specific to the field. Field codes are instructions and characters that generate a field's result. For example, if you inserted a date field, the field code would instruct Word to insert the current date in the location where you inserted the field. The field code would also instruct Word to automatically update the date each time the document is opened.

A field can be blank, ready to be filled in, or it can contain default text or numbers that change each time you open the document that contains the fields.

The office manager at Lakewood Mountains Resort conducts a weekly meeting for all mangers. For each meeting, he prints out an agenda that lists the topics of discussion and contains room for the managers to take notes. For his convenience, he has inserted a date field at the top of the agenda, which automatically displays the current date every time he opens and prints the agenda.

Word has many other fields to choose from.

Type of field	Example of what the field will display
Information	The name of the author of a document
Equation and Formula	The result of an arithmetic expression
Links and Reference	The insertion of an AutoText entry

You can view the different types of available fields by displaying the Field dialog box. On the Insert menu, click Field.

In this exercise, you insert a date field at the top of an agenda, and you test the field.

Open

1   On the Standard toolbar, click the Open button. Navigate to the Lesson01 folder in the Word Expert Practice folder, and double-click the file LMR Weekly Agenda 01.

2   Click the center of the blank line below the text *LMR Weekly Agenda*.

3   On the Insert menu, click Field.

The Field dialog box appears.

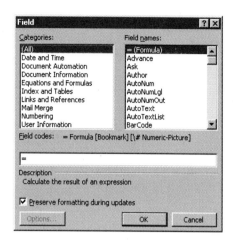

4   In the Categories list, click Date And Time.

5   In the Field Names list, click Date.

6   Click OK.

The current date appears below the text *LMR Weekly Agenda*.

7   Save the document as **LMR Weekly Adgenda 01 Edited**, and close it.

Word saves and closes the file.

8   In the bottom-right corner of the Windows taskbar, double-click the time.

The Date/Time Properties dialog box appears.

9   Modify the calendar so that it is one week into the future, and click OK.

10   Open LMR Weekly Agenda 01 Edited.

Notice that the date has changed.

11   Close the document, and change your computer's date back to the current date.

To modify the calendar, you move the mouse pointer to a number on the calendar, and click the number. If you need to change the month, in the top-right section of the Date/Time Properties dialog box, click the down arrow to the right of the month currently displayed. Select the month you want, and click OK.

important

You'll need to adjust the time on a computer occasionally. When the system's battery is weak (typically after a prolonged period in which the computer is not turned on), the displayed time might be incorrect. Also, Microsoft Windows might adjust the clock incorrectly in regions that do not observe Daylight Savings Time. However, you should rarely, if ever, need to adjust the date. The date is changed in this exercise solely to provide a way for you to note the change in the Date/Time field.

W2000E.1.1

Applying Paragraph and Section Shading

Shading can be used to emphasize an aspect of a document or call attention to specific information. It can also help call attention to special titles or headings. Word allows you to add shading to selected text in a document. To shade text, select the text to be shaded, and on the Standard toolbar, click the Tables and Borders button. Click the Shading Color down arrow, and then click a color. Your selected text or paragraph takes on the color you selected.

If the color you selected makes the text difficult to read, you can use the Borders And Shading dialog box to make your shading lighter. When you print a shade, the printer creates the shade by applying dots of color at varying densities, depending on the shading percentage that you specify. For example, a 5% shade has fewer dots that a 65% shade. Word can also arrange these dots of color into different patterns, such as vertical, horizontal, and diagonal lines.

W2000E.4.2

Moving, Resizing, and Deleting a Picture

Word has an extensive Clip Art Gallery with hundreds of ready-to-use images, including buttons, cartoons, pictures, and backgrounds. The Clip Art Gallery even includes sound and motion clip files. You can insert a picture from the Clip Art Gallery or from another source into your document. After you insert a picture into a Word document, you can move, size, and delete the picture.

The picture doesn't need to stay where you first inserted it. After you view the placement of the picture, you might decide that the picture should be moved up or down or a little to the left or right. You might decide that the picture would really look better on a different page. You move a picture in Word by positioning the mouse pointer over the picture until the pointer becomes a four-headed pointer and dragging the picture to a new location.

The Clip Art Gallery does not display pictures in their actual size, so when you insert a picture from the Clip Art Gallery, the picture might be a lot larger or smaller than you thought it would be. Word allows you to resize a picture to any size. You change the size of the picture by dragging the **sizing handles** (as shown below) in the appropriate direction.

Sizing Handles

Sizing handles are the small white squares located at the corners and sides of a picture or object. They are used for resizing. To display the sizing handles, click the picture. If you drag a corner sizing handle, you'll resize the entire picture proportionally. If you drag one of the middle sizing handles on one of the sides of the picture, you'll make the picture either wider or narrower, taller or shorter.

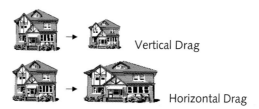

Vertical Drag

Horizontal Drag

If you decide that you no longer want a particular picture, or if you inserted one by mistake, you can delete it. Simply click the picture and press Delete.

In this exercise, you move and resize two pictures and delete a picture.

> You can size a picture more precisely by changing the measurements on the Size tab of the Format Picture dialog box. To display the Format Picture dialog box, right-click the picture, and click Format Picture.

Open

1 On the Standard toolbar, click the Open button. Navigate to the Lesson01 folder in the Word Expert Practice folder and double-click the file Hiking 01.

2 Click the picture of a hiker.

The sizing handles appear around the picture.

> You can quickly display the Picture toolbar by right-clicking a picture, and on the shortcut menu, clicking Show Picture Toolbar.

3 Drag the bottom-right sizing handle down and to the right about 1.5 inches.

The picture is larger. Notice that the text has shifted to the right to accommodate the larger size of the picture.

4 Drag the hiker picture under the sentence that starts with the text *The weather in the mountains.*

5 Press the right arrow key a few times to center the picture, as shown below.

> You can move a picture in smaller increments by pressing and holding down the Ctrl key while pressing the desired arrow key.

> Notice that the text is wrapping around the picture in a square configuration. This is because the Square text-wrapping style has already been applied to this picture.

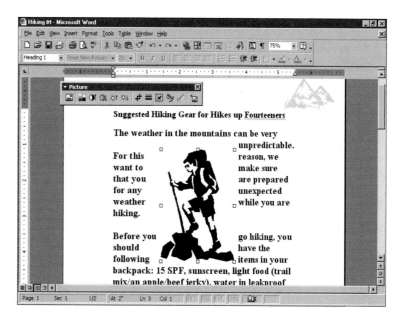

6   Drag the mountain picture to page 2, under the second column.

7   Insert a column break before the text *General hiking*.

> You can quickly insert a column break by pressing Ctrl+Shift+Enter.

8   Click the mountain picture.

9   Drag the top-left sizing handle up and to the left about two inches.

The mountain picture is enlarged.

10   Click the leaf picture.

> You'll work more with this picture in the next exercise.

11   Press Delete.

The picture is deleted.

Keep this file open for the next exercise.

Editing Clip Art

Have you ever scrolled through the Clip Gallery window in search of the perfect picture but didn't find it? As a result, you probably settled for one that would suffice. But perhaps the picture that you selected as being "close enough" would have been perfect if it were a different color or if it looked just a bit different. Fortunately Word lets you make changes to many clip art pictures.

A clip art picture can be a **GIF** (Graphics Interchange Format), **TIF** (Tag Image File Format), **WMF** (Windows Metafile Format), **BMP,** or **JPG** file. A BMP is a file that identifies graphics stored in a bit-map file format. A JPG is a graphic stored as a file in the JPEG (Joint Photographic Experts Group) format. To find out the file name and format of a particular clip art picture, position the mouse pointer over a picture in the Insert ClipArt window. A ScreenTip will appear displaying the file name and file format of the clip. You can only edit pictures that have the .wmf extension.

You can edit a WMF picture after you insert it in a document. First you right-click the picture and on the shortcut menu that appears, click Edit Picture. The picture appears in its own window with boundary lines around it and the Edit Picture toolbar to its left. If you zoom in on the picture and click it, sizing handles will appear around an individual shape or line within the picture. This is because the picture is made up of several objects that have their own shapes and colors.

To edit a picture, you first select the shape or line objects within the picture. While the objects are selected, you use the Drawing toolbar to change the fill color or line color, add a shadow or 3-D effect, or rotate the object. If you don't like a particular object within the image, you can delete it. You can also use the sizing handles around the objects to make them smaller or larger. You can even move the objects to new locations by dragging them. If you don't like how the picture looks after editing, you can return the picture to its original state. At the end of the Edit Picture toolbar, click the Reset Picture button. This will delete all the edits you made to the picture.

When you are finished editing the image, on the Edit Picture Toolbar, click the Close Picture button. The modified image will appear in its original place in your document.

W2000E.6.6

Controlling Text Wrapping

Word can **wrap** text around a picture. Wrapping occurs when you move a picture over text and the text moves to make room for the picture, as you saw in the previous exercise. You can control how text wraps around the picture. Word has six different text-wrapping styles that you can use.

Style	Description
Square	The picture is "framed" by text. The text forms a square around the picture.
Tight	The picture's shape is outlined by text.
Behind Text	The picture appears to be behind the text. The text does not wrap around the picture.
In Front Of Text	The picture appears to be on top of the text. The text does not wrap around the picture.
Top And Bottom	The picture has text above it and below it; however, the picture does not have text to the left or right of it.
Through	The picture is "hugged" by text from all different directions.

In this exercise, you set the wrapping to Behind Text for one picture and to Tight for another picture.

1   If the Picture toolbar is not displayed, on the View menu, point to Toolbars, and click Picture.

2   Select the picture of the mountains on the second page.

3   Drag the picture to the center of the page.

Text Wrapping

4   On the Picture toolbar, click the Text Wrapping button.

5   Click the Behind Text option.

The picture appears to be behind the text.

You can also use the Right and Left arrow keys to move pictures that are selected. Use these arrow keys to "nudge" the picture in small increments.

6   Scroll to page 1.

7   Click the picture of the hiker.

Text Wrapping

8   On the Picture toolbar, click the Text Wrapping button to display the text wrapping options.

9   Click Tight.

The text no longer forms a square around the picture. The text now outlines the outer shape of the picture.

10   Press the down arrow key to even out the wrapping.

tip

Notice that the text to the right of the picture is farther away than the text to the left of the picture. You can make the text wrapping even on both sides. On the Picture toolbar, click the Text Wrapping button, and click the Edit Wrap Points option. After you click Edit Wrap Points, the picture will be surrounded by small squares called **selection handles**. Selection handles are used for diagonal, vertical, or horizontal resizing. Drag the selection handle of your choice in the desired direction and watch how the wrapping changes. When you're finished, click anywhere outside of the picture to deselect it.

11   Save the document as **Hiking 01 Edited**, and close it.

Word saves and closes the file.

Lesson Wrap-Up

In this lesson, you learned how to control widows and orphans; how to insert fields; how to move, size, and delete pictures; and how to control text wrapping around a picture.

If you are continuing to the next lesson:

●   On the File menu, click Close.
    If you are prompted to save the changes, click No.
    Word closes the file.

If you are not continuing to other lessons:

●   On the File menu, click Exit.
    If you are prompted to save the changes, click No.
    Word closes.

Lesson Glossary

BMP   (Windows bitmap) A file format created by Microsoft that is commonly used for photographs and illustrations.

field   A location on a document that can automatically update information. A field is generated by a code that is specific to the field.

field code Instructions and characters that generate a field's result.

GIF (Graphics Interchange Format) A file format that can be viewed in a Web browser.

JPG (Joint Photographic Experts Group) A file format that is used to efficiently compress and store images that include thousands or even millions of colors. The JPG format is supported by most Web browsers.

orphan A word or a broken sentence that appears on its own line at the bottom of a page.

selection handles Small black squares located around a picture or an object that are used for diagonal, vertical, or horizontal resizing.

sizing handles Small white squares located at the corners and sides of a picture or an object that are used for diagonal, vertical, or horizontal resizing.

TIF (Tagged Image File Format) An older file format used to compress and store color images. It is not recognized by Web browsers.

widow A word or broken sentence that appears on its own line at the top of a page.

WMF (Windows Metafile) A file format created by Microsoft that provides "hinting" information to allow images to be resized without a loss in quality. The WMF format can also store multiple objects within a single picture file. The WMF format is not recognized by Web browsers.

wrap To surround a picture with text.

Quick Quiz

1   Describe what the text around a picture looks like if the Top And Bottom wrapping style has been applied to it.

2   Where can you locate a list of the different types of fields available in Word?

3   What is an orphan?

4   Which Clip Art picture format can be edited in Word?

5   What must you do to display sizing handles on a picture?

important

In the Putting It All Together section below, you must complete Exercise 1 to continue to Exercise 2.

Putting It All Together

Exercise 1: Open the LMR Wait Staff Test 01 file. Resize the waiter picture so that it is about one inch smaller. Change the text wrapping to Top And Bottom. Move the waiter picture so that it is centered, the text *LMR Wait Staff* is above it, and the text *Test* is below it. Delete the chef picture. Save the file as **LMR Wait Staff Test 01 Edited**.

Exercise 2: Using the file LMR Wait Staff Test 01 Edited, turn on widow and orphan control. Insert the Time field to the right of the text *Start time*. Save the file.

LESSON 2

Using Advanced Document Formats

After completing this lesson, you will be able to:

✔ *Create new styles.*

✔ *Use existing styles.*

✔ *Use sample text to create a style.*

✔ *Apply styles.*

✔ *Update a current style.*

✔ *Delete a style.*

✔ *Find and replace styles.*

✔ *Find and replace formatting.*

✔ *Create alternating footers.*

✔ *Create a different first-page footer.*

✔ *Use column breaks.*

Microsoft Word 2000 provides several ways for you to build on the skills you've acquired for formatting documents. Have you ever formatted a heading with multiple formatting attributes such as font, font size, or font color, and wished that you could use that same formatting for other headings throughout the document without having to go through the steps to apply the formatting each time? Word lets you do just that. You can apply multiple formatting attributes to paragraphs and characters and then quickly apply those same attributes to text throughout the document.

You've probably used the Find And Replace dialog box to search for words but wanted to know how you could narrow your search. Word lets you search through a document for formatting attributes, special characters, and non-printing characters, and then replace them with alternates.

You probably already know how to add page numbers in the footer of your document—but you can do much more with headers and footers. When you use Word, you can create alternating headers or footers and create a different header or footer on the first page of a document.

In this lesson, you will learn how to name, apply, update, and delete formatting attributes and how to find and replace formatting, special characters, and non-printing characters. You also will create alternating footers and a different first-page footer. Finally, you will learn how to create watermarks and use column breaks.

Sample files for the lesson

To complete the procedures in this lesson, you will need to use the practice files LMR Weekly 02, LMR Employee Handbook 02, and Welcome Pamphlet 02 in the Lesson02 folder in the Word Expert Practice folder located on your hard disk. These documents were created for the employees of Lakewood Mountains Resort and include updates of current events, guidelines to follow, a checklist for certain duties, and an internal memo listing salaries of various employees. You'll also insert a graphic named Leaf 02.

Reviewing Styles

In the following exercises, the Standard and Formatting toolbars have been separated. For additional information on how to separate the toolbars, see the "Using the CD-ROM" section at the begining of this book.

You might already know that a **style** is a named set of formatting attributes. After you create a style, you can use it to apply multiple formatting characteristics to text simply by clicking the name of the style in the Style list. Styles save you time when you format a document and help you maintain a consistent format within the same document and from document to document. For example, the ready-made Normal style applies left-alignment to text and a 12 point, Times New Roman font.

The chief benefit of using styles is convenience. If you don't apply a style, you'll have to change all the attributes separately. If you apply a style to many different locations in a document and then decide to change the style, you need to change the style only once. The change will be updated in every location of the document that has that style applied. You can use **character styles** and **paragraph styles** to format text. A character style contains only character formatting attributes such as bold, underline, and font style characteristics. A paragraph style can contain both paragraph formatting attributes (such as spacing and indentation) and character formatting attributes. The difference between a paragraph style and a character style is that a paragraph style affects all the text in a paragraph, while a character style affects only selected characters or words.

The Style Organizer is explained later in this lesson.

Styles are specific to individual documents; if you create a style, it is added only to the open document. To use a style in a different document, you copy the style from the current document to the other document by using the Style Organizer. To make styles available to all documents that you create, you use the Style Organizer to copy styles to Word's global template, which is used each time you create a new document. By default, the global template is named Normal.dot.

W2000E.2.4

To access the Style list on the Formatting toolbar, click the Style list down arrow.

Creating New Styles

Word includes several built-in styles that you can use. A few of these styles can be found in the Style list on the Formatting toolbar, and a complete list is in the Style dialog box, as shown in the following illustration. Word provides styles that create bullets, headings, body text, salutations and closings for letters, and more.

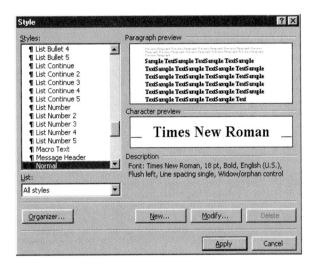

Even though Word provides more than 100 ready-made styles, they only scratch the surface of the thousands of ways you can format characters and paragraphs. Consequently, you might want to create your own styles. For instance, the events coordinator at Lakewood Mountains Resort wanted an interesting heading for her weekly bulletin. She reviewed Word's built-in styles and liked the font size for the Heading 1 style, but she didn't like its font. She liked the font of Heading 2, but she didn't like that it was italicized. So she decided to create a style with a new name that would apply the precise heading format that she wanted.

You can create a style "from scratch" by defining your own formatting attributes, or you can use an existing style and build on or modify that style to create a new style. For example, if you like the Normal style, but not the particular font size, you can use the existing Normal style to create a new style in which only the font size is changed. The Normal style still exists, but you will have created a new style based on the Normal style. When you create a new style, it is stored within the current document.

In this exercise, you use the New Style dialog box to create and name a style for the headings in the LMR Weekly bulletin.

Open

1   On the Standard toolbar, click the Open button. Navigate to the Lesson02 folder in the Word Expert Practicer folder, and double-click the file LMR Weekly 02.

2   On the Format menu, click Style.

The Style dialog box appears.

3   Click the New button.

The New Style dialog box appears.

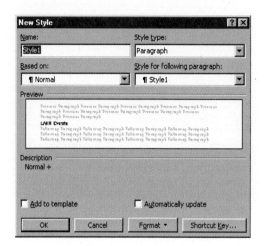

4   In the Name box, type **LMR A Head**.

Notice that Paragraph is already selected in the Style Type box.

5   Click the Format button.

A list of formatting characteristics appears.

6   Click Font.

The Font dialog box appears.

7   In the Font list, scroll down, and click Verdana.

8   Select the number in the Size box, and type **28**.

9   Click the Font Color down arrow, click the Blue-Gray square (second row, second to the last square), and then click OK.

The font attributes are specified, and the Font dialog box closes.

10 Click the Format button, and click Numbering.

The Bullets And Numbering dialog box appears.

Bullets can take a variety of forms, such as icons, pictures, and any symbols.

11 On the Bulleted tab, click the second bullet style in the second row, and click OK twice to accept the selections and to return to the Style dialog box.

The style is created.

12 In the Style dialog box, click the Close button.

You will apply the LMR A Head style later in this lesson.

13 On the Formatting toolbar, click the Style down arrow.

The LMR A Head style appears in the list.

14 Click anywhere in the text of the document.

Keep this file open for the next exercise.

Using Existing Styles

Often you create a style that has characteristics similar to an existing style. For example, you might create two similar headings with different font sizes.

Lakewood Mountains Resort
Lakewood Mountains Resort

You can create a new style that includes some or all of the formatting characteristics of an existing style by formatting the new style based on the existing style. Using this method, you create the new style without modifying the definition of the existing style. This approach makes it unnecessary to define every attribute that you want to use for the new style. Instead, you modify or add only those attributes that are different from the existing style.

In this exercise, you create and name a style based on an existing style. Then you use the new style as the basis for creating another style. Both new styles will be applied to the LMR Weekly Bulletin in later exercises.

1   On the Format menu, click Style.

The Style dialog box appears.

2   Click the New button.

The New Style dialog box appears.

3   Type **LMR B Head** in the Name box.

4   Click the Based On down arrow, scroll if necessary, and then click the LMR A Head style.

You will base your new style on the LMR A Head style.

5   Click the Format button.

A list of formatting characteristics appears.

6   Click Font.

The Font dialog box appears.

7   Select the number in the Size box, type **18**, and then click OK.

A smaller font size is now selected.

8   Click the Format button again.

A list of formatting characteristics appears.

9   Click Numbering.

The Bullets And Numbering dialog box appears.

If you select None, Word won't number items in a list.

10   Click None, and click OK.

The Bullets And Numbering dialog box closes.

11   Click the Format button again.

12   Click Tabs to change the tab settings in this style.

The Tabs dialog box appears.

13   In the Tab Stop Position box, type **2**.

14   Click the Set button, and click OK twice.

The LMR B Head style is created.

15   Click the Close button.

LMR B Head is added to the Style list, and the Style dialog box closes.

Keep this file open for the next exercise.

Using Sample Text to Create a Style

Perhaps the easiest method for creating a style is to specify text that you have already formatted as the basis for a new style. This approach creates a style using sample text and is sometimes called creating a style "by example." To use this technique, you format text in a paragraph of your document or simply select text that you've already formatted, and then record the formatting characteristics as a new style.

If the style is a paragraph style, you can define the style using either the New Style dialog box or by simply typing the new style name in the Style box on the Formatting toolbar. To create a character style from sample text, you must use the New Style dialog box.

In this exercise, you format a paragraph and use it as a sample to create a paragraph style. You then format a character and use it as a sample to create a character style.

1   Select the text *Don't forget to RSVP to the picnic and party invitation!*

2   On the Format menu, click Font.

The Font dialog box appears.

3   Scroll up through the Font list, and click Comic Sans MS.

4   Click the Font Color down arrow, click the Plum square (fourth row, second to last square), and click OK.

The font and color change in the selected paragraph, and the Font dialog box closes.

5   Click in the Style box on the Formatting toolbar.

The current style is selected.

6   Type **Text!**, and press Enter.

The Text! style is created.

7   On the Formatting toolbar, click the Style down arrow.

The new style appears in the Style list.

8   Select the letter *D* in the word *Don't*.

9   Using the Font Size list on the Formatting toolbar, change the font size to 26 points.

10   On the Format menu, click Style.

The Style dialog box appears.

11   Click the New button.

The New Style dialog box appears.

12   Type **Large Letter** in the Name box.

13   Click the Style Type down arrow, and click Character.

14   Click OK.

The Large Letter style is created.

15   Click the Close button.

The New Style dialog box closes, and the character style is created and added to the Style list.

Keep this file open for the next exercise.

Styles in the Style list are alphabetized. To find the new Text! style, you might have to scroll down.

Applying Styles

By now you have viewed Word's ready-made styles, and you have a small library of useful styles to choose from. You've also taken the time to create several styles of your own, so you can apply multiple formatting attributes to selected text simply by clicking a style name in the Style list. The following table explains how you can apply styles to change formatting within a document.

To	Do this
Apply a style to text that you type	Click to position the insertion point on a blank line, select a style in the Style list, and then type. The text that you type will automatically appear in the style that you selected.
Apply a style to an entire paragraph	Click anywhere in the paragraph, and click the style in the style list.
Apply a style to multiple consecutive paragraphs	Select all the paragraphs that you want to apply the style to, and click the desired style in the style list.
Apply a style to a character or specific text	Select only the specific text or character, and click the desired style in the style list.

In this exercise, you apply the styles that you created in previous exercises to paragraphs and characters in the LMR Weekly Bulletin.

1   Click the text *LMR Events*.

2   On the Formatting toolbar, in the Style list, click LMR A Head.

The style is applied.

3   Using the same method as described in steps 1 through 2, apply the LMR A Head style to the following headings: *Lunch Specials*, *New Employees*, and *Job Openings*, as shown below.

> You will have to scroll to the second page to change all the headings.

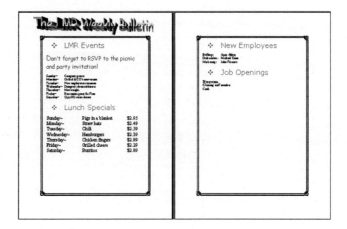

4 Scroll up and select all of the text between (but not including) *Don't forget to RSVP to the picnic and party invitation!* and *Lunch Specials*.

5 In the Style list on the Formatting toolbar, click LMR B Head.

   The LMR B Head style is applied.

6 Scroll to page 2, and apply the LMR B Head style to all of the text between *New Employees* and *Job Openings* and the text below *Job Openings*.

   The LMR B Head style is applied to the selected text.

7 Click the blank line under the heading *New Employees*, press Enter to create space for a new heading, and press the up arrow key once.

8 In the Style list, scroll down and click Text! to select a new style for the heading you will type in the blank space.

9 Type **Welcome!**, and press Enter.

   The style is applied as you type.

10 Select the *W* in the word *Welcome*, and apply the Large Letter style to it.

11 Click anywhere in the document to deselect the text.

   Your document should look similar to the following.

The LMR Weekly Bulletin title was created using the WordArt feature. To learn more about WordArt, see Lesson 8, "Working with Graphics," in the Microsoft Word 2000 Step by Step Courseware Expert Skills Student Guide.

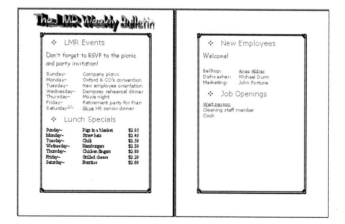

Keep this file open for the next exercise.

tip

You can type just the first letter of a style in the Style box to quickly display the style in the Style list on the Formatting toolbar. You also can type the name of the style in the Style box to apply a style without having to locate it in the Style list.

Adding a Style to the Normal Template

After you create a style, you can make that style available to any new document that you create. On the Format menu, click Style. In the Style dialog box, click the Organizer button to display the Organizer dialog box. A list of all the styles in the current document will appear. Simply click the style that you want to be available in new documents, and click the Copy button. The style will move to the To Normal.dot list, which makes it available in the Normal template. When you open a new blank document and click the Style down arrow, the new style will appear.

If you no longer want the style to appear in the Style list, display the Organizer dialog box, click the style in the To Normal.dot list, and click the Delete button. Click Yes to confirm the deletion.

The Style list in the Normal template displays Word's default styles, so when you add a style to the Normal template, in effect, you're making that style one of Word's default styles.

Updating a Current Style

After you have applied a style to a particular type of heading, you might decide that the style needs some fine-tuning. Maybe the color is lighter than you expected, or perhaps the font size is too large. Whatever the problem, Word lets you modify any style at any time. When you modify a style, Word instantly updates the original style applied to paragraphs or characters throughout the document.

As is true for creating and applying styles, you can modify styles by specifying formatting either in the Style dialog box or by using the Formatting toolbar.

important

If you click a style in the Style list and the Modify Style dialog box appears, this means this style was modified at some point—whether you intended to modify it or not. (It is possible that you could have accidentally modified a style without realizing it.) If the Modify Style dialog box appears and you really do not want to modify the style, you should click the Reapply The Formatting Of The Style To The Selection option to reapply the style instead of modifying it.

In this exercise, you modify the LMR A Head style and the Large Letter style in the LMR Weekly Bulletin.

1   Scroll to page 1, and click the heading *Lunch Specials*.

2   On the Format menu, click Bullets And Numbering.

3   Click None, and click OK.

    The bullet is removed from the style.

4   On the Formatting toolbar, click the Style box, and press Enter.

The Modify Style dialog box appears.

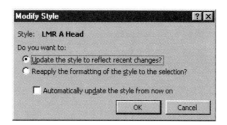

5   Click OK to update the style.

All the LMR A Heads now appear without a bullet.

6   Select the *D* in the word *Don't* at the top of the first page.

7   Using the Font Size list on the Formatting toolbar, change the font size to 36 points.

If you scroll to the text *Welcome!* on page 2, you'll see that the font size of the *W* in *Welcome!* has also changed to 36 points.

8   On the Formatting toolbar, click the Style box, and press Enter.

The Modify Style dialog box appears.

9   Click OK to update the Large Letter style.

Keep this file open for the next exercise.

Deleting a Style

You cannot delete Word's ready-made styles.

You can delete styles you no longer use. However, if you delete a style that is currently applied to text in a document, the text will no longer be formatted according to the style and will take on the style characteristics of corresponding paragraphs.

In this exercise, you delete the Large Letter style.

1   On the Format menu, click Style.

The Style dialog box appears. The Large Letter style is already selected.

2   Click the Delete button.

An alert box appears, asking if you are sure that you want to delete the style.

3   Click Yes.

The style is deleted.

4   In the Style dialog box, click the Close button.

The letter *D* in the word *Don't* and the letter *W* in the word *Welcome* are now in the same style as their corresponding text.

5   Save the document with the name **LMR Weekly 02 Edited**.

Word saves the file.

Keep this file open for the next exercise.

W2000E.2.1

A few examples of Art borders you might find useful include holiday borders (candy corn, holly and ivy), festive borders (balloons and noise makers), shapes (stars and hearts), food (apples and cupcakes), and various interesting line designs.

Creating Page Borders

You can spice up the appearance of a document by adding page borders. For example, the LMR Weekly file in the previous exercise uses borders to add color and draw people's attention to the flyer. Word has many decorative and festive page borders that you can add. Simply click Borders And Shading on the Format menu, and click the Page Border tab in the Borders And Shading dialog box. In the Style list, click a line style and format it by choosing a color and width. Or you can click a border from the Art list. The Art list has preformatted page borders. When you click a page border, Word displays a preview in the Borders And Shading dialog box. After you've made your selection, click OK. The border will appear outside the page margins of your document. In the screen below, apples were chosen as the page border. Notice that in the preview box you can select where you wish to place the borders. In this example, all four page borders were selected. In the Preview box, you can click the diagram or use the buttons to apply borders to the top, bottom, and sides. To completely frame your document with the border, you select all four buttons in the Preview box, or click the diagram until a four-sided border appears.

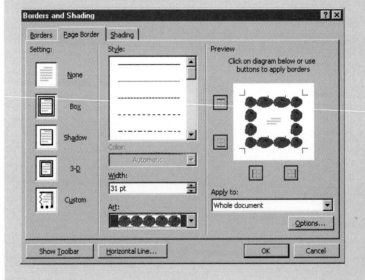

Finding and Replacing Styles

W2000E.2.6

Suppose you've created several styles for a document and then decide that certain paragraphs in your document would look better with a different style that you've already created. For instance, the events coordinator at Lakewood Mountains Resort created three styles for the three different levels of headings that she uses in brochures. Later she decided that the subheadings would look better with the main headings style. In turn, she decided that the style for the heading under the subheading would look better with the subheading style. She could visually scan each page for the styles that she wants to change, but depending on the size of the document, visually scanning each page could take a lot of time. Fortunately, the Find And Replace dialog box in Word provides an option that you can use to search for a specific style and replace it with a different style.

You can replace all occurrences of a certain style, or you can let Word find each instance of the style and then change the style individually. In other words, if you don't want to replace the style, you can instruct Word to skip a particular instance and find the next instance. If you decide to replace a particular instance of a style with a different style, simply click the Replace button. Word will replace the style and continue searching for the next instance.

In this exercise, you find specific paragraphs that have the LMR B Head style applied and change the style to LMR List Bullet.

1   Move the insertion point to the top of page 2.

2   On the Edit menu, click Replace.

You can also press F5 to display the Find And Replace dialog box.

The Find And Replace dialog box appears.

3   Click the More button.

Additional options appear in the dialog box.

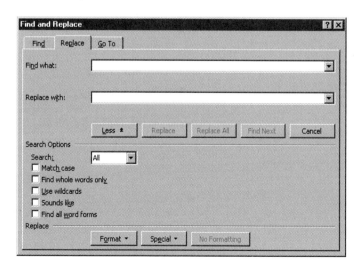

4   Click the Format button.

A format list is displayed.

5   Click Style.

The Find Style dialog box appears.

6   Scroll down, click the LMR B Head style, and then click OK.

The text *Style: LMR B Head* appears in the Find What box.

7   Click the Replace With box.

8   Click the Format button.

9   Click Style.

The Replace Style dialog box appears.

10   Scroll down, click the LMR List Bullet style, and then click OK.

The text *Style: LMR List Bullet* appears under the Replace With box.

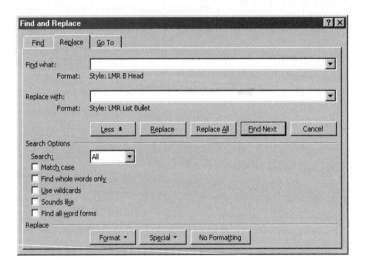

W2000E.2.6

You might have to move the Find And Replace dialog box out of the way to see the text in the document. Drag the title bar of the Find And Replace dialog box to move it to another place on your screen.

11   Click the Find Next button until the text *Wait Person* is selected in the document.

12   Click the Replace button until all of the items below the Job Openings heading are changed to the LMR List Bullet style.

An alert box appears, informing you that Word has finished searching the document.

13   Click OK.

Keep this file and the Find And Replace dialog box open for the next exercise.

Finding and Replacing Formatting

Finding styles is just one search you can perform using the Find And Replace dialog box; Word also allows you to find and replace specific formats such as font size and paragraph spacing, tab formatting (including tab spacing and tab types), foreign language formats, and text wrapping formats for frames used on Web pages. Specialized searches such as these help you fine-tune what you are looking for so that you can cut down on the time you spend searching.

For example, the human resources manager at Lakewood Mountains Resort decided that she no longer likes the font color that she used on the LMR Weekly bulletin, so she used the Find And Replace dialog box to change all occurrences of the font color to a new color.

In this exercise, you find the blue-gray text and change it to dark teal.

important

After you perform a search, you need to clear the options that you specified. Otherwise, Word will incorporate the old search criteria into any new search that you perform.

1 Click the Find What dialog box, and click the No Formatting button.

The LMR B Head style is no longer a search criterion.

2 Click the Replace With box, and click the No Formatting button.

The LMR List Bullet style is no longer a search criterion.

3 Click the Find What box again.

4 Click the Format button, and click Font.

The Find Font dialog box appears.

Since you chose a specific color, Word searches for any font that is blue-gray.

5 Click the Font Color down arrow, click the Blue-Gray square (second row, second to last square), and then click OK.

The text *Font Color: Blue-Gray* appears under the Find What box.

6 Click the Replace With box.

7 Click the Format button, and click Font.

8 Click the Font Color down arrow, click the Dark Teal square (first row, fourth from the last square), and then click OK.

The text *Font Color: Dark Teal* appears under the Replace With box. Word will replace any font that is Blue-Gray with Dark Teal.

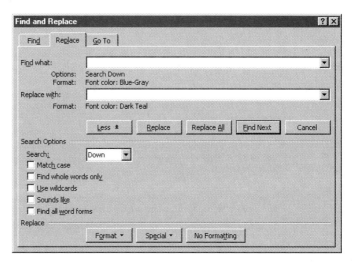

9 Click the Replace All button.

An alert box appears, informing you that seven replacements were made.

10 Click OK.

11   In the Find And Replace dialog box, click the Close button.

12   View the changes in the document, then save and close the document.

Word saves and closes the document.

W2000E.2.6

An em dash is a dash that is the width of the capital letter M, and an en dash is a dash the width of a capital N.

Finding and Replacing Special and Non-Printing Characters

You can also perform a search on special and non-printing characters. Some of the special characters that you can replace include em dashes and en dashes. Some of the non-printing characters you can replace include paragraph marks, tab characters, any characters, any digits, any letters, and column and section breaks.

The manager of the employee cafeteria at Lakewood Mountains Resort announced that the specials on next week's menu will be $2.22 in honor of his father's birthday (February 2, 1922). The human resources manager updates the prices for the lunch specials on the LMR Weekly bulletin by using the non-printing characters option called Any Digit in the Find And Replace Dialog box. Word finds each occurrence of any digit in the document, and when the manager clicks the Replace button, Word replaces it with a 2.

Creating Alternating Footers

For a further example of headers, look at the headers throughout this book, located at the top of every page.

In Word documents, you'll often find a **footer** that displays the same information at the bottom of every page in the document, or a **header** that displays the same information at the top of every page. However, you can provide additional information by alternating the information in the footer or header on every other page. This is a common practice in book publishing. When you open a book, you see two pages at once—a left page and a right page. Every left page has an even page number, while every right page has an odd number. To take advantage of this page layout, most book publishers provide different information at the top or bottom of even-numbered and odd-numbered pages. For example, the human resources manager at Lakewood Mountains Resort created an employee handbook with the name of the book in even-page footers and the name of the chapter in odd-page footers.

tip

In book publishing, it is traditional practice to place the title of a work on the left (even-numbered) pages and the title of the chapter or section on the right (odd-numbered) pages. Why? In Western cultures, the eye is trained to read from left to right. The arrangement of a book title on the left page and the chapter title on the right page causes the reader to digest general header or footer information first and then more specific header or footer information.

When you display information such as a chapter title in the even-numbered or odd-numbered footer, the reader can use the footer to quickly find a particular chapter.

In this exercise, you create alternating footers in a document.

Open

1   On the Standard toolbar, click the Open button. Navigate to the Lesson02 folder in the Word Expert practice folder, and double-click the file LMR Employee Handbook 02.

2   Scroll down to the bottom of page 1, and double-click the footer to open it.

The Header And Footer toolbar appears.

Page Setup

3   On the Header And Footer toolbar, click the Page Setup button.

The Page Setup dialog box appears.

4   In the Headers And Footers section of the dialog box, select the Different Odd And Even check box.

The Preview section now shows two pages instead of one.

5   Click OK.

6   Click to the right of the number 1 at the bottom of the page, press Tab six times, and type **Chapter 1 Using the Handbook**.

7   Scroll to the page 2 footer.

Insert Page Number

8   Click the footer, and click the Insert Page Number button on the Header And Footer toolbar.

The number 2 appears in the footer.

9   Click to the left of the number 2, type **LMR Employee Handbook**, and press Tab seven times.

10 Click the Close button on the Header And Footer toolbar.

11 Scroll through the document to see how the footers alternate.

Keep this file open for the next exercise.

W2000E.2.2
W2000E.4.1

Creating a Different First-Page Footer

Occasionally, the first page of a chapter might display only the chapter's title or a few lines of text that summarize what the chapter will cover. In any case, it's pretty standard to format the first page differently than other pages, usually by providing more white space at the top of the first page. To add some visual appeal to a sparse chapter-opening page, you can design a footer for the first page that is different from the rest of the document's footers.

In this exercise, you create a different footer for the first page of the LMR Employee Handbook and enhance it by changing the font size of the page number and inserting a picture into the footer.

1 To display the Drawing toolbar, on the View menu, click Toolbars, and then click Drawing.

2 Double-click the footer on the first page to open the Header And Footer toolbar.

The Header And Footer toolbar appears.

Page Setup

3 On the Header And Footer toolbar, click the Page Setup button.

The Page Setup dialog box appears.

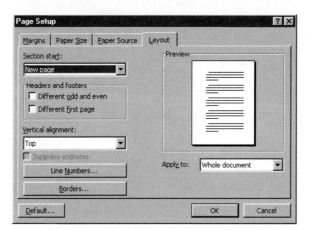

4 In the Headers And Footers section of the dialog box, select the Different First Page check box, and click OK.

Insert Page Number

5 Click the Insert Page Number button to insert the page number for the first page.

6 Select the number 1, and, using the Size list, increase the font size of the number to 36 points.

7 Click to the right of the number 1, and on the Insert menu, point to Picture, and click From File.

The Insert Picture dialog box appears.

> When you make changes that may affect the entire layout of a document, (for example, inserting pictures might move text downward), it's a good idea to scroll through the document before you save it to make sure the changes and layout of the document are what you intended.

8 Navigate to the Lesson02 folder and double-click the Leaf 02.bmp file.

The graphic is inserted to the right of the number 1.

9 Right-click the graphic, and click Copy.

10 Move the insertion point to the left of the number 1.

Paste

11 On the Formatting toolbar, click the Paste button.

The graphic is placed on both sides of the number.

12 Save the file as **LMR Employee Handbook 02 Edited**, and close the document.

W2000E.2.5

Creating a Watermark

A **watermark** is an image that appears on top of or behind document text, and can appear on every page of a document. A watermark can be a word, a symbol, a drawn object, or a graphic. Watermarks are often used to show that a document is authentic. For example, paychecks will often have watermarks on the back of the check with the paper company logo. The presence of the watermark verifies the check is authentic and is used to discourage people from counterfeiting checks. Watermarks are also used to mark a document as confidential or as company property. The human resources manager at Lakewood Mountains Resort places a "Confidential" watermark on memos that deal with sensitive information—such as employee pay increases.

You can put a watermark on every page of a document. To create a watermark, click View on the menu bar, and, on the View menu, click Header And Footer. Insert the watermark text or picture into the header or footer box. If the watermark is a picture, simply insert it and it will appear where you position it. If the watermark is text, you need to create a text box by clicking the Text Box button on the Drawing toolbar and then typing the text inside it.

Once the image or text is positioned, click the Close button on the Header And Footer toolbar. You can also use the WordArt button to create more graphically interesting text. WordArt is a ready-made collection of text designs, called WordArt styles. You can access the WordArt dialog box by clicking the Insert WordArt button on the Drawing toolbar.

> Because you can rotate a WordArt object, WordArt is especially useful if you want a text watermark to appear diagonally across every page.

W2000E.2.7

Using Column Breaks

Columns can enhance the readability of a document, and in some cases save you space. Columns in a Word document break just like pages. When the text in a column reaches either the bottom of a page or the next section break, the text continues at the top of the next column on that page. When the text reaches the bottom of the last column on a page, the text moves to the top of the first column on the next page. If you have a column break in certain places, you can override an automatic column break that Word creates by inserting a manual break. You can also delete a column break.

Word makes it easy to delete column breaks. Simply position the insertion point to the left of the column break marker, and on your keyboard, press Delete. The column break marker will no longer appear. You can also double-click the column break marker to select it and, on your keyboard, press Backspace to delete the column break.

The marketing manager at Lakewood Mountains Resort is putting together a welcome pamphlet for the resort. After she completed her draft, she thought it looked flat and wanted to spice it up, so she created columns. Now all the resort's highlights are listed in columns, but she's still not satisfied. She wants the Recreation paragraph to begin on the second page.

In this exercise, you change a column break so that the Recreation paragraph begins on the second page.

Show/Hide ¶

If the Show/Hide ¶ button isn't displayed, on the Standard toolbar, click More Buttons to display more buttons, and click the Show/Hide ¶ button.

If you position the insertion point before the two paragraph marks between *The Adventures* paragraph and the *Recreation* paragraph, the *Recreation* paragraph will be moved below the first line of the first column on the next page.

1   On the Standard toobar, click the Open button. Navigate to the Lesson02 folder in the Word Expert Practice folder, and double-click the file Welcome Pamphlet 02.

2   On the Standard toolbar, click the Show/Hide ¶ button.

     All formatting marks appear in the document.

3   Scroll to the paragraph with the heading *Recreation*.

4   Position the insertion point at the beginning of the word *Recreation*.

5   On the Insert menu, click Break.

     The Break dialog box appears.

6   In the Break dialog box, click the Column Break option.

7   Click OK.

     The Recreation paragraph is moved to the top of the first column on the next page, and a column break marker is shown under *The Adventures* paragraph.

8   On the Standard toolbar, click the Show/Hide ¶ button.

     The formatting marks are removed.

9 On the Standard toolbar, click the Zoom down arrow, and click Two Pages.

Both pages are shown.

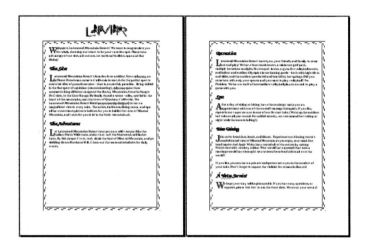

10 On the Standard toolbar, click the Zoom down arrow, and click 100%.

The view of the document returns to 100%.

Lesson Wrap-Up

In this lesson, you learned how to create, apply, update, and delete styles; how to find and replace styles, formats, and special and non-printing characters; how to create alternating footers and a different first-page footer; and how to create a watermark and insert column breaks. This lesson also covered how to create a WordArt object.

If you are continuing to the next lesson:

● On the File menu, click Close.

If you are prompted to save changes, click No.

Word closes the file.

If you are not continuing to other lessons:

● On the File menu, click Exit.

If you are prompted to save changes, click No.

Word closes.

Lesson Glossary

character styles Pre-defined character formatting attributes such as bold, underline, and font style that can be applied to selected characters or words, without affecting the entire paragraph.

header Information—such as a page number, title, chapter, date, or author's name—that appears at the top of each page in a document.

footer Information—such as a page number, title, chapter, date, or author's name—that appears at the bottom of each page in a document.

paragraph styles Paragraph formatting attributes (such as spacing and indentation) and character formatting attributes that can be applied to all of the text in one or more selected paragraphs.

style A named set of formatting instructions. You use a style to apply multiple formatting characteristics to selected text by clicking a style name in the Style list.

watermark Words, symbols, drawn objects, or graphics that appear on top of or behind document text and can appear on every page of a document.

Quick Quiz

1 How do you delete a column break?

2 Do you have to select a paragraph to apply a style to it? Explain.

3 What is a watermark?

4 What are the two types of styles?

5 Name three formats that you can perform a search and replace on.

6 Can you create a character style from sample text using the same steps you use to create a paragraph style from sample text? Explain.

7 If you don't want to look through all the changes that you specified to find and replace, which button in the Find And Replace dialog box do you click?

8 If you create a style in one document, will it automatically be available in another document? Explain.

9 What must you do to clear the previously used Find And Replace formatting criteria?

important

In the Putting It All Together section below, you must complete Exercise 1 to continue to Exercise 2.

Putting It All Together

Exercise 1: If necessary, start Word. Open the Cleaning Staff Manual 02 file. Add the List style from the Style dialog box to the Style list on the Formatting toolbar. Create a Paragraph style called A Head, using the text *Bathroom*. Make the font bold and embossed, make the font size 48, and make the color dark blue (first row, third to last color square). Apply the A Head style to the text *Kitchenette* and *Bedroom*. Delete the C Head style. Select the subheading style and change its font size to 28 and update the style throughout the document. Save the file as **Cleaning Staff Manual 02 Edited**.

Exercise 2: Replace all embossed text with shadowed text. Set the first page footer so that it does not display a number. Save the file.

LESSON 3

Working with Tables and Lists

After completing this lesson, you will be able to:

✔ *Embed and modify worksheets in a table.*

✔ *Link Excel data as a table.*

✔ *Sort table data.*

✔ *Sort lists and other paragraphs.*

Ledgers, calculators, scratch paper, and even abacuses used to be common tools for people who "crunched" numbers all day long. The introduction of computers and software programs such as Microsoft Word and Microsoft Excel made the time-consuming task of calculating lists of data much easier. Not only can you calculate, modify, and sort data, but you also can insert Excel worksheets into Word tables and link Excel data as a table in a Word document. A **table** organizes related data in a row-and-column format.

Occasionally, the tables that you can create in Word are not sufficient to meet your needs. For example, the office manager at Lakewood Mountains Resort needs to create a budget for the employee holiday party and summer picnic. Both of these budgets will include complex formulas and contain large amounts of data that will be hard to manage in a Word table, so she decides to use Excel. Excel not only allows her to create more complex tables than Word, but it also makes creating tables and performing calculations within tables easier because Excel has many additional formatting and calculation features. For example, typing numbers in a table is quicker if you don't have to type dollar signs, commas, and decimal points in each entry. Using Excel, you can type the data in a table and then format all of the data at once to insert dollar signs, commas, and decimal points.

Working with formulas is also easier in Excel than in Word. Using Excel, you can type a formula just once and apply that formula to data in other cells. (A **cell** is the intersection of a row and a column.) If you want to use a formula in more than one cell in a Word table, you must retype the formula in each cell.

You can take advantage of Excel's powerful functions while working in Word by inserting and linking Excel worksheets in Word documents. When you insert an Excel worksheet in a Word document, the worksheet is displayed as a table.

In this lesson, you will learn how to insert and link Excel worksheets into Word documents. You will then learn how to modify worksheets in a table. You will also learn how to sort table data as well as lists and paragraphs.

Sample files for the lesson

To complete the procedures in this lesson, you will need to use the files LMR Revenue 03, LMR 3rd Quarter Revenue 03.xls, and LMR Weekly 03 in the Lesson 03 folder in the Word Expert Practice folder located on your hard disk.

W2000E.3.1
W2000E.3.4

In the following exercises, the Standard and Formatting toolbars have been separated. For additional information on how to separate the toolbars, see the "Using the CD-ROM" section at the beginning of this book.

Embedding and Modifying Worksheets in a Table

The sales manager at Lakewood Mountains Resort is reviewing second-quarter revenues in a table that he created in a Word document, and he realizes that he spends a lot of time typing numbers and calculations. He wants to use an Excel worksheet to make his task easier; however, he wants to display the information as a table in a Word document. Using an Excel worksheet facilitates the manager's job because he can use Excel's features for displaying numbers in currency format and he can quickly create formulas to calculate sales totals. When he is finished creating the Excel worksheet, the sales manager simply inserts, or embeds, the worksheet into the table in his Word document.

When you embed an Excel worksheet in a Word document, you can use all of Excel's tools and commands to modify the data in the embedded worksheet. In other words, even though the embedded worksheet is displayed as a table, you can still work with it as you would any Excel worksheet.

When you embed objects in Word documents, you can elect to embed a new object or to create an **embedded object** from an existing file. To embed a new object into a Word document, use the Create New tab in the Object dialog box. When the object is inserted into Word, you can double-click it to add or edit data for the object. To embed an existing object, use the Create From File tab in the Object dialog box. When the object is inserted, it can be resized and moved as desired.

In this exercise, you embed an Excel worksheet into a Word document and you insert data from the original Word table by pasting the contents of the Word table into the embedded Excel worksheet.

Open

1   On the Standart toolbar click the Open button. Navigate to the Lesson03 folder in the Word Expert Practice folder, and double-click the file LMR Revenue 03.

If the insertion point is outside the table, the Table menu will not be activated.

2   Click anywhere in the table.

3   On the Table menu, point to Select, and click Table.

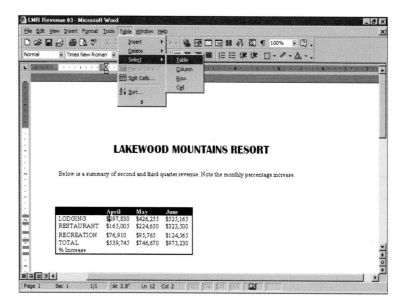

The entire table in the document LMR Revenue is selected.

Copy

4   On the Standard toolbar, click the Copy button.

The Word table is copied.

5   On the Table menu, point to Delete, and click Table.

The Word table is deleted.

6   On the Insert menu, click Object.

The Object dialog box appears, and the Create New tab appears.

7   Scroll down the Object Type list, and click Microsoft Excel Worksheet.

A quick way to insert an empty Excel worksheet in a Word document is by clicking the Microsoft Excel Worksheet button on the Standard toolbar and selecting the desired number of rows and columns that you want.

Microsoft Excel Worksheet

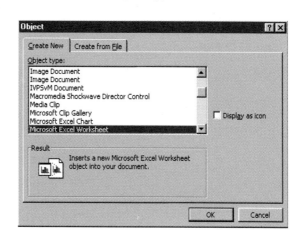

8 Click OK.

An Excel worksheet is embedded in the Word document.

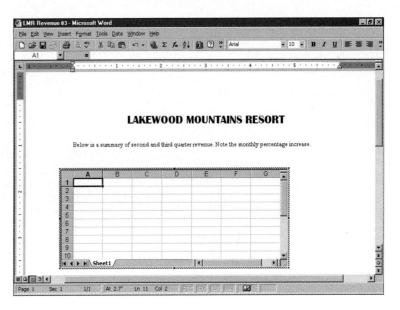

Paste

9 On the Standard toolbar, click the Paste button.

The data from the Word table is inserted in the Excel worksheet.

10 On the Format menu, point to Column, and click AutoFit Selection.

The worksheet columns are narrowed to fit the numbers in each column, but notice that the columns are not widened to fit the text.

11 Position the mouse pointer over the vertical line between the column A heading and the column B heading until the mouse pointer turns into a resizing pointer.

Resizing pointer

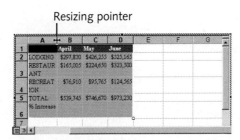

12 Drag the vertical line to the right until the text fits in the column.

13 On the Format menu, point to Row, and click AutoFit.

Excel automatically decreases the height of the cells to fit the data in each row.

14 Use the resizing handle located in the middle of the gray edge along the bottom of the Excel worksheet to drag the border up until the gray edge is displayed below row 7.

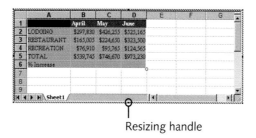

Resizing handle

15 Use the resizing handle located in the middle of the gray edge along the right side of the Excel worksheet to drag the border to the left until the gray edge is displayed in column E.

The Excel worksheet should look similar to the following illustration.

For more information on using Excel Worksheets, see Lesson 2, "Editing and Formatting Worksheets," in the Microsoft Excel 2000 Step by Step Courseware Core Skills Student Guide.

Resizing handle

16 On the File menu, click Save As.

The Save As dialog box appears.

17 Rename the file **LMR Revenue 03 Edited**.

18 Click Save.

The file is saved as LMR Revenue 03 Edited.

Keep this file open for the next exercise.

W2000E.3.2

A function is a sequence of steps performed by a program.

Performing Calculations in a Table

When you refer to a particular cell in a table, you combine the column letter with the row number. For example, the first cell in the first column of a table is referred to as *A1*. *A1* is the cell name, or **cell reference**. When you perform calculations in tables, you can use cell references rather than the numbers stored in a cell. For example, the formula =A1+A2 will add the values of the first two cells in the first column. Referring to a cell using the cell reference rather than its contents ensures that the formula can be easily updated even if the cell's contents change.

Word provides predefined formulas called **functions** to make performing calculations easier. You can use a function to create totals and averages and to determine the minimum and maximum values in a group of cells. For example, the function =SUM(ABOVE) will produce a total of all the cells above the cell that contains the function.

(continued)

continued

To create a formula in a Word table, you click the cell that will contain the formula. On the Table menu, click Formula to display the Formula dialog box. In the Formula dialog box, type the desired formula. Or if you want to use a formula predefined by Word, you can simply click the Paste Function down arrow, click the function that you want, and then type the cell references to be used in the Formula box. You can also select how the numbers will be displayed. Cells can be formatted with $ signs, commas, and decimal points, for example. To make your selection, click the Number Format down arrow, and then click the desired number format. Click OK to close the Formula dialog box.

When you type a formula in the Formula bar, you must first type an equal sign (=); otherwise Excel will consider what you type to be text, not a formula.

Suppose you want to calculate the percentage increase for Lakewood Mountains Resort's revenues. If you use the Word table, you first perform the calculation to figure out the May percentage increase that you formatted in the previous exercise: You position the insertion point in cell C6, and click Formula on the Table menu. In the Formula box, you type =(C5/B5)-1, in the Number Format down box, you click the down arrow, select 0% in the list, and then click OK.

To figure out the June increase, you have to position the insertion point in cell D6, and then repeat the steps, except in the Formula text box, you type the formula =(D5/C5)-1. If you use an Excel worksheet, however, you select cell C6, type =(C5/B5)-1 in the Formula box, and then press Enter. Next, you simply copy the function to the next cell by clicking the fill handle at the bottom-right corner of the cell and dragging to the next cell.

Linking Excel Data as a Table

W2000E.3.3

An embedded object is an object that is inserted in a Word document, but is created and edited in an application other than Word. Although you can modify an emebedded object, the changes you make to it are not applied to the original object, which is called the source object and is stored in a seperate file. Because the source object can't be modified directly in Word, you have to re-embed the object each time changes are made to the source object. If you are using an object that is updated frequently, you should link the object instead. A **linked object** is an object that is created and edited in an application other than Word but is connected to a Word document so that you can double-click the object in Word to open the source object. In other words, linked objects remain stored in the source file. As a result, when the source file is modified, the changes can be updated in the Word document.

You can link either a portion of an Excel worksheet or an entire worksheet to a Word document. When you link the data from an Excel worksheet, the data can be displayed in Word as a table or as an **icon**. An icon is a picture that represents the Excel worksheet. When you double-click the icon or the table, Excel is activated, and the file that is represented by the icon is opened. Each time you update the Excel worksheet, the linked table in Word can also be updated.

The sales manager at Lakewood Mountains Resort saved the third-quarter revenue projections in an Excel worksheet because the numbers are still being finalized. He needs to send a memo with the second-quarter figures as well as the third-quarter projections. Because the third-quarter numbers will continue to change, he doesn't want to embed the worksheet in the Word document. Instead, he will link the Excel worksheet to his prepared memo and later modify the third-quarter revenues without having to modify the original document.

In this exercise, you link an Excel worksheet to a Word document and modify the worksheet.

1   In the document LMR Revenue 03 Edited, click anywhere outside the table.

2   Press Ctrl+End.

    The insertion point moves to the end of the document.

3   On the Insert menu, click Object.

    The Object dialog box appears.

4   Click the Create From File tab.

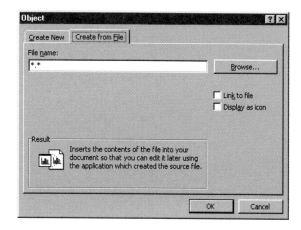

5   Click the Browse button.

    The Browse dialog box appears.

6   Navigate to the file LMR 3rd Quarter Revenue 03.xls in the Lesson03 folder, and click the file.

    You can also double-click the file name to quickly insert it in the File Name box.

7   Click the Insert button.

    The Object dialog box is displayed again and the file name LMR 3rd Quarter Revenue 03.xls appears in the File Name box.

8   In the Object dialog box, select the Link To File check box, and click OK.

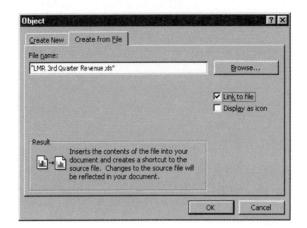

You can also represent the linked object as an icon in the Word document by selecting the Display As Icon check box in the Object dialog box. You can choose your own icon by clicking the Change Icon button in the Object dialog box (this button is displayed only after you select the Display As Icon check box), and then making a selection in the Change Icon dialog box.

9   Double-click the second table.

Excel is activated, and the original document (LMR 3rd Quarter Revenue 03.xls) is opened.

10   In the Excel worksheet, click cell C3.

11   In the Formula Bar, select the number 5, and type **0**.

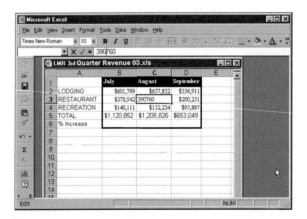

Notice that the value in cell C5 has changed as well. When you changed the data in cell C3, you changed the information but not the formula in the cells. When you decreased the number in cell C3, the formula subtracted this number from the total. The reverse would have happened if you had increased the number in cell C3.

12   Press Enter.

The value in cell C3 is now $390,760, and the total in cell C5 is $1,200,826.

13   To verify that the changes made in the Excel worksheet are reflected in the linked Excel table, click the LMR Revenue 03 Edited button on the taskbar to display the Word document.

Save

14   On the Standard toolbar, click the Save button to save changes made to the Word document.

15   Exit Excel. If you are prompted to save the changes, click No.

tip

To link a portion of an existing Excel worksheet, open the desired worksheet and copy the columns and rows that you want to link to the Word document. Open the Word document and click where you want the Excel data to appear. On the Edit menu, click Paste Special to display the Paste Special dialog box. In the As list, click Microsoft Excel Worksheet Object. Click the Paste Link option, and click OK.

W2000E.1.3

Sorting Table Data

After you have performed calculations in a table, you might later want to rearrange how the data is presented. Word makes it easy to sort data within a table. You can sort all the data in a table or you can sort specific rows or columns by highlighting the row or column you want to sort. The data in the other rows and columns won't be changed. You can sort in ascending or descending numeric order, or by ascending or descending alphabetical order.

In this exercise, you sort the data in the second-quarter revenue table to list the revenue categories with the smallest revenues first.

Open

1   On the Standard toolbar, click the Open button. Navigate to the Lesson03 folder in the Word Expert Practice folder, and double-click the file LMR Revenue 03.

2   Click anywhere inside the table.

3   On the Table menu, click Sort.

    The Sort Text dialog box is shown.

Word cannot sort the table until you click the table or select specific rows to be sorted.

4   In the Sort Text dialog box, click the Sort By down arrow, and click April.

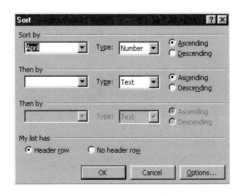

5   In the Sort By section, click the Type down arrow, and click Number, if necessary.

Notice that the table moved all the rows to correspond with the changes in the April column. Recreation revenues are listed first, then restaurant revenues, and then lodging revenues. The % Increase row is moved to the top of the table because there are no values in the row.

6   Click the Ascending option, if necessary, and click OK.

The numbers in the table are listed in ascending order, from smallest to largest revenues.

	April	May	June
% Increase			
RECREATION	$76,910	$95,765	$124,565
RESTAURANT	$165,005	$224,650	$323,500
LODGING	$297,830	$426,255	$525,165
TOTAL	$539,745	$746,670	$973,230

7   On the File menu, click Close. If you are prompted to save changes, click No.

Word closes the file.

W2000E.1.3

Sorting Lists and Other Paragraphs

On occasion you might want to sort lists. For example, your manager might ask you to catalog responsibilities and duties for new employees. After you create the document, you decide that the information should be listed in alphabetical order. You don't have to redo the document. Word can alphabetize the list for you.

Creating lists in Word is easy. You can display bulleted or numbered lists in Word simply by starting the list with a number or an asterisk. Word formats each subsequent item as a list entry and enters the appropriate character—number or bullet, for example—each time you press Enter.

After you create a list, Word can sort it for you. Because you press Enter after typing each list item, the item is treated as a separate paragraph. Word can sort paragraphs by text, number, or date starting with the first word, number, or date in the paragraph. You can sort paragraphs in ascending or descending numeric order, and dates in ascending or descending date order. You sort lists and other paragraphs just as you sort data in tables—by using the Sort Text dialog box.

In this exercise, you sort a list in the Lakewood Mountains Resort weekly newsletter.

1   On the Standard toobar, click the Open button. Navigate to the Lesson03 folder, and double-click the file LMR Weekly 03.

2   Select the list under the heading *Employee Lunch Specials*.

3   On the Table menu, click Sort.

The Sort Text dialog box is displayed.

4   Click the Sort By down arrow, and click Paragraphs.

You can quickly create lists by selecting all of the items and clicking the Bullets button or the Numbering button on the Formatting toolbar.

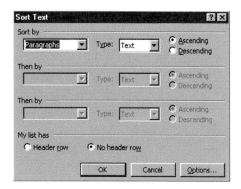

Notice that when you click the Type down arrow, you can also choose to sort the list by date or text.

5   Click the Type down arrow, and click Number.

6   If necessary, click the Acending option, and click OK.

The employee lunch specials are now listed in order of their cost, with the least expensive specials listed first.

7   On the File menu, click Close.

If you are prompted to save changes, Click No.

Word closes the file.

Lesson Wrap-Up

In this lesson, you learned how to insert an Excel worksheet as a Word table, how to modify worksheets and perform calculations within a table, how to link Excel data as a table, how to sort data in a table, and how to sort lists and paragraphs.

If you are continuing to other lessons:

● On the File menu, click Close if any of the files you used in this lesson are still open.

   If you are prompted to save changes, click No.

   Word closes the files.

If you are not continuing to other lessons:

● On the File menu, click Exit.

   Word closes.

Lesson Glossary

cell A small rectangular box that is the intersection of a column and a row in a table. You can type text and numbers, and perform calculations, in each cell.

cell reference The column letter and row number that corresponds to a particular cell; the cell name.

embedded object An object that is created and edited in an application other than Word and then inserted into a Word document. The object is not automatically modified if changes are made to the source file.

functions Predefined sequences of steps, usually involving calculations, performed by a program, such as calculating the sum of a column of data in a table.

icon For a linked object, a picture that represents the object.

linked object An object that is created and edited in an application other than Word and is represented in the Word document but remains stored in the source file.

table A structure that contains rows, columns, and cells. Tables are used to organize text and numbers as well as to calculate values.

Quick Quiz

1   How do you insert an Excel worksheet into a Word document?

2   What is an embedded object?

3   How do you sort a list using Word?

4   How do you activate Excel tools in an Excel worksheet that has been embedded in a Word document?

5   What is a linked object?

6   What is a cell reference?

important

In the Putting It All Together section below, you must complete Exercise 1 before continuing to Exercise 2.

Putting It All Together

Exercise 1: Open LMR Revenue 03, position the insertion point below the existing table, and link the file LMR 3rd Quarter Revenue 03.xls to the Word document.

Exercise 2: In the LMR 3rd Quarter Revenue 03 workbook that you just linked to the Word document in the previous exercise, change the numbers as follows:

> In the Lodging row, change July to $597,333, and change August to $623,947. In the Restaurant row, change July to $600,896, and change August to $640,062. In the Recreation row, change July to $136,100, and change August to $150,478.

Close the Excel worksheet to display the information as a table in the Word document. Save the document as **LMR Revenue 03 Updated** and close it.

LESSON 4

Using Charts

After completing this lesson, you will be able to:

✔ *Create a chart.*

✔ *Modify a chart.*

✔ *Import data into a chart.*

Although tables and lists are useful in organizing data, you might find that you need to do more with data than just organize it. Data is often easier to interpret when it's in a graphical format (such as a bar chart or line graph) rather than in a table format. Traditionally the terms *chart* and *graph* were used to differentiate certain kinds of graphical data. For example, a graphic that represented data as trend lines was called a line graph, while a graphic that represented data as bars was called a bar chart. In Microsoft Word 2000, the word **chart** to refers to all types of graphical data.

To create a chart in a Word document, you use Microsoft Graph 2000. Microsoft Graph 2000 is a supplementary application available in Word 2000 and other Microsoft Office 2000 applications. Microsoft Graph 2000 makes it easy to create and modify charts to suit different presentations. For example, you could use a chart to present income and expense data in a visual format or to compare sales from month to month. You can change the shape, size, and color of charts. You can also create a chart by using existing data from Word tables, Microsoft Excel worksheets, and other documents.

In this lesson, you will learn how to create and modify charts, and import data into a chart.

Sample files for the lesson

To complete the procedures in this lesson, you will need to use the files named LMR Revenue_Spring 04, LMR Revenue_Summer 04, and LMR Revenue_Summer 04.xls in the Lesson04 folder in the Word Expert Practice folder located on your hard disk.

W2000E.4.3

To view the available chart types, you must first insert a chart in a Word document. Then click the Chart Type down arrow to display the chart type icons or click Chart Type on the Chart menu to display the Chart Type dialog box.

Each standard chart type has two or more *sub-types* (additional selections). When you select a chart sub-type in the Chart Type dialog box, a description of the chart sub-type appears in the Chart Sub-Type section of the Chart Type dialog box.

Creating a Chart

Charts that you create with Microsoft Graph are embedded as objects in Word documents. When you start Microsoft Graph, a sample chart and **datasheet** are displayed in the Word document. A datasheet is a table that contains the data presented in the chart. When you make changes to the datasheet, the changes are reflected in the chart.

You can create several different chart types using Microsoft Graph. The following table lists the available standard chart types and their icons and descriptions.

Chart Type	Icon	Description
Column		Presents data in vertical columns and compares values across categories.
Bar		Presents data in horizontal bars and compares values across categories.
Line		Presents data in lines and displays trends over time or across categories.
Pie		Displays the relationship of each value to a total as a fractional slice.
XY (Scatter)		Compares pairs of values and displays values as single data points optionally connected by lines.
Area		Displays the trend of values over time or categories.
Doughnut		Displays data in the same way as a pie chart does, but can contain multiple series.
Radar		Displays changes in values relative to a center point.
Surface		Displays data across two dimensions in a continuous curve.
Bubble		Describes connections between concepts without emphasizing a structural sequence.
Stock		Presents data in columns and displays data in a High-Low-Close model.
Cylinder		Displays data in columns with a cylindrical shape.
Cone		Displays data in columns with a conical shape.
Pyramid		Displays data in columns with a pyramid shape.

A datasheet resembles a table. Like a table, a datasheet is made up of a series of **columns** and **rows**. Columns are identified by letters, and rows are identified by numbers. A **cell** is the box that is the intersection of a column and a row. You use cells to type data that you want to include in a chart into the datasheet. A datasheet reserves a row and column for headings that you supply.

A **row heading** is the numbered grey area to the left of a row. To select an entire row, you click the row heading. A **column heading** is the lettered or numbered area at the top of each column. To select an entire column, you click the column heading. To select the entire datasheet, you click the Select All button, which is located in the top-left corner of the datasheet. After you create a chart, you click a blank area of the Word document to hide the related datasheet and show just the chart. To display the datasheet so that you can modify the chart, you double-click the chart.

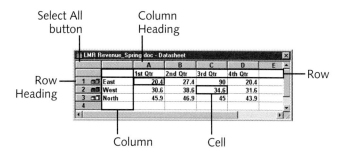

In the following exercises, the Standard and Formatting toolbars have been separated. For additional information on how to separate the toolbars, see the "Using the CD-ROM" section at the beginning of this book.

When you insert a new chart in a Word document, Word displays a column chart along with sample data in the datasheet, including sample row and column headings. The sample data is intended to help guide you in entering your own data. After you insert a chart, the first step is to change the datasheet contents. When you change the values in the datasheet, the chart changes to reflect the new values.

The accountant at Lakewood Mountains Resort is preparing to meet with the owners of the resort, who want to know how the resort's various departments performed during the second quarter. The accountant created a Word document that shows this information in a table, but she wants to make a chart to present the data to the owners.

In this exercise, you create a chart for the accountant to use in her presentation.

Open

1   On the Standard toolbar, click the Open button. Navigate to the Lesson04 folder in the Word Expert Practice folder, and double-click the file LMR Revenue_Spring 04.

2   Press Ctrl+End.

The insertion point moves to the end of the document.

3   On the Insert menu, click Object.

The Object dialog box appears, with the Create New tab displayed.

> **Depending on the programs installed on your computer, your list of object types might differ from the illustration.**

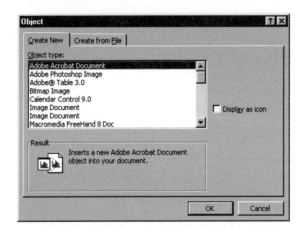

4   Scroll down the Object Type list, click Microsoft Graph 2000 Chart, and then click OK.

A sample chart and datasheet appear.

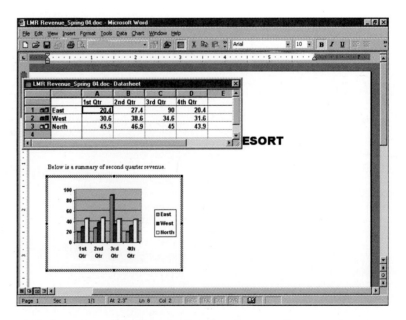

5   Click the Select All button on the datasheet, and press Delete.

The sample data is deleted.

6 In row 1 (in the column before column A), in the second cell, type **LODGING**, and press Enter.

The heading is entered, and the insertion point moves to the cell below *LODGING*.

Notice that the words *RESTAURANT* and *RECREATION* don't fit completely in the cells in the datasheet.

7 Type **RESTAURANT**, and press Enter.

The insertion point moves to the cell below *RESTAURANT*.

8 Type **RECREATION**, and press Enter.

The insertion point moves to the cell below *RECREATION*.

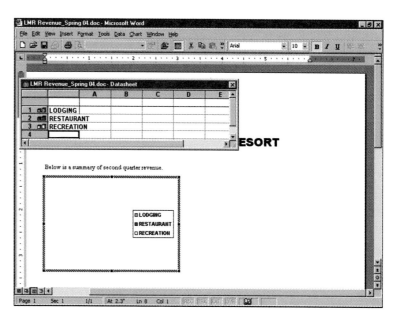

Resize Pointer

9 In the datasheet, position the mouse pointer over the vertical line between the blank column heading and the column A heading until the mouse pointer turns into a double-headed resize pointer, and drag the vertical line to the right until the words fit within the column.

10 In column A, in the row above row 1, click the cell, type **April**, and then press Tab.

April is added to the chart, and the insertion point moves one cell to the right.

11 Type **May**, and press Tab.

May is added to the chart, and the insertion point moves one cell to the right.

12 Type **June**, and press Enter.

June is added to the chart, and the insertion point moves down one cell.

Move the insertion point from row to row by pressing Enter. Move the insertion point from column to column by pressing Tab. (Use Shift+Tab to move backward, or Shift+Enter to move up a row.) You can also use the arrow keys to move up, down, left, and right in the datasheet.

13   Click the first empty cell in the second row (column A). Type the data in the table shown below into the chart's datasheet. (Be sure to include the dollar signs and commas.)

	April	May	June
LODGING	$297,830	$426,255	$525,165
RESTAURANT	$165,005	$224,650	$323,500
RECREATION	$76,910	$95,765	$124,565

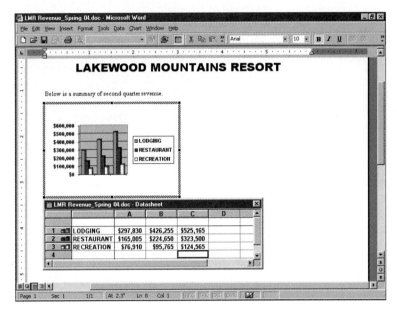

Notice that when you click outside the chart, the datasheet no longer appears, but the chart remains displayed. To activate the datasheet, you just double-click the chart.

14   Save the document as **LMR_Revenue_Spring 04 Edited**.

Keep this file open for the next exercise.

W2000E.4.3

Modifying Charts

You aren't limited to the chart type that Word provides when you insert a chart object, nor are you limited to the default formatting for the chart. You can change to a different, more suitable type of chart if you want, and you can change other elements in the chart, including fill colors and patterns, fonts and font sizes, and more. The following table explains several modifications you can make to a chart.

Select	To
Chart Type	Display the same data in a different chart format. For example, the same data can be displayed as a bar chart, bubble chart, or a pie chart.
Color, pattern, lines, fills, and borders	Modify the format of the chart. For example, you can add a border around the chart, change a fill color (the color inside a closed area) or pattern, or change the color of the data (series) in a chart.
Font	Change the appearance of text in a chart by changing the font style and font size.
Gridlines	Add or remove vertical and horizontal gridlines on several chart types. By default, a chart shows horizontal gridlines only.

You can change gridlines so that they appear in more frequent increments, or you can remove gridlines completely.

(continued)

continued

Select	To
Title	Add and modify chart titles, as well as titles of the **axes** within charts. Axes are lines that provide a frame of reference or comparison in a chart by identifying incremental values on the chart. For example, when you first insert a chart object, the sample column chart displays horizontal gridlines in increments of 20. The vertical, or **value axis** is typically called the y-axis. The horizontal, or **category axis** is known as the x-axis. In a three dimensional system, a z-axis is also used to show depth.
Legend	Modify the text and formatting of the **legend**. The legend is text that describes or explains the graphic. On a graph or map, the legend is the key to the patterns, colors, or symbols used in bars, lines, slices of a pie, and other representations of chart values.

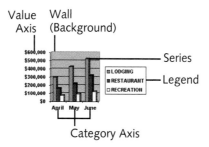

To change the formatting for a chart, you first click the part of the chart that you want to modify. You then make changes by clicking buttons that appear on the Standard toolbar when a chart is activated and the datasheet is displayed, or by clicking the appropriate menu commands.

If a button that you need does not appear on the Standard toolbar when a chart is activated, click the More Buttons button at the end of the toolbar.

More Buttons

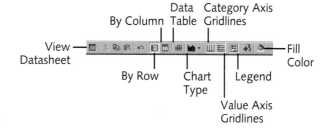

When you work with a chart, the Standard toolbar remains in the Word window, but includes additional buttons for modifying the chart, as shown below. The following table explains the purpose of each button.

Button	Button Name	Purpose
	View Datasheet	Displays or hides the view of the datasheet.
	By Row	Charts values according to the data entered in rows of the datasheet (the default).
	By Column	Charts values according to the data entered in columns of the datasheet. For example, if you click the By Column button for the chart you created in the previous exercise, Word would display columns for LODGING, RESTAURANT, and RECREATION, rather than for April, May, and June.
	Data Table	Displays a row-and-column table of the data used to create the chart. Although this table is similar to the datasheet, it is a component of the chart itself, whereas the datasheet is used to create data values for the chart.
	Chart Type	Changes the current chart to a different type of chart, such as a line to a pie chart.
	Category Axis Gridlines	Displays vertical gridlines for the category axis.
	Value Axis Gridlines	Displays horizontal gridlines for the value axis. This option is turned on by default.
	Legend	Turns on or off the display of the legend. The legend is turned on by default.
	Fill Color	Changes the fill color of a selected area of the chart, such as the wall (background) or a **series**.

A series comprises the values in a chart that are represented pictorially as bars, lines, pie slices, or other pictorial representations.

In this exercise, you change the chart type and several colors in the LMR Revenue Chart.

1   If necessary, double-click the chart to activate it.

2   On the View menu, point to Toolbars, and click Formatting.

    The Formatting toolbar is removed from view, and additional buttons for modifying the chart appear.

If you dragged the datasheet out of the way, you'll need to double-click the chart before you can proceed with the steps in this exercise.

3   On the Standard toolbar, click the View Datasheet button.

    The datasheet is closed.

View Datasheet

You can also close the datasheet by clicking the Close button in the top-right corner of the datasheet.

Chart Type

4 On the Standard toolbar, click the Chart Type down arrow.

The list of chart types appears.

3-D Bar Chart

5 Click the 3-D Bar Chart button (the second button in the second row of the list).

The chart type changes to a 3-D bar chart.

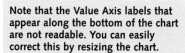

Note that the Value Axis labels that appear along the bottom of the chart are not readable. You can easily correct this by resizing the chart.

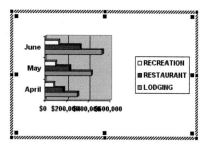

6 On the right border of the chart, drag the middle sizing handle to the right until you can easily read the numbers at the bottom of the chart.

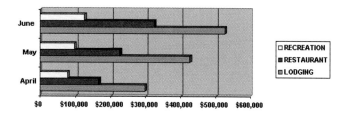

7 Click the gray background of the chart.

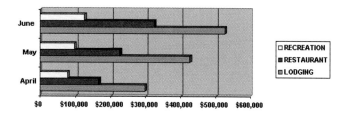

Fill Color

8 Click the Fill Color down arrow.

The Fill Color palette appears.

9 Click the Sea Green square (third row, fourth column).

The background of the chart changes to sea green.

10 Click any of the yellow bars that represent Recreation Revenue on the chart.

All of the yellow bars that represent Recreation Revenue are selected.

11 On the Standard toolbar, click the Fill Color down arrow.

The Fill Color palette appears.

12 Click the Light Green square (bottom row, fourth column).

The series bars for Recreation Revenue change to light green.

13 Save and close the document.

Word saves and closes the document.

tip

You can double-click different areas of the chart to select the part of the chart you want to modify. When you double-click an area of the chart, the Format dialog box, with which you can edit the chart, is displayed. Where you double-click in the chart determines what kind of Format dialog box appears. For example, if you double-click a bar in the chart, the Format Data Series dialog box is displayed with multiple tabs, letting you decide how to modify the bar in the chart. If you double-click the background of the chart, the Format Walls dialog box appears, and you can choose from the Patterns tab to change the background color or modify the chart border.

W2000E.4.4

Importing Data into a Chart

In the previous exercise, you typed data into cells of a datasheet to define a chart. But if the data that you need already exists in a worksheet, you don't need to type the data again. Word makes it easy to add data to a chart by importing existing data from an Excel worksheet. When you **import** existing data into a Word chart, you copy the contents of an Excel worksheet into the Word chart's datasheet.

After you import an Excel worksheet into a chart datasheet, you might find that some numbers don't fit in the cells because they are longer than the space provided for them in the cell. These numbers are represented with number signs (#). To restore the numbers, position the mouse pointer between the column headers until it turns into a double-headed resize pointer and then drag to widen the column.

Copy

Paste

You can also import Word table data into a chart by copying and pasting. Select the data you want to copy from the Word table, and on the Standard toolbar, click the Copy button. Click the cell in the datasheet where you want the top-left cell of the imported data to be displayed, and on the Standard toolbar, click the Paste button to import the data. You can use this same approach to copy a selected range of cells from an Excel worksheet.

In this exercise, you import data from an Excel worksheet into a chart in a Word document. You then add a data table to the chart, resize the chart, change the font size for the data table, and add more horizontal gridlines to the chart.

Open

1   On the Standard toolbar, click the Open button. Navigate to the Lesson04 folder in the Word Expert Practice folder, and double-click the file LMR Revenue_Summer 04.

2   Press Ctrl+End.

The insertion point moves to the end of the document.

3   On the Insert menu, click Object.

The Object dialog box appears, with the Create New tab selected.

4 Scroll down the Object Type list, click Microsoft Graph 2000 Chart, and then click OK.

A sample chart and datasheet appear.

Import File

5 On the Standard toolbar, click the Import File button.

The Import File dialog box appears.

6 Navigate to the Word Expert Practice folder, if necessary, and double-click the LMR Revenue_Summer 04 Excel workbook file.

Word displays the Import Data Options dialog box. The Excel workbook contains three worksheets, so you can use this dialog box to select the worksheet that contains the data you want to import.

Notice that in the Import Data Options dialog box, you can choose to import a range of cells or an entire worksheet. To import a range, first select the worksheet that contains the range in the Select Sheet From Workbook list, click the Range option, type the range in the Range box, and then click OK.

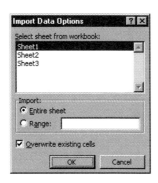

7 Click OK to accept the default worksheet, Sheet 1.

8 The data from the Excel worksheet appears in the datasheet (overwriting the sample data), and the data is displayed as a column chart.

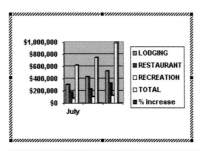

View Datasheet

9 On the Standard toolbar, click the View Datasheet button.

The datasheet is closed.

Data Table

10 On the Standard toolbar, click the Data Table button.

A data table appears in the chart. However, the table is too small and only a portion of its contents fit within the chart.

11   Drag the chart's bottom-right resizing handle down and to the right until the chart area is about twice its original size, as shown below.

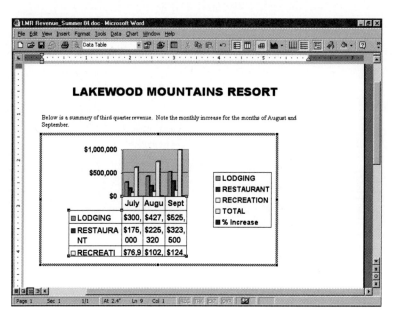

The data table is more readable, but some of the table is still out of view. You can correct this problem by changing the font size for the data table.

12   Double-click anywhere in the data table.

The Format Data Table dialog box appears.

13   If necessary, click the Font tab.

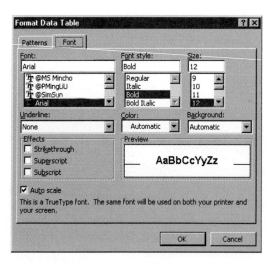

14   Double-click the Size box, type **8**, and then click OK.

The font size changes and all of the data table contents appear within the chart.

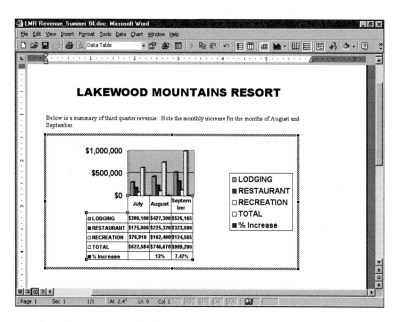

15   On the Chart menu, click Chart Options, and click the Gridlines tab.

The Chart Options dialog box displays options for changing gridlines.

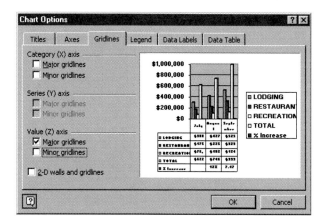

16   In the Value (Z) Axis section, select the Minor Gridlines check box, and click OK.

The chart displays horizontal gridlines at every $100,000 increment, making it easier to understand the values represented by the columns.

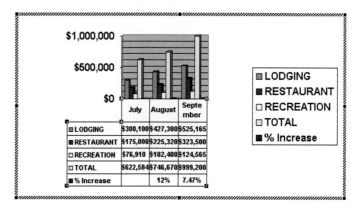

17   On the File menu, click Save As, and save the file as **LMR Revenue_Summer 04 Edited**.

Lesson Wrap-Up

In this lesson, you learned how to create and modify a chart and how to import data into a chart.

If you are continuing to other lessons:

● On the File menu, click Close.
Word closes the file.

If you are not continuing to other lessons:

● On the File menu, click Exit.
Word closes.

Lesson Glossary

axes   Lines that provide a frame of reference or comparison in a chart for plotting points. The vertical, or value, axis is typically called the y-axis. The horizontal, or category, axis is known as the x-axis. In a three dimensional system, the z-axis is used to show depth.

category axis   The horizontal axis used to plot data on a bar, column, or line chart.

cell   The intersection of a row and column on a datasheet where users can enter data. The cell is displayed as a small box on a datasheet.

chart   A graphical representation of data, displayed in pictorial, rather than numeric, form.

columns   Vertical arrangements of a series of text or numbers in a datasheet. For example, a continuous series of cells running top to bottom on a datasheet.

column heading The gray lettered or numbered area at the top of a column in a datasheet.

datasheet A table that contains the data displayed in a chart.

import In a Word chart, to copy the contents of an Excel worksheet or other object into the chart's datasheet.

legend Text that describes or explains the graphic. On a graph or map, the legend is the key to the patterns, colors, or symbols used.

rows Horizontal arrangement of a series of text or numbers in a datasheet. For example, a continuous series of cells running left to right on a datasheet.

row heading The numbered gray area to the left of a row in a datasheet.

series The values in a chart that are represented pictorially as bars, lines, pie slices, or other pictorial representations.

value axis The vertical axis used to plot data on a bar, column, or line chart.

Quick Quiz

1   Why would you want to put information or data into chart format?

2   How do you import an Excel worksheet into a Word chart?

3   How do you modify a chart?

4   What's the name of the object in a datasheet in which you type data for a chart?

5   How can you easily move the insertion point back and forth between cells in a datasheet?

6   How do you insert a chart into a Word document?

important

In the Putting It All Together section below, you must complete Exercise 1 to continue to Exercise 2.

Putting It All Together

Exercise 1: If necessary, start Word. Create a chart to display the second-quarter expenses for the retail stores at Lakewood Mountains Resort. Use the following information:

	April	May	June
Gift Shop	$9,310	$7,940	$8,457
Restaurant	$10,874	$9,986	$10,045
Rentals	$4,000	$3,967	$5,870

Save the document as **LMR Retail Expense**.

Exercise 2: Change the chart that you created in Exercise 1 to a 3-D bar chart. Change the color of the Gift Shop bars to red, change the Restaurant bars to indigo, and change the Rentals bars to light blue. The background of the chart should be green, and the chart area should be orange. Add minor, vertical gridlines to the chart. Save the document.

LESSON 5

Customizing Word

After completing this lesson, you will be able to:

✔ *Move and organize toolbars.*

✔ *Add and remove toolbar buttons.*

✔ *Create a custom toolbar.*

✔ *Customize menus.*

✔ *Customize keyboard shortcuts.*

When you use Microsoft Word 2000, you don't have to be satisfied with the existing settings for displaying toolbars, buttons, and menus. You can easily customize dozens of options so that Word works in the way that *you* want to work. When you start Word, the Standard and Formatting toolbars appear below the menu bar. Word places the Standard and Formatting toolbars on one row to give you a larger work area. However, you can separate the toolbars so that they are on different rows. This customization allows you to see more buttons on each toolbar and gives you room to add other buttons to the toolbars. And of course, you can display additional toolbars when you need them. For example, if you are creating tables in a document, you might want to display the Tables And Borders toolbar so that you can use the buttons on the toolbar rather than having to navigate through the Table menu and its submenus.

You've probably noticed that Word modifies menus as you work. When you first use a menu, Word displays a short version of the menu, which lists the commands that people use most frequently. If you click the arrows that appear at the bottom of a menu, or if you simply display the short menu and wait a few seconds, the full menu appears, showing all available commands for that menu. As you click commands on the full menus, Word recognizes that you will probably want to use these commands again and adds them to the short version of the menus. In this way, the menus become personalized for the way you work. You can turn off personalized menus or reset them to their default settings.

In this lesson, you will learn how to move and resize a toolbar, add buttons to a toolbar, remove buttons from a toolbar, create a custom toolbar, add items to a menu, remove items from a menu, and create a custom menu.

 **Sample files for the lesson**

To complete the procedures in this lesson, you will need to use the practice file Tailspin Ad 05 in the Lesson05 folder in the Word Expert Practice folder located on your hard disk.

W2000E.6.7

Customizing Toolbars and Menus

Toolbars can appear in two ways: floating or docked. A **floating toolbar** is not attached to the top, bottom, left side, or right side of the Word window. You can move a floating toolbar and change its size and shape. A **docked toolbar** is connected to the top, bottom, left side, or right side of the Word window. You can move and resize a docked toolbar, but not as easily as you can move and resize a floating toolbar. The following illustration shows the Formatting toolbar when it is floating.

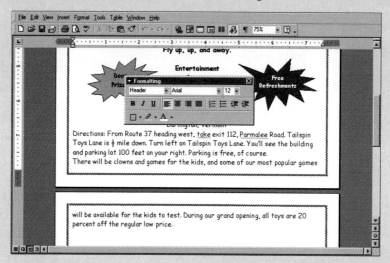

All toolbars can be floating or docked, although they are initially displayed as one or the other. To dock or move a floating toolbar, drag it by its title bar to a different location or to any edge of the Word window. To change a docked toolbar to a floating toolbar, position the mouse pointer over the vertical **move handle** at the left end of the toolbar until the mouse pointer changes to a four-headed arrow (move pointer), and then drag the toolbar to the desired location.

Move handle ———
Move pointer ———

You can also move a floating toolbar by clicking an empty area of the toolbar and dragging the toolbar to the desired location.

Moving and Organizing Toolbars

To change the size of a floating toolbar, position the mouse pointer on any edge of the toolbar and then drag in the desired direction to reduce or enlarge the height or width of the toolbar. To change the length of a docked toolbar, position the pointer on the vertical move handle at the left end of the toolbar until the four-headed move pointer appears, and drag the handle to the left or right until the toolbar is the size that you want it to be.

In the following exercises, the Standard and Formatting toolbars have been separated. For additional information on how to separate the toolbars, see the "Using the CD-ROM" section at the beginning of this book.

You also have control over the way personalized menus appear. Chiefly, if you don't like the way personalized menus add commands as you use them, you can turn off this feature so that the full menus appear when you click the name of a menu on the menu bar. To display full menus, on the Tools menu, click Customize, and click the Options tab. Clear the Menus Show Recently Used Commands First check box, and close the Customize dialog box.

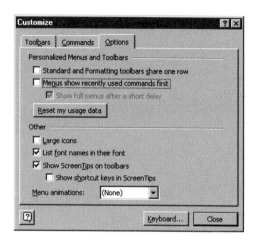

If you want to continue to use the personalized menus but want to return the menus to their original settings (so that they display the same commands as when you first installed and used Word), you can easily do so. Click the Options tab of the Customize dialog box, and click the Reset My Usage Data button.

In this exercise, you resize the Formatting toolbar. Then you change the location of the Formatting toolbar so that it floats in the document. Next you move the toolbar so that it is anchored to the right edge of the Word window, and then you return the Formatting toolbar to its original location. Finally you turn off the display of personalized menus and view the result.

New Blank Document

> You must display at least one document for the Standard and Formatting toolbars to appear in full.

1   If a blank document is not currently displayed, on the Standard toolbar, click the New Blank Document button.

2   If the rulers are not displayed in the Word window, on the View menu, click Ruler.

    The ruler appears on the screen under the Formatting toolbar and on the left side of the screen.

3   Position the mouse pointer on the vertical move handle at the left end of the Formatting toolbar until the four-headed arrow appears.

    The toolbar can now be resized or moved.

> Moving a toolbar to the right is useful if you want to add another toolbar (especially a custom toolbar) to the left of the current toolbar. Moving a toolbar to the left is useful if you want to make room for additional buttons at the right end of the toolbar. Creating custom toolbars and adding toolbar buttons are covered later in this lesson.

4   Drag the move handle to the right about one inch.

    The Formatting toolbar moves one inch to the right.

5 Position the mouse pointer on the vertical move handle at the left end of the Formatting toolbar, and then drag it down about two inches.

The Formatting toolbar floats in the document window.

6 Click the title bar of the floating Formatting toolbar, and drag it to the right edge of the Word window.

The Formatting toolbar is anchored against the right edge of the Word window.

Because the toolbar is docked vertically rather than horizontally, the move handle appears at the top of the toolbar.

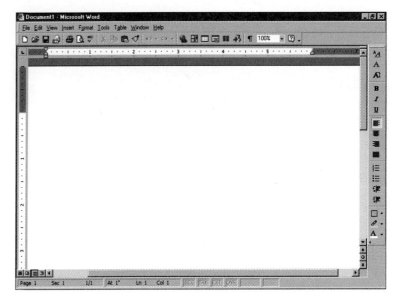

7 Click the move handle at the top of the toolbar, and drag it back to its original location so that the Formatting toolbar once again appears anchored below the Standard toolbar, as shown below.

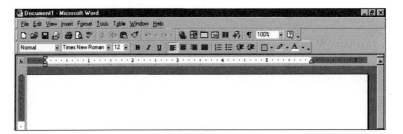

The Formatting toolbar returns to its original location between the Standard toolbar and the horizontal ruler.

8   Click the Format menu.

Word displays the short version of the Format menu.

Your menu might show additional
commands that you or another
person has used recently.

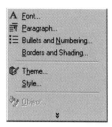

9   On the Tools menu, click Customize, and click the Options tab, if necessary.

10   Clear the Menus Show Recently Used Commands First check box, and click Close.

The personalized menus are turned off, and the dialog box closes.

11   Click the Format menu.

The short menu no longer appears first. Instead, all commands on the Format menu appear when you display this menu.

Adding and Removing Toolbar Buttons

Most toolbars have many buttons that do not appear on the toolbar when it is displayed. You can use these additional buttons to customize the toolbars with buttons for tasks that you perform frequently. For example, if you like to format headings in **small caps** format, you can do so by selecting the text that you want to format, and on the Format menu, clicking Font, and then selecting the Small Caps check box. However, it's much easier to add a toolbar button that automatically formats selected text in the small caps format. That way, changing the format is just one click away.

You can use the small caps format to add professionalism and attractiveness to headings and other text in your documents.

When you use small caps, the uppercase letters are displayed as large capital letters and lowercase letters as small capital letters, as shown below.

LAKEWOOD MOUNTAINS RESORT

You can add buttons to Word toolbars two ways.

To identify a particular button, position the mouse pointer over the button. A yellow ScreenTip appears, telling you the name or function of the button.

- You can click the More Buttons arrow at the right end of a docked toolbar (or click the down arrow in the top-left corner of a floating toolbar).

- You can use the Customize dialog box to add buttons. Right-click anywhere on the menu bar or on a toolbar, and then click Customize to display the Customize dialog box. Click the Commands tab if necessary, and then in the Categories list on thc left side of the dialog box, click the Category for which you want to add a button. In the list of commands on the right side of the dialog box, drag the button or list item from the dialog box onto the desired toolbar at the location where you want it to appear. As you drag, the pointer includes a button icon to indicate that you are adding a button. A black I-beam appears when you have positioned the button at a location on a toolbar where it can be added, as shown on the following page.

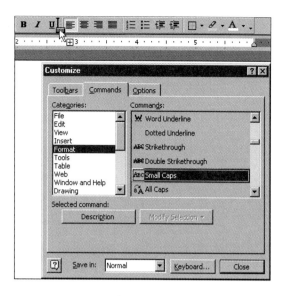

When you use the Customize dialog box to move or remove buttons, you do not have to select a specific tab in the dialog box.

Just as you can add buttons to toolbars, you can remove them from toolbars. Removing toolbar buttons is especially useful if a toolbar contains buttons that you rarely use and you want to use that space to add other buttons. For example, the Standard toolbar contains a button called Document Map, which is useful to view the organization of headings in a long document. However, many people never use this button. You might want to remove this button and replace it with a button that inserts a page break automatically.

Instead of dragging the button off the toolbar, you simply select the button and drag it to the new location. If the Customize dialog box is not open, hold down the Alt key and drag the button to a different location or, to move it, drag the button into the Word window.

You can use the Add/Remove Buttons menu to choose the buttons for a toolbar. To view the Add/Remove buttons menu, click the down arrow at the end of the toolbar, and then click Add/Remove Buttons. Click the name of the button that you want to remove.

You can also use the Customize dialog box to remove a button from a toolbar.

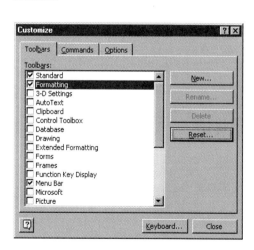

With the Customize dialog box open, you can click a button and drag it off the toolbar.

In this exercise, you remove a button from a toolbar, add buttons to a toolbar, use the new buttons to add formatting to a document, and then reset the toolbar to its default settings.

Open

1   On the Standard toolbar, click the Open button. Navigate to the Lesson05 folder in the Word Expert Pracitce folder, and double-click the Tailspin Ad 05.

2   At the right end of the Standard toolbar, click the More Buttons arrow, and click Add Or Remove Buttons.

A list of buttons appears.

3   In the list of buttons, click Document Map.

The Document Map button no longer appears on the Standard toolbar.

4   Right-click anywhere on the menu bar or a toolbar, and at the bottom of the shortcut menu that appears, click Customize.

The Customize dialog box appears.

> You can also display the Customize dialog box by pointing to Toolbars on the View menu and then clicking Customize, or by clicking Customize on the Tools menu.

5   In the Customize dialog box, click the Commands tab.

The Categories and Commands lists appear.

6   In the Categories list, click Format.

The commands in the Format category appear in the Commands list.

7   Scroll down the Commands list until you can see Small Caps.

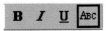

Underline

8   Drag Small Caps from the Commands list and position it on the Formatting toolbar to the right of the Underline button.

The Small Caps button appears on the Formatting toolbar.

9 In the Categories list, click Edit.

The commands in the Edit category appear in the Commands list.

Redo

10 Drag the Repeat button from the Commands list and position it on the Standard toolbar to the right of the Redo button.

The Repeat button appears on the Standard toolbar.

11 In the Customize dialog box, click Close.

The Customize dialog box closes.

12 Scroll down so that you can see the bottom half of the document, and select the lines of text that read *Entertainment, Prizes, Great Food.*

Small Caps

13 On the Formatting toolbar, click the Small Caps button.

The selected text appears in small caps.

14 In the *When* line that follows, select *a.m.*

Repeat

15 On the Standard toolbar, click the Repeat button.

Word repeats the small caps formatting for the selected text.

16 Right-click anywhere on the menu bar or on a toolbar, and at the bottom of the shortcut menu that appears, click Customize.

The Customize dialog box appears.

> When you click the name of a toolbar, make sure to keep the check box selected if you want the toolbar to remain displayed. Just select the name of the toolbar, not the check box to the left of the name.

17 Click the Toolbars tab, and in the list of toolbars, make sure that Standard is selected.

18 Click the Reset button, and click OK.

A dialog box appears, and you must click OK to verify that you want to reset the toolbar.

The Standard toolbar is reset to its default setting. The Document Map button reappears on the toolbar, and the Repeat button no longer appears.

> Notice that the document doesn't change, even though you pulled the button down onto the document.

19 On the Formatting toolbar, drag the Small Caps button off the toolbar and onto the document.

The Small Caps button no longer appears on the Formatting toolbar.

Leave the Customize dialog box open for the next exercise.

Creating a Custom Toolbar

Although modifying an existing toolbar is the quickest way to make a toolbar more efficient, Word also allows you to create a new toolbar from scratch. If you are using commands from many different toolbars, you might want to create your own custom toolbar that has all the buttons you need in one place so you don't have to open various toolbars and search for buttons.

For example, if you are working on a long document that contains several pictures and drawing objects, you might want to build your own custom toolbar that contains buttons for creating page breaks, creating column breaks, wrapping text around pictures and objects, and creating or changing fill colors of objects. If you place all of these buttons on one custom toolbar, they will all be in a convenient, central location. You won't have to move from toolbar to toolbar, nor will you need to use menus for such commands as page breaks and column breaks.

In this exercise, you create a custom toolbar, use the custom toolbar to add formatting to a document, and then delete the custom toolbar.

1   On the Toolbars tab in the Customize dialog box, click the New button to display the New Toolbar dialog box.

2   In the Toolbar Name box, type **Flyer**.

3   Verify that the Make Toolbar Available To box displays Normal or Normal.dot, and click OK.

If you click the Make Toolbar Available To down arrow and select a document (or the title of the document you are currently using), the toolbar you create will only be available when you open this document.

An empty floating toolbar is displayed next to the Customize dialog box.

4   In the Customize dialog box, click the Commands tab.

The Categories and Commands lists appear in the dialog box.

5   In the Categories list, click Insert.

The Insert commands appear in the list of commands.

6   In the Commands list, drag Page Break onto the Flyer toolbar.

The Page Break button appears on the Flyer toolbar.

7   In the Commands list, drag Insert Column Break to the right of the Page Break button on the Flyer toolbar.

The Insert Column Break button appears on the Flyer toolbar.

8   In the Categories list, click Format.

The Format commands appear in the list of commands.

Drop Cap refers to a large capital letter at the beginning of a text block that occupies the vertical depth of two or more lines of regular text.

9 In the Commands list, scroll down until you can see Drop Cap, and drag Drop Cap to the right of the Column Break button on the Flyer toolbar.

The Drop Cap button appears on the Flyer toolbar.

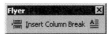

10 In the Customize dialog box, click Close.

The Customize dialog box closes.

11 Near the bottom of the document, click to the left of the word *Directions*.

Page Break

12 On the Flyer toolbar, click the Page Break button.

Word inserts a page break at the location of the insertion point.

Columns

13 Select all the text on page 2, and on the Standard toolbar, click the Columns button. On the Columns menu, click the second column.

Word formats the second page in two-column format.

14 Click at the start of the line that begins *There will be clowns*, and on the Flyer toolbar, click Insert Column Break.

Word inserts a column break at the location of the insertion point.

15 At the start of the second page, select the letter *D* in *Directions*.

Drop Cap

16 On the Flyer toolbar, click Drop Cap.

Word displays the Drop Cap dialog box.

17 In the Position section of the dialog box, click Dropped, and click OK.

Word formats the letter *D* as a drop cap.

18 Click anywhere outside the drop cap to deselect it.

The second page of your document should look similar to the following illustration.

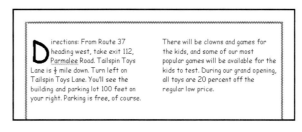

19   Right-click anywhere on the Flyer toolbar, and click Customize on the shortcut menu.

The Customize dialog box appears.

20   Click the Toolbars tab.

21   In the Toolbars list, scroll down, and select the word Flyer, and click the Delete button.

An alert box appears, asking if you are sure that you want to delete the toolbar.

22   Click OK to confirm the deletion.

The Flyer toolbar is deleted.

Keep the Customize dialog box open for the next exercise.

> You can also delete a custom menu by opening the Customize dialog box, selecting the Custom menu, and then dragging the menu onto the document.

Customizing Menus

You can also use Word to modify menus to suit your needs. You can add or delete commands on an existing menu, or create a custom menu from scratch. You create a custom menu in essentially the same way that you create a custom toolbar. That is, you use the Customize dialog box to create a new menu, name the custom menu, and then add commands to it as desired.

> You can delete only menus that you create; you cannot delete menus that come with Word.

When you no longer need a custom menu, you can delete it. To delete the custom menu, open the Customize dialog box, right-click the custom menu that you want to delete, and then click Delete on the shortcut menu.

In this exercise, you add and delete menu commands and create a custom menu.

1   In the Customize dialog box, click the Commands tab.

The Categories and Commands lists appear.

2   In the Categories list, click Web.

The Web commands are displayed in the Commands list.

> To pick a new button image for a menu command, open the Customize dialog box, click the menu bar that contains the command with the image that you want to change, right-click the command, and then click Change Button Image on the shortcut menu. A list of button images will appear. You can click a new button image from this list.

3 In the Commands list, drag Start Page to the word *Insert* on the menu bar, and then position the command above the Break command on the menu, as shown below.

If the Customize dialog box is in your way, you can move it by dragging the title bar.

4 In the Customize dialog box, click Close.

The Customize dialog box closes.

5 On the menu bar, click Insert.

The Insert menu should look similar to the following illustration.

As you saw when you added buttons to a toolbar, a black I-beam shows you where an item will be inserted on a menu.

You can also remove a menu by holding down the Alt key and dragging the menu into the Word window.

6 Right-click the menu bar or a toolbar, and click Customize.

The Customize dialog box appears.

7 On the menu bar, click Insert, and drag the Start Page command from the Insert menu onto the document.

The Start Page command is removed from the Insert menu.

Notice once again that the document does not change, even though the command was dragged onto the document.

8 On the menu bar, click Insert.

The Insert menu closes.

9 In the Customize dialog box, make sure that the Commands tab is selected, and in the Categories list, scroll to the bottom, and click New Menu.

New Menu appears in the Commands list.

> If you want to reset a menu back to its original default settings, open the Customize dialog box, on the menu bar, right-click the menu that you want to reset, and then click Reset on the shortcut menu.

10   Drag New Menu from the Commands list to the end of the menu bar.

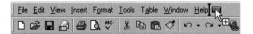

The menu option, New Menu, appears at the end of the menu bar.

11   On the menu bar, right-click New Menu, and on the shortcut menu, in the Name box, select the text *New Menu*, type **Custom,** and then press Enter.

The shortcut menu is closed, and the menu is renamed.

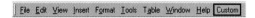

12   On the menu bar, click Custom.

A blank menu appears under the Custom menu.

13   In the Categories list, scroll up, and click View.

The View commands appear in the Commands list.

> If the Custom menu disappears as you drag, hover the mouse pointer over the word Custom on the menu bar for a moment until the menu reappears.

14   In the Commands list, scroll down, and drag Zoom 100% onto the empty menu on the Custom menu.

The Zoom 100% command appears on the Custom menu.

15   In the Commands list, drag Fit To Window onto the Custom menu, below the Zoom 100% command.

The Fit To Window command appears on the Custom menu.

16   In the Commands list, scroll down, and drag Comments to the Custom menu, below the Zoom 100% and Fit To Window commands.

Keep the Customize dialog box open for the next exercise.

Customizing Keyboard Shortcuts

Word also allows you to customize keyboard shortcuts. A **keyboard shortcut** is one or more keys that you press on the keyboard to complete a task. For example, instead of clicking the Bold button on the Formatting toolbar, you can press Ctrl+B to make selected text bold. You might want to customize a keyboard shortcut for a command that doesn't already have a keyboard shortcut or if you find that an existing keyboard shortcut is awkward. For example, pressing Ctrl+B can be a bit of a reach for users who have small hands or who have arthritis. Some users might want to assign Ctrl+Alt+X as the keys for making text bold because this is an easy key combination to press on the keyboard. To create or modify a keyboard shortcut for a command, display the Customize dialog box, and click the Keyboard button. The Customize Keyboard dialog box will appear, which you can use to type the keyboard shortcut for a particular command.

You might want to assign a keyboard shortcut for a style that you use frequently so that you don't have to display the Style list and select the style name each time that you want to apply the style. To apply a keyboard shortcut to a style, display the Customize dialog box, and click the Keyboard button. In the Customize Keyboard dialog box that appears, scroll down through the Categories list until you see the Styles category. Click this category, and click the name of the style to which you want to apply a keyboard shortcut. You can use this technique to select other categories and the desired command within the selected category.

In this exercise, you customize a keyboard shortcut for the Close File command, which does not have a shortcut key by default.

1   In the Customize dialog box, click the Keyboard button.

     The Customize Keyboard dialog box appears.

When you create a keyboard shortcut, you can save the shortcut in the Normal template and use the keyboard shortcut in all your documents. If you only want to use the keyboard shortcut in the current document, in the Customize Keyboard dialog box, in the Save Changes In box, click the current document name. You can learn more about the Normal Template in Lesson 3, "Using Templates and Wizards," in the Microsoft Word 2000 Step by Step Courseware Core Skills Student Guide.

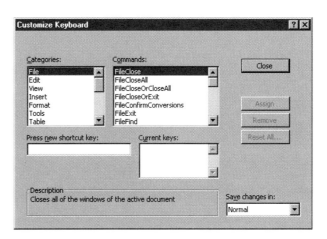

2   Verify that File is selected in the Categories list and that FileClose is selected in the Commands list.

3   Click in the Press New Shortcut Key box.

4   With the insertion point in the Press New Shortcut Key box, press Alt+C.

If the keyboard shortcut already exists, Word will alert you with a message below the Press New Shortcut Key box. Notice that the keyboard shortcut is unassigned.

5   Click the Assign button.

The shortcut key combination is assigned to the command.

6   Click the Close button.

The Customize Keyboard dialog box closes.

7   In the Customize dialog box, click Close.

The Customize dialog box closes.

8   Save the document as **Tailspin Ad 05 Edited** in the Lesson05 folder.

9   Press Alt+C.

The keyboard shortcut that you assigned closes the current document.

10   Right-click the menu bar or a toolbar, and click Customize.

The Customize dialog box appears.

11   Click the Keyboard button.

The Customize Keyboard dialog box appears.

12   In the Customize Keyboard dialog box, make sure that the following are selected: *File*, *FileClose*, and *Alt+C*.

13   Click the Remove button.

The shortcut key combination is deleted.

14   Click Close.

The Customize Keyboard dialog box closes.

15   In the Customize dialog box, click Close.

The Customize dialog box closes.

tip

You can also use Word to modify a **ScreenTip** (the tip that appears when you rest the mouse pointer on a button). You can modify toolbar ScreenTips to include shortcut key combinations in addition to the name or function. In the Customize dialog box, click the Options tab, and select the Show Shortcut Keys In ScreenTips check box. After you select the check box and close the dialog box, when you move the mouse pointer over the button, the ScreenTip appears with the name of the button and the keyboard shortcut. This approach is useful to help remind you of a particular keyboard shortcut.

You'll learn more about macros in Lesson 7, "Using Macros."

Modify Command Settings

After you've made changes to toolbars or menus, you might want to modify the command settings. For example, you might want to add certain items, such as macros and fonts that do not have ready-made buttons, to the toolbar. Word makes changing command settings easy.

To create a custom button, in the Customize dialog box, click the Commands tab, and click the desired category in the Categories list. Drag a command from the Commands list to the desired toolbar. If you want to modify the new button, such as changing the button's default icon, right-click the button on its toolbar to display the shortcut menu, or click the Modify Selection button in the Customize dialog box, and either click Edit Button Image or point to Change Button Image, and then click the desired icon.

You can also modify command settings on a menu. If you add commands to a ready-made menu, for example, you might want to change the name of the menu. To change the name of a menu, open the Customize dialog box, and on the menu bar, right-click the menu that you want to change to display the shortcut menu. On the shortcut menu, type the new name in the Name box, and press Enter.

You can also change the way commands appear on a menu. To modify commands on a menu, open the Customize dialog box, and click the menu that contains the command that you want to change. Right-click the menu command, and click the option that you want on the shortcut menu.

Lesson Wrap-Up

This lesson covered how to modify and customize toolbars, menus, keyboard shortcuts, and command settings.

If you are continuing to other lessons:

1   Right-click the menu bar or a toolbar, and click Customize.

   The Customize dialog box appears.

2   On the menu bar, click the Custom menu, and drag the menu off the menu bar and onto the work area.

   The menu is removed form the menu bar.

If you are not continuing to other lessons:

1   Right-click the menu bar or a toolbar, and click Customize.

   The Customize dialog box appears.

2   On the menu bar, click the Custom menu, and drag the menu off the menu bar and onto the work area.

   The menu is removed form the menu bar.

3   On the File menu, click Exit.

   Word closes.

Lesson Glossary

docked toolbar A toolbar that is attached to any side of the Word window.

floating toolbar A toolbar that is not attached to a side of the Word window.

keyboard shortcut A combination of one or more keys that you press on the keyboard to complete a task.

move handle The vertical bar at the left end of a docked toolbar. The move handle can be used to move a toolbar to the left or right on its current row, to a different location within the document window (as a floating toolbar), or to a different side of the Word window.

ScreenTip A help item that briefly explains what an element is. ScreenTips appear when the mouse pointer is held over a button or screen element for a few seconds.

small caps A formatting style in which uppercase letters are displayed as large capital letters and lowercase letters are displayed as small capital letters.

Quick Quiz

1   Identify the two ways that toolbars can be positioned.

2   What is a quick way to display the Toolbars menu?

3   Why might you want to customize a menu?

4   How can you add a new button to a toolbar?

5   How do you change a docked toolbar to a floating toolbar?

6   How do you customize keyboard shortcuts?

7   How do you resize or move a docked toolbar to a different position on its current row?

8   How do you dock a floating toolbar?

Putting It All Together

Exercise 1: Create a toolbar named **Practice** that includes the following commands and menu items, from left to right:

New E-Mail Message, New Blank Document, Cut, Paste, Hide Spelling Errors, Insert Table, Check Box, Format menu. Dock the toolbar along the left side of the Word window, and then delete the toolbar.

Exercise 2: Create a menu named **Practice 02** at the left end of the Standard toolbar that includes the following commands, beginning at the top of the menu.

In the Categories list, click Insert to find the Page Number and Time commands. Use the Web category to find the Start Page and Search The Web commands, and use the Borders category to find the Borders And Shading command. Then delete the menu.

Merging Documents for Mailing

After completing this lesson, you will be able to:

✔ *Understand mail merge.*

✔ *Create a main document.*

✔ *Create a data source.*

✔ *Add merge fields and merge documents.*

✔ *Sort data records.*

✔ *Filter records.*

✔ *Merge documents with a different data source.*

✔ *Generate mailing labels.*

You'll often find that you need to send a document that you created in Microsoft Word 2000 to multiple recipients. If the document is a letter to your clients or to prospective customers, you'll want to include each customer's name and address near the top of the first page of the letter, along with a personalized greeting line. If you're sending the letter to only three or four customers, it's easy enough to create the original letter, save it, and then save additional copies of the letter so that each copy contains the personalized address and greeting.

If you want to send the letter to more than a few people, manually entering the address and personalized greeting on separate copies of the letter doesn't take advantage of Word's capabilities. With Word, you can type a form letter or other document that you want to send to a group of recipients and then **merge** (combine) the letter with a list of addresses or other personalized information for each recipient.

Instead of creating a separate copy of each letter on your hard disk (which can waste hard disk space if you send the document to hundreds or thousands of recipients), Word saves the merge information (names and addresses) for all the recipients in a separate database. Then when you're ready to print a copy of the document for each recipient, Word merges the address information into each document at the time of printing. Of course, you can preview the way Word will merge the document during printing to make sure that you get the format that you want. After you create the address information once and store it in a database that Word can use, you can merge this same information into other printed letters or even into mailing labels and envelopes.

In this lesson, you will learn how to create a main document, create a data source, add merge fields to a main document, sort and **filter** data source records prior to merging, and then merge a main document with a data source to create printed form letters.

Sample files for the lesson

To complete the procedures in this lesson, you will need to use the practice files LMR Letter 06 and LMR Teacher Database 06 in the Lesson06 folder in the Word Expert Practice folder located on your hard disk. You'll use these files to merge documents for mailing.

Understanding Mail Merge

Because you'll usually merge address and other personalized information into printed documents that can be mailed to recipients, the procedure for performing these steps in Word is called **mail merge**. The mail merge process involves two files: the **main document** and the **data source**.

> A field is a location in a document that can automatically update information. A field is generated by a code that is specific to the field. You can learn more about fields in Lesson 1, "Using Advanced Paragraph Formatting."

A main document is a file that contains text that does not change, such as the body of a form letter. The main document also contains **fields** called **merge fields**, which are text entries that are not printed but indicate where Word should insert personalized information. In a main document, merge fields appear surrounded by double arrows (or "chevron" merge characters) to help distinguish them from the body of the document (such as the content of a letter). For instance, suppose that you type the following merge fields at the top of a main document (a form letter).

```
<<FirstName>> <<LastName>>
<<Company>>
<<Address1>>
<<Address2>>
<<City>>, <<State>> <<Zip>>
```

Word can then use these merge fields to insert the appropriate personalized text in the format you specify, as shown below.

> Amy Isaacson
> Lakewood Mountains Resort
> 1501 Bryant's Gap Trail
> Room 104
> Erewhon, CA 84501

The data source file contains personalized text that will change on each printed copy of the letter. In this example, the names and addresses near the top of each letter change on each letter. When you create a data source, you assign a name to each field. This field name matches a merge field in the main document. For example, the field name *FirstName* in the data source matches the <<FirstName>> merge field in the main document. By matching the field name in a data source with a merge field that appears in a main document, Word inserts personalized information at specified locations in the merged document. All the fields—such as a name, building, address, city, state, postal code, or phone number—for a particular address form a **record**.

You can insert merge fields at multiple locations within a document, and not just at the address line. For instance, suppose that the beginning of your form letter contains the following merge fields and text.

October 21, 2000

<<FirstName>> <<LastName>>
<<Company>>
<<Address1>>
<<Address2>>
<<City>>, <<State>> <<Zip>>

Dear <<FirstName>>,

I would like to invite you to the grand opening of the Emerald Wing at Lakewood Mountains Resort.

Notice that the <<FirstName>> merge field appears at two different locations in the main document.

Each copy of the printed document would be similar to the following; however, each copy would contain unique personalized information.

October 21, 2000

Amy Isaacson
Lakewood Mountains Resort
1501 Bryant's Gap Trail
Room 104
Erewhon, CA 84501

Dear Amy,

I would like to invite you to the grand opening of the Emerald Wing at Lakewood Mountains Resort.

W2000E.5.1

Creating a Main Document

You must create a main document before you can create a data source file—unless the data source comes from a pre-existing external file or database, which you will learn about later in this lesson. You can create four different kinds of main documents with Word's mail merge feature: form letters, mailing labels, envelopes, and **catalogs**. A catalog is any document that contains recurring fields, such as an inventory parts list.

You could create a main document that contains fields for part number, part description, and quantity. You could then merge the main document (the catalog) with a data source that contains a list of part numbers, descriptions, and stock-on-hand-quantities. You would then have an inventory list that tells you the parts and quantities for materials that you have in stock.

In the following exercises, the Standard and Formatting toolbars have been separated. For additional information on how to separate the toolbars, see the "Using the CD-ROM" section at the beginning of this book.

The form letter is the most common type of main document used with mail merge. The body of the letter is the same for each recipient, but personalized information, such as names and addresses, change based on the contents of the data source file. You can create a form letter by using a previously created letter and entering field codes into it, or by creating a new main document.

To create a new document, on the Tools menu, click Mail Merge. In the Mail Merge Helper dialog box, in the Main Document section, click the Create button. Choose the type of document you want to create. An alert box appears, asking if you want to use the open document (the active window) as the main document or create a new one. You can create a new document by clicking New Document in the alert box, and then in the Mail Merge Helper dialog box, clicking Edit to edit the new document.

At Lakewood Mountains Resort, the marketing manager wrote a letter to the members of Science Teachers of America. The teachers were at the resort for a three-day retreat, and now the marketing manager wants to follow up with them. She wrote a letter that she wants to send to each teacher, all of whom work at different schools.

In this exercise, you create a main document that can be used to send follow-up information to the teachers.

Open

1   On the Standard toolbar, click the Open button. Navigate to the Lesson06 folder in the Word Practice folder, and double-click the file LMR Letter 06.

2   On the Tools menu, click Mail Merge.

The Mail Merge Helper dialog box appears.

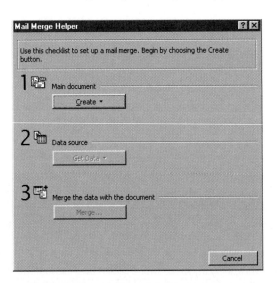

If you change your mind and don't want the document to be a mail merge main document, in the Mail Merge Helper dialog box, in the Main Document section, click Create. Select Restore To Normal Word Document, and in the alert box, click Yes. Your document is once again a normal document.

3   In the Mail Merge Helper dialog box, in the Main Document section, click the Create button.

The Create list appears.

4   In the Create list, click Form Letters.

An alert box appears, asking if you want to use the open document (the active window) as the main document, or create a new one.

5   In the alert box, click the Active Window button.

The Mail Merge Helper dialog box appears, and in the Data Source Section, the Get Data button appears.

Leave the dialog box open for the next exercise.

W2000E.5.2

You can use the Create Data Source dialog box to choose the fields that you want to include for each record in your data source file.

Creating a Data Source

After you create the main document, the letter is almost ready to be merged. But first you need to create a database of names and addresses. The database is referred to as the *data source*. The data is stored in rows in a table format, with each row containing a complete record and each column containing a field. The first row in the table is called the *header row*, and each column begins with a header that is a field name. When you create a data source, the Create Data Source dialog box displays one record at a time. You use this dialog box to add each record to the data source file.

After you have created your data source and you save the file, an alert box appears, asking if you want to add data to the database or add merge fields to the main document. You can click the Edit Data Source button to add data to the database, or click the Edit Main Document button to add merge fields to the main document. If the main document is already created, you can click the Edit Data Source button to type the data to be merged. If your letter isn't created yet, you can click the Edit Main Document button to type the letter.

In this exercise, you use the Mail Merge Helper to create a data source file.

1   In the Mail Merge Helper dialog box, in the Data Source section, click the Get Data button.

    The Get Data list appears.

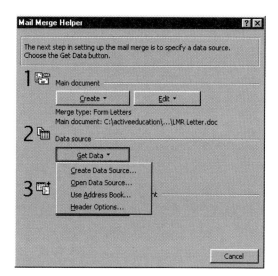

2   In the Get Data list, click Create Data Source.

The Create Data Source dialog box appears.

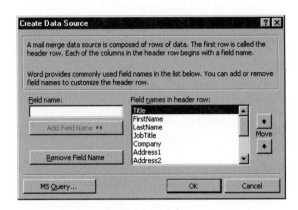

3   In the Field Names In Header Row list, make sure that Title is selected, and click the Remove Field Name button.

The Title field name is removed.

4   In the Field Names In Header Row list, click JobTitle, and click the Remove Field Name button.

The JobTitle field name is removed.

5   Using the same steps, remove the following field names: Company, Address2, Country, HomePhone, and WorkPhone.

The field names are removed.

After you add a new field, you can press Enter instead of clicking the Add Field Name button each time.

6   To add the field name School, in the Field Name box, type **School**, and click the Add Field Name button.

School is added at the bottom of the Field Name list.

If you want to use more than one word to describe a field, make sure that you do not use a space between the words. Word does not accept spaces in field names. You can combine words (capitalizing each word to distinguish them) or use an underscore (_) to separate the words—for example, *StreetAddress* or *Street_Address*.

7   To move School to below the LastName field, make sure that School is selected, and click the up arrow button in the Move section to the right of the Field Names In Header Row list. Click the up arrow repeatedly until the School field is positioned below the LastName field.

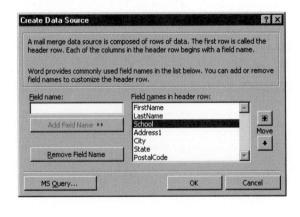

8   In the Create Data Source dialog box, click OK.

The Save As dialog box appears.

9   In the File Name box, type **LMR Database 06**, and click the Save button.

An alert box appears, asking if you want to add data to your database, or add merge fields to your main document.

10   In the alert box, click the Edit Data Source button.

The Data Form dialog box appears, as shown below.

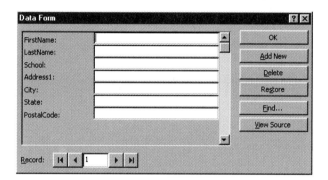

11   Type **Jon** in the FirstName box, and press Enter.

12   Type **Grande** in the LastName box, and press Enter.

13   Type **Thomas Jefferson Junior High School** in the School box, and press Enter.

14   Type **9876 Thomas Jefferson Pkwy.** in the Address1 box, and press Enter.

15   Type **Glendale** in the City box, and press Enter.

16   Type **AZ** in the State box, and press Enter.

17   Type **84337** in the PostalCode box.

18   Click the Add New button, or press Enter to display a new blank record.

19   Add the following records to the database.

Anne Paper
Millsburg Senior High School
456 South Rd.
Millsburg CT 80004

John Rodman
West Junior/Senior High School
5678 Ford Ave.
Cambridge KY 90210

(There are more records to enter on the next page.)

You can double-check your entries to verify spelling and correct addresses by clicking the View Source button in the Data Form dialog box to display all data source records in a table format. Changes you make in the table will be reflected in the data source. To return to the data form, on the Mail Merge toolbar, click the Data Form button.

Data Form

Sherri Hart
Georgetown Elementary School
1234 Nugget Ave.
Georgetown CO 84590

Anas Abbar
Tucker Junior High School
7899 38th St.
Tucker IL 50025

Diane Tibbott
East High School
91011 W. Pearl Ave.
San Diego CA 68144

Sean Alexander
Glory High School
987 Main St.
Leadville CO 87540

After you have finished entering your records, and before you click OK, you can scroll back and forth to check the records by using the Record buttons at the bottom of the Data Form dialog box.

Record

20   Click OK in the Data Form dialog box.

The data source is created and the Data Form dialog box closes.

Keep this file open for the next exercise.

W2000E.5.4

Adding Merge Fields and Merging Documents

Merging documents, the final step in the mail merge process, prepares the main document to be printed. Merging adds merge information to the main document so that data source records will be printed in the desired merge manner. You use the Mail Merge toolbar to insert merge fields and merge the information.

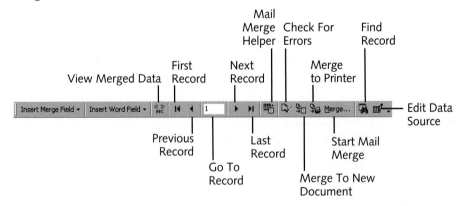

As part of this process, you must type merge fields at the desired locations within the main document. The merge fields tell Word where to insert fields from the data source file into the main document when copies of the main document are merged and printed.

You are almost ready to merge the form letters for the Lakewood Mountains Resort marketing manager.

In this exercise, you insert merge fields into the LMR Letter 06 document and merge the document with a database to prepare the letters for printing and mailing.

Show/Hide ¶

Notice that the Mail Merge toolbar appears below the Formatting toolbar.

1   On the Standard toolbar, click the Show/Hide ¶ button.

Formatting marks are shown throughout the document.

2   Click the third blank line below the *Lakewood Mountains Resort* heading, and on the Mail Merge toolbar, click the Insert Merge Field button.

A list of field names is shown.

> Insert Merge Field ▼
>
>   FirstName
>   LastName
>   School
>   Address1
>   City
>   State
>   PostalCode

3   In the list of field names, click FirstName.

The FirstName merge field is inserted into the document. Notice that the merge field has the same font size, style, and color of the text in the body of the letter.

4   Press the Spacebar once, click the Insert Merge Field button to display the list of field names, and then click LastName.

The LastName merge field is inserted into the document.

5   Press Enter to position the insertion point at the beginning of the next line.

6   Click the Insert Merge Field button to display the list of field names, click School, and then press Enter.

The School merge field is inserted into the document.

7   Using the same procedure as the one described in the above steps, insert the following merge fields into the third and fourth lines of the address block. Observe the comma and space following the City merge field, and add two spaces following the State merge field.

<<Address1>> <<City>>, <<State>> <<PostalCode>>

8   Click to the right of the word *Dear*, and press the Spacebar once.

9   Click the Insert Merge Field button to display the list of field names, and click FirstName.

The FirstName merge field is inserted into the document.

To make letters less formal, you can omit the LastName field from the salutation line.

10   Press the Spacebar once, click the Insert Merge Field button to display the list of field names, and then click LastName.

The Last Name merge field is inserted into the document.

11   Type a comma after the LastName field.

Check For Errors

12   On the Mail Merge toolbar, click the Check For Errors button to review the document before merging.

The Checking And Reporting Errors dialog box appears.

13   In the Checking And Reporting Errors dialog box, click the Simulate The Merge And Report Errors In A New Document option, and click OK.

An alert box is displayed, indicating that no errors were found.

14   In the alert box, click OK.

The alert box closes.

View Merged Data

15   On the Mail Merge toolbar, click the View Merged Data button.

The document appears with the information from the first record (Jon Grande).

Next Record

16   On the Mail Merge toolbar, click the Next Record button.

The document is displayed with the information from the second record (Anne Paper).

> Now that the merge fields are inserted in the letter, you are ready to merge the documents.

17   On the Mail Merge toolbar, click the View Merged Data button.

The main document file is displayed with the merge fields.

18   Save the file as **LMR Letter 06 Edited**.

Merge To New Document

19   On the Mail Merge toolbar, click the Merge To New Document button.

The files are merged, and the first record (Jon Grande) is displayed in a new document window. Scroll through the document to see the seven customized letters.

×
Close

20   Save the new file as **LMR Teacher Letters**, and in the top-right corner of the Word window, click the Close button.

Word saves and closes the document.

Keep the file LMR Letter 06 Edited open for the next exercise.

W2000E.5.3

Sorting Data Records

After you create a data source, you can organize the data in the same data source in several ways. For example, when you create a large mailing of form letters, it might be helpful if you sort all records by last name or by postal code. In fact, the U.S. Postal Service requires that envelopes in a **bulk mail** shipment be sorted in ZIP code order. Bulk mail is generally at least 250 pieces of mail that have identical information in each letter and envelope.

Sorting data records alphabetically is also helpful. For example, when the marketing manager writes an internal employee letter directed at all employees, she can personalize the letter by adding the employee's name. She alphabetizes the data records by last name so that she can save time when she files them in the employee mail slots, because the mail slots are also alphabetized by last name.

In this exercise, you sort the LMR database in ascending alphabetical order.

Mail Merge Helper

1   On the Mail Merge toolbar, click the Mail Merge Helper button.

The Mail Merge Helper dialog box appears.

2   In the Mail Merge dialog box, in the Merge The Data With The Document section, click the Query Options button.

The Query Options dialog box appears.

3   In the Query Options dialog box, click the Sort Records tab.

4   Click the Sort By down arrow, and click LastName.

Notice that all fields in your database are displayed in the Sort By list.

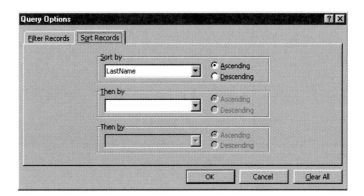

5   In the Query Options dialog box, verify that Ascending is selected to sort the records from A to Z, and click OK.

The Mail Merge Helper dialog box appears.

6   In the Merge The Data With The Document section, click Merge.

The Merge dialog box appears.

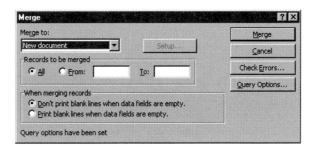

7   In the Merge dialog box, click Merge.

The records are merged to a new document and the multiple letters in the new document appear in alphabetical order by last name. Scroll through and close the document without saving changes.

Show Hide ¶

8   On the Standard toolbar, click the Show/Hide ¶ button.

The formatting marks are no longer displayed in the document.

Keep the file LMR Letter 06 Edited open for the next exercise.

Filtering Records

One of the more useful features of mail merge is the ability to use a database (data source) for a variety of different projects. You may want to use only part of a data source. Mail merge makes it easy to do this.

For example, suppose that your employer wants you to send a brochure to everyone who has used services provided by your company in a specific postal code range. Records in your company's database have hundreds, if not thousands, of postal codes, but you don't have to create a new database for your brochure. Instead, you can find the specific addresses that you need by sorting through the entire database and using the addresses of people who fall into your specific postal code range.

You don't have to create a new database with the selected records; you can simply filter out the records you don't want. For instance, the marketing manager at Lakewood Mountains Resort decided to send her form letter only to teachers from Colorado. She can sort and filter data records by the State field (CO) so that only the records for Colorado teachers are merged in the letters.

To filter data, in the Mail Merge Helper dialog box, click the Query Options button, and click the Filter tab. When you click the Field down arrow, a list of fields that you created is shown. When you click the desired field, the insertion point moves to the Compare To box. In the Compare To box, type the specific name, address, postal code, and so on that you want to sort. The merge will compare all data in the chosen fields and merge only those records that match the **query** rule.

A query is the process of extracting specified data from a database and presenting it for use.

You can further detail your search with the Comparison down arrow. When you click the Comparison down arrow, a list of search options appears. Suppose that you had a database of thousands of people from across the nation, but you only want to send information to certain people. For example, in the Field list, you might click LastName, in the Comparison list, select Equal To, and in the Compare To box, type Smith. Letters will only be sent to people whose last name is Smith. If you chose Not Equal To, letters would be sent to all last names except Smith. Less Than would send the letters to names starting with A–Smith. Greater Than sends the letters to last names that start Smith–Z. Less Than Or Equal To sends letters A–Smith. Greater Than Or Equal To sends letters Smith–Z.

You can use the Comparison lists for numbers as well as alphabetical listings.

If Is Blank is selected in the Comparison section, letters that don't have the field will be selected. Is Not Blank shows all the documents with the field. For example, if some of the addresses in your database use the title field, and a few don't, you can use Is Blank to select all the names that don't use the title field. Or you can use Is Not Blank to select all the names with the title field.

In this exercise, you merge records of teachers who are from Colorado.

Mail Merge Helper

1 On the Mail Merge toolbar, click the Mail Merge Helper button.

   The Mail Merge Helper dialog box appears.

2 In the Mail Merge Helper dialog box, in the Merge The Data With Document section, click the Query Options button. If necessary, click the Filter Records tab.

   The Filter Records tab of the Query Options dialog box appears.

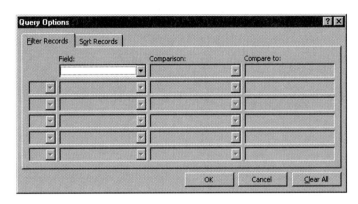

3 Click the Field down arrow, scroll down, and click State.

   Equal To is selected in the Comparison list, and the insertion point moves to the Compare To box.

4 In the Compare To box, type **CO**, and click OK.

   The merge will compare all data in the State field to CO, and merge only those records that match the query rule. The Mail Merge Helper dialog box reappears.

5 In the Mail Merge Helper dialog box, and in the Merge The Data With The Document section, click Merge.

   The Merge dialog box appears.

Only two of the seven records are used because only two of the teachers are from Colorado.

6 In the Merge dialog box, click the Merge button.

   The files are merged, and the merged information is sent to a new document file.

7 Scroll through the records, and close the document without saving it.

   Keep the file LMR Letter 06 Edited open for the next exercise.

Close

W2000E.5.6

Merging Documents with a Different Data Source

At this point in the lesson, you've merged documents with a data source created in Word. But what if you or somebody else in your organization has already created a database in a different application? Word can accommodate this situation. Specifically, Word's mail merge feature lets you merge a main document with data sources from many different types of applications, such as Microsoft Access, Microsoft Excel, Microsoft FoxPro, or the Address Book from Microsoft Outlook or Microsoft Outlook Express. You use the Mail Merge Helper dialog box to perform the merge. The precise steps to follow will vary slightly depending on the source of the data.

For example, suppose that the marketing manager at Lakewood Mountains Resort already created an Excel worksheet with the names and addresses of the teachers who participated in the science retreat. The marketing manager can merge the Excel worksheet with a letter created in Word to generate a personalized letter for the teachers who came to the retreat.

In this exercise, you merge the file LMR Letter 06 with a list created in Excel.

Open

1   On the Standard toolbar, click the Open button. If necessary, navigate to the Lesson06 folder in the Word Expert Practice folder, and double-click the file LMR Letter 06.

2   On the Tools menu, click Mail Merge.

    The Mail Merge Helper dialog box appears.

3   In the Mail Merge Helper dialog box, in the Main Document section, click the Create button, and click Form Letters.

    An alert box appears, asking if you want to use the open document (the active window) as the main document or create a new document.

4   Click the Active Window button in the alert box.

5   In the Data Source section, click the Get Data button, and click Open Data Source.

    The Open Data Source dialog box appears.

6   In the Open Data Source dialog box, click the Files Of Type down arrow, and click MS Excel Worksheets.

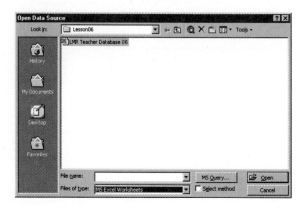

You can specify a range of cells in the dialog box, such as A1:C5, to display only information in the cells A1 through C5. For this lesson, you'll need the entire worksheet. You can find more information about worksheets in Lesson 1, "Learning Worksheet Fundamentals," in the Microsoft Excel 2000 Courseware Core Skills Student Guide.

While Word processes the information from the data source, you might have to wait a few moments for the alert box to appear.

Notice that the field names are the column headers from the Microsoft Excel worksheet.

7   Navigate to the Lesson06 folder, and double-click the file LMR Teacher Database 06.

The file opens, and a Microsoft Excel dialog box appears, asking if you want to insert the entire spreadsheet.

8   Click OK.

An alert box appears, explaining that there are no merge fields in the main document.

9   In the alert box, click the Edit Main Document button.

LMR Letter 06 appears, along with the Mail Merge toolbar.

10   Click three lines below the Lakewood Mountains Resort header, and on the Mail Merge toolbar, click the Insert Merge Field button to display the list of field names.

11   In the list of field names, click Name, and press Enter.

The Name merge field is inserted, and the insertion point appears at the beginning of the line below the first inserted field name.

12   Click the Insert Merge Field button to display the list of field names, click School, and then press Enter.

The School merge field appears, and the insertion point is positioned at the beginning of the next line.

13   Click the Insert Merge Field button, click Street_Address, and press Enter.

The Street_Address merge field is displayed, and the insertion point is positioned at the beginning of the next line.

14   Click the Insert Merge Field button, and click City_State_Zip_Code in the list of field names.

The City_State_Zip_Code merge field is inserted in the document.

15   Click after the word *Dear*, and press the Spacebar once.

16   Click the Insert Merge Field button, and click *Name*.

The Name merge field is inserted in the document.

17   Type a comma after the Name field.

Merge To New Document

18   On the Mail Merge toolbar, click the Merge To New Document button.

The documents are now merged, and the first record (Anas Abbar) appears in a new document window. Scroll through the document to see the seven customized letters.

Close

19   Save the new file as **LMR Teacher Letters Updated**, and in the top-right corner of the Word window, click the Close button.

Word closes the document.

Keep the file LMR Letter 06 open for the next exercise.

W2000E.5.5

Generating Mailing Labels

If you've already created a data source, you can use it to print mailing labels as well as to create form letters or other mail merge documents. Avery and other label and stationery companies provide sheets of mailing labels that you can insert into your printer to create mailing labels. By using a data source to print mailing labels, you can avoid typing addresses on separate envelopes. The process for creating mailing labels is similar to the mail merge process, except that you don't have to create a main document.

To create mailing labels, in the Mail Merge Helper dialog box, click Create, and click Mailing Labels. In the alert box, click Active Window, and in the Data Source section, click the Get Data button. Navigate to your data source, and select the data. Another alert box appears with the Set Up Main Document button. You click this button to specify the mailing label format. When you click the button, the Label Options dialog box appears and lets you choose the size and format of your labels. After the label size is selected, Word generates the labels in what looks like a table on your screen. The lines in the table do not print, but they represent the dimensions of the labels that will be printed.

In this exercise, you create mailing labels with the Excel workbook called LMR Teacher Database 06.

New Blank Document

1   On the Standard toolbar, click the New Blank Document button.

A new, blank document window appears.

2   On the Tools menu, click Mail Merge.

The Mail Merge Helper dialog box appears.

3   In the Mail Merge Helper dialog box, in the Main Document section, click Create.

The Create list appears.

4   In the Create list, click Mailing Labels.

An alert box appears, prompting you to choose a place for the main document.

5   In the Alert box, click Active Window.

If you want to merge from your Outlook Address Book, in step 6, click Use Address Book instead of Open Data Source.

6   In the Mail Merge Helper dialog box, in the Data Source section, click the Get Data button, and click Open Data Source in the list.

The Open Data Source dialog box appears.

7   Click the File Type down arrow, and click MS Excel Worksheets (*.xls). Navigate to the Lesson06 folder, and double-click LMR Teacher Database 06.

The Microsoft Excel dialog box appears.

8   In the Microsoft Excel dialog box, click OK to select the entire worksheet.

An alert box appears.

9   In the alert box, click the Set Up Main Document button.

The Label Options dialog box appears so that you can specify the mailing label format.

10   In the Label Options dialog box, scroll down the Product Number list, and click *8460 – Address*.

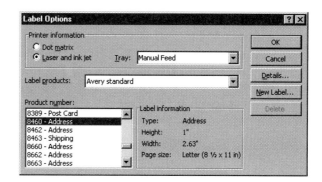

11   Click OK.

The Create Labels dialog box appears.

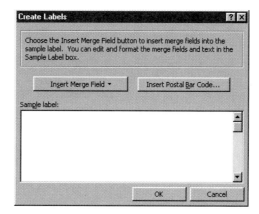

12   In the Create Labels dialog box, click the Insert Merge Field button.

The list of field names appears.

13   Click Name in the list, and press Enter.

The Name merge field is inserted into the sample label, and the insertion point is positioned at the beginning of the next line in the address block.

14   Click the Insert Merge Field button to display the list of field names, click *School*, and then press Enter.

The School merge field is inserted into the sample label.

15   Repeat the procedure for inserting merge fields to add the third and fourth lines of the address block.

16   When you are finished entering merge fields, click OK.

The Mail Merge Helper dialog box reappears.

17   In the Merge The Data With The Document section, click Merge.

The Merge dialog box appears.

18   In the Merge dialog box, click the Merge button.

The mailing labels appear in a new document.

Anas Abbar Tucker Junior High School 7899 38th Street Tucker, IL 50025	Jon Grande Thomas Jefferson High School 9876 Thomas Jefferson Pkwy Glendale, AZ 84337	Anne Paper Millsburg Senior High School 456 South Rd. Millsburg, Ct. 80004
John Rodman West Junior/Senior High School 5678 Ford Ave. Cambridge, KY 90210	Diane Tibbott East High School 91011 W. Pearl Ave. San Diego, CA 68144	Sherri Hart Georgetown Elementary School 1234 Nugget Ave. Georgetown, CO 84590
Sean Alexander Glory High School 987 Main St. Leadville, CO 87450		

A bar code is a special identification code printed as a set of vertical bars with various widths. The postal code is represented by the bar code and is scanned by the Post Office to sort mail faster.

tip

You can also add a **bar code** to the label by selecting the Delivery Point Barcode check box in the Labels tab of the Envelopes And Labels dialog box.

19   On the File menu, click Close to close the document. If you are prompted to save changes, click No.

Word closes the document without saving the changes.

Lesson Wrap-Up

In this lesson, you learned how to merge documents for mailing, how to sort and filter data in a data source, how to merge a document with a data source created in an application other than Word, and how to create mailing labels from a mailing list.

If you are continuing to other lessons:

● On the File menu, click Close to close any open documents. If you are prompted to save the changes, click No.
Word closes the document without saving the changes.

If you are not continuing to other lessons:

● On the File menu, click Exit. If you are prompted to save changes, click No.
Word closes.

Lesson Glossary

bar code A special identification code printed as a set of vertical bars with various widths. The postal code on mailing labels can be represented by a bar code, which is scanned by the Post Office to sort mail faster.

bulk mail A mailing of at least 250 pieces that contain identical information. Bulk mail must be sorted in ZIP code order.

catalog Any document that contains recurring fields that are suitable for a merge, such as an inventory parts list.

data source A file that contains personalized text, such as a database of names and addresses, that will change on each printed copy of the letter. With Word's mail merge feature, you can use one data source for many different main documents.

fields In a data source, single items of information, such as a first name, a last name, or a street address.

filter Criteria applied to a data source so that only those records that match the criteria appear in the list.

mail merge A feature in Word that allows you to create a document, such as a form letter, and customize each printed version of the document—typically by inserting personalized information from a list, database, or other data source.

main document A file that contains text that does not change, such as the body of a form letter. The main document also contains merge fields, which are text entries that are not printed but indicate where Word should insert personalized information.

merge The combining of two or more items, such as lists, in an ordered way without changing the structure of each item.

merge fields Text entries that are not printed, but indicate where Word should insert personalized information.

query The process of extricating specified data from a database and presenting it for use in a document.

record A set of related information in a data source. For example, all the information about one recipient on a mailing list is a record.

Quick Quiz

1   If you want to use mail merge with a document you have already created, what do you need to do to begin the process?

2   How do you create a data source in mail merge?

3   What is a main document?

4   When would you click Open Data Source in the Get Data list?

5   How do you begin the process of sorting data in a data source?

6   The mail merge process uses two files. What are they?

important

In the Putting It All Together section below, you must complete Exercise 1 to continue to Exercise 2.

Putting It All Together

Exercise 1: Use Mail Merge to personalize the LMR Letter 06 in the Lesson06 folder for five of your friends and associates.

Exercise 2: Sort the mailing list from Exercise 1 by ZIP code.

LESSON 7

Using Macros

After completing this lesson, you will be able to:

✔ *Record a macro.*

✔ *Assign a macro.*

✔ *Run a macro.*

✔ *Edit a macro.*

✔ *Copy a macro.*

✔ *Rename a macro.*

✔ *Delete a macro.*

The marketing manager at Lakewood Mountains Resort is feeling overwhelmed with work. Her two assistants are on vacation, so she has to handle all interdepartmental correspondence, as well as respond to clients. She's creating three newsletters for the next three months. Although the newsletters are for different months, they contain much of the same information, and she's feeling the strain of having to enter the information repeatedly. Fortunately Microsoft Word 2000 provides a way to avoid this extra work.

With Word, she can create a **macro** to reduce keyboard steps. A macro is a series of commands and instructions that are performed collectively as a single command. For example, the marketing manager sends mailings to people on the resort's mailing list about once per week. Instead of having to perform each step to create a main document and open a data source, she can create a macro to save time and reduce the steps that are involved to perform a task. All the marketing manager has to do is click the macro. She performs this single step, and Word takes care of the rest.

> When you record a macro, Word displays a Stop Recording toolbar, which you can use to temporarily pause or stop macro recording.

Macros can be used to automate a variety of tasks, such as specifying page layout formats, applying special formatting characteristics to text, defining columns, and setting up tables. To create a macro easily, you **record** a sequence of keystrokes and mouse clicks. Word also includes a scaled-down version of Microsoft **Visual Basic**, which you can use to edit macros that you've created. Visual Basic is a programming language that can be used with Word and other Microsoft Office applications to help customize the way you work.

In this lesson, you will learn how to record a macro, assign the macro to a toolbar, run the macro in a Word document, edit and copy the macro, rename the macro, and delete the macro you created.

 **Sample files for the lesson**

To complete the procedures in this lesson, you will need to use the practice file LMR Promotion Memo 07 in the Lesson07 folder in the Word Expert Practice folder on your hard disk.

W2000E.6.2

In the following exercises, the Standard and Formatting toolbars have been separated. For additional information on how to separate the toolbars, see the "Using the CD-ROM" section at the beginning of this book.

Recording a Macro

When you record a macro, Word starts a utility that converts your keystrokes and mouse clicks into Visual Basic commands. A version of Visual Basic, called **Visual Basic for Applications (VBA)** comes with Word. All the macros that you create are stored as a **module,** or a collection of program code, within a Visual Basic **project.** A project is a Visual Basic program that can be stored in a Word document or template. The term *module* is specific to Visual Basic. Within Word, a macro module is called a **macro project item**. If you create multiple macros for a document or template, all the macros are stored collectively within a single macro project item.

The important point to keep in mind is that a macro is not a separate file. It is a block of Visual Basic programming code stored as part of a macro project item. The project item, in turn, is stored in a Visual Basic project, which is stored in a Word document or template. The following diagram illustrates the way that three macros (named Macro1, Macro2, and Macro3) might be stored.

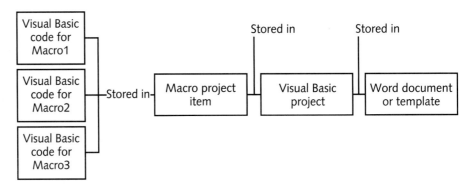

If the document that is active when you record the macro is based on the **Normal template,** the Visual Basic project and the macros (collectively, the macro project item) contained within it are stored in the Normal template (Normal.dot) file. The Normal template is a collection of page, paragraph, and character formats that you regularly use when you create or edit a document. Although you can create or use other templates for documents, Word uses the Normal template by default. So when you start Word or click the New Blank Document button, Word creates a new, blank document based on the Normal template. For this reason, the Normal template is called a **global template** because all the styles, macros, and other formatting stored in the template are available to all documents that use the Normal template.

If the active document is based on another template, you can store the macro in that template, in which case it will be available only to documents that are based on that template. You can also save a macro so that it is available only to the current document.

Before you record a macro, it's a good idea to write down the sequence of operations and the commands and actions that the macro will perform. By writing down the steps that you want the macro to perform, you won't omit any step during the recording and consequently will reduce the chance that you will have to re-record or edit the macro.

You can take your time when you record the macro. The speed at which you perform each step isn't related to the speed at which the macro runs. Instead, Word performs the steps at the full speed of your computer's CPU when you run the macro.

Word does not record the movement of the mouse pointer within a document window, so you should use the keyboard to select text and to move the insertion point. You can, however, use the mouse to select menu commands, to click toolbar buttons, and to scroll through the document window while you are recording a macro.

You usually create a macro to save time and reduce the steps that you must complete to perform a task. As a result, you'll usually want to assign a macro to a toolbar, menu, or shortcut key so that the macro can be executed quickly.

At Lakewood Mountains Resort, the human resources manager is working on a memo to the resort's accountant to notify the accountant about title and salary changes for different employees. The human resources manager wants to insert tables into the memo, but she wants to create a macro to automate table insertion.

In this exercise, you create a macro that inserts a table in a document.

Open

1   On the Standard toolbar, click the Open button. Navigate to the Lesson07 folder in the Word Expert Practice folder, and double-click the file LMR Promotion Memo 07.

2   Click the blank line below the *Wait Staff* heading, and on the Tools menu, point to Macro, and then click Record New Macro.

    The Record Macro dialog box appears.

A macro name cannot include spaces and cannot be longer than 32 characters. You can also type a brief description of the macro in the Description box.

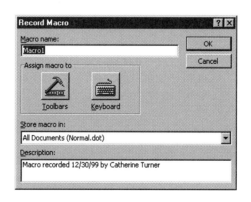

3   In the Record Macro dialog box, in the Macro Name box, type **Table**, and click OK.

    The mouse pointer now includes a cassette tape icon, and the Stop Recording toolbar appears in the document window. The cassette icon indicates that the macro is being recorded. Word will record all your keystrokes and mouse clicks from this point forward until you click the Stop Recording button on the Stop Recording toolbar.

In the Record Macro dialog box, in the Store Macro In box, notice that the macro will be stored globally because All Documents (Normal.dot) appears by default. You can select other ways to store the macro by clicking the Store Macro down arrow and clicking another option. For example, you could store the macro in the Elegant Memo template, or you could store the macro so that it is available only in the current document.

Tables And Borders

4   On the Standard toolbar, click the Tables And Borders button.

The Tables And Borders toolbar appears.

Insert Table

5   On the Tables And Borders Toolbar, click the Insert Table button.

The Insert Table dialog box appears.

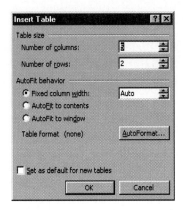

6   In the Insert Table dialog box, type **5** in the Number Of Columns box, type **2** in the Number Of Rows box, and click OK.

A five-column-by-two-row table appears below the Wait Staff heading.

7   Hold down the Shift key, press the Down arrow key, and then press the Right arrow key four times.

Word selects the entire table.

Shading Color

8   On the Tables And Borders toolbar, click the Shading Color down arrow.

A color palette appears.

9 Click the Blue-Gray square (fifth row, seventh square).

The table is colored blue-gray.

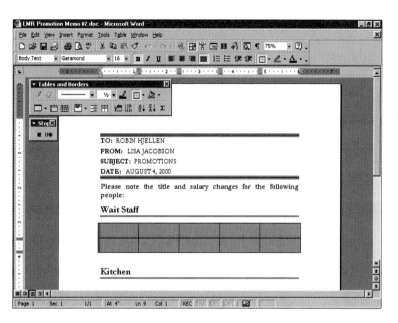

Remember: You use the arrow keys on the keyboard instead of the mouse because mouse movements in a document cannot be recorded in a macro.

10 Press the Up arrow key once, and press the Down arrow key.

Word deselects the table and positions the insertion point in the first cell.

11 In the first cell, type **Name**, and press Tab.

The insertion point moves to the second cell in the first row.

12 In the second cell, type **Old Title**, and press Tab.

The insertion point moves to the third cell in the first row.

13 Type **New Title**, and press Tab.

The insertion point moves to the fourth cell in the first row.

14 Type **Old Salary**, and press Tab.

The insertion point moves to the fifth cell.

15 Type **New Salary**, press and hold the Shift key, and then press the Left arrow key fourteen times until the first row is entirely selected.

Word selects all cells in the first row.

Drawing

16 On the Standard toolbar, click the Drawing button.

The Drawing toolbar appears.

17 On the Drawing toolbar, click the Font Color down arrow, and select the Light Turquoise square (fifth row, fifth color).

Move the Tables And Borders toolbar and the Drawing toolbar if they are in your way.

The font color for the first row of text changes to light turquoise.

Stop Recording

18 On the Macro toolbar, click the Stop Recording button.

The Macro toolbar disappears, and the cassette recorder icon no longer appears as part of the mouse pointer.

Close

19 Click anywhere outside the table to deselect it, and in the top-right corners of the Drawing and Tables And Borders toolbars, click the Close buttons.

Keep this file open for the next exercise.

Below is the list of steps used to create this macro:

- Click the Tables And Borders button.
- Click the Insert Table button.
- Type **5**.
- Type **2**.
- Click OK.
- Hold down the Shift key.
- Press the down arrow key.
- Press the right arrow key four times.
- Click the Shading Color down arrow.
- Click the Blue-Gray square.
- Press the up arrow key once.
- Press the down arrow key once.
- Type **Name**.
- Press Tab.
- Type **Old Title**.
- Press Tab.
- Type **New Title**.
- Press Tab.
- Type **Old Salary**.
- Type **New Salary**.
- Press Tab.
- Press and hold the Shift key.
- Press the left arrow key 14 times.
- Click the Drawing button.
- Click the Font Color down arrow.
- Click the Light Turquoise square.

Assigning a Macro

The human resources manager uses the macro she made to help her create a main document and open a data source at least twice a day. By creating the macro, she saves herself time and reduces the steps that must be completed to create a main document and open a data source. She currently runs the macro from the Record Macro dialog box, but accessing the dialog box is time consuming. Instead, she can assign the macro to a toolbar of her choice, like the Standard toolbar, which she always has open in the Word window.

You can assign a macro to a toolbar or menu before or after you record the macro. If you aren't sure how you want to assign your macro, you can create it first and assign it to a toolbar or menu later.

If you want to assign the macro to a keyboard shortcut, you can do so before or after you record the macro. To assign a macro to a keyboard shortcut before you record the macro, in the Record Macro dialog box, click the Keyboard button, and then type a key combination. To assign a macro to a keyboard shortcut, after you've recorded the macro, on the Tools menu, click Customize. Click the Commands tab, scroll down through the Categories list, click Macros, and then click the Keyboard button. In the Categories list, click Macros. In the Macros list on the right, click the name of the macro. Click in the Press New Shortcut Key box, and press the key combination that you want to use.

In this exercise, you assign the Table macro to the Standard toolbar.

> An example of a key combination is Ctrl+B. By pressing these two keys, you can apply the Bold attribute to selected text.

1   On the Tools menu, click Customize.

The Customize dialog box appears.

2   In the Customize dialog box, click the Commands tab, if necessary.

3   In the Categories list, scroll down, and click Macros.

Available macros appear in the Commands list on the right.

4   In the Commands list, click Normal.NewMacros.Table.

> Depending on the programs installed in your computer, your list of commands might differ from the illustration.

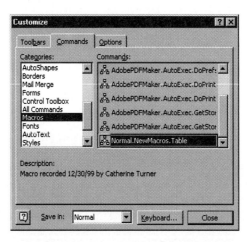

Tables and Borders

5   Drag the command to the Standard toolbar, and position the command to the left of the Tables And Borders button.

The macro button appears on the Standard toolbar to the left of the Tables And Borders button.

6   In the Customize dialog box, click Close.

The Customize dialog box closes.

Keep this file open for the next exercise.

W2000E.6.2

Running a Macro

Now that you have created your macro and assigned it to a toolbar button, you are ready to run it. To run a macro, position the insertion point at the location in your document where you want to run the macro. Then simply click the macro name on the toolbar or menu that you assigned it to, or press the key combination (if you assigned the macro to a keyboard shortcut). You won't see the actual steps involved in creating the macro; you'll see just the result.

In this exercise, you run the Table macro.

1 Click the blank line below the *Kitchen* heading.

2 On the Standard toolbar, click the macro button that you just created.

The same table is inserted. Notice that the text is selected in the first row.

Your document should look similar to the following illustration.

Be sure you click the line below the Kitchen heading, and not the line containing the Kitchen heading. If you are unsure where to place the insertion point, on the Standard toolbar, click the Show/Hide ¶ button to display the formatting marks. Place the insertion point before the paragraph mark in the blank line under the *Kitchen* heading.

Show/Hide ¶

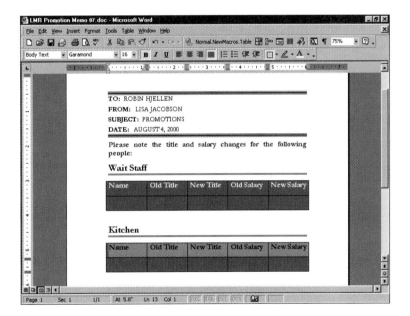

3 Save the document as **LMR Promotion Memo 07 Edited**.

Keep this file open for the next exercise.

tip

To run a macro from the Macros dialog box, position the insertion point where you want the result of the macro to be displayed. On the Tools menu, point to Macro, and then click Macros. In the Macros dialog box, click the macro name in the Macro Name box, and then click the Run button (or double-click the macro name).

W2000E.6.2

Editing a Macro

If you run a macro and then discover that the macro doesn't do exactly what you want, you can always re-record it, however; if a macro contains several steps, re-recording the macro can be time consuming and error prone. Since a macro is stored in the document or template as part of a Visual Basic project, you can use the **Visual Basic Editor** to make minor changes to the macro. For example, the Lakewood Mountains Resort human resources manager isn't completely satisfied with the Table macro because it doesn't deselect the text in the first row of the table. She wants to edit the macro so that the text is deselected.

> Students are introduced to a simple Visual Basic instruction in the following exercise. A detailed discussion of the Visual Basic programming language is beyond the scope of this course.

To start the Visual Basic Editor, point to Macro on the Tools menu, and click Macros. In the Macros dialog box that appears, click the name of the macro that you want to change, and then click the Edit button. When you display a macro in the Visual Basic Editor, you'll see several programming language commands that will probably be unfamiliar to you. It isn't necessary to know Visual Basic to edit a macro. If you know the steps that you used to record a macro, you can use the Visual Basic editor to identify clues that will help you understand which commands perform which steps in the macro. You can then modify a Visual Basic program command by changing one or a few words within the command.

For example, suppose that you see this command in the Visual Basic Editor:

```
Selection.MoveRight Unit:=wdCharacter, Count:=9,
Extend:=wdExtend
```

Although this command might not be immediately understandable to you, it will begin to make more sense if you know what steps were used when the macro was recorded. In this case, one of the macro steps selected a block of text nine characters long. If you run the macro and discover that you really want the macro to select a block of text 12 characters long, you can edit this Visual Basic command to change *Count:=9* to *Count:=12*. The macro will then run as you intended it to.

Consider another example. Suppose that your macro includes the following Visual Basic command:

```
Selection.Font.Bold = wdToggle
```

Let's say you realize that, when you recorded the macro, you clicked the Bold button on the Standard toolbar when you meant to click the Italic button. You can edit this command to read as follows:

```
Selection.Font.Italic = wdToggle
```

As you become more familiar with commands that appear in the Visual Basic Editor and what the commands do, you can often edit a macro by adding your own commands to the macro module.

In this exercise, you edit the Table macro to deselect text as the last macro step.

1   On the Tools menu, point to Macro, and click Macros.

The Macros dialog box appears.

2   In the list of macros in the Macros dialog box, click Table, and click the Edit button.

The macro instructions are displayed in the Visual Basic Editor window.

> Notice that the Project and Properties windows also appear on the screen.

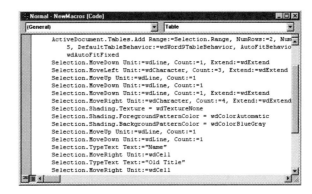

3   In the Visual Basic Editor window, use the Down arrow key to move the insertion point to the end of the code, and click to the left of the text *End Sub*.

> Notice that after you type *Selection.*, a list of commands appears. You can scroll through the list and select the MoveRight command, or you can continue typing.

4   Type **Selection.MoveRight**.

5   Press Enter.

Verify that *End Sub* is still displayed at the end of the code.

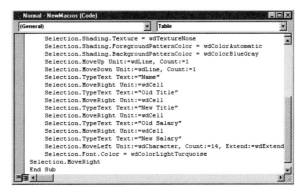

The instruction is inserted. The new instruction will move the insertion point to the right when you run the macro, and in the process, deselect the text.

> Notice the results of the edits that you made in the Visual Basic Editor window; the first row in the table is no longer selected.

6   On the File menu, click Close And Return To Microsoft Word.

The Visual Basic Editor closes, and the macro is saved with the change. LMR Promotion Memo 07 Edited is the active window.

7   Click the first blank line below the Customer Service heading.

8   On the Standard toolbar, click the macro button.

Word inserts the table and deselects the text in the first row.

X
Close

9   Save and close the document.

W2000E.6.3

Copying Macros

If you create a document using a template other than Normal.dot, any macros that you create and save to the Normal template will not be available in the new document because it uses a different template. For example, suppose that you use the Elegant Memo template to create a memo. You then realize, as you create the memo, that you want to use a macro that you created and saved as part of the Normal template. You don't have to re-record the macro to do this; instead, you can copy the macro to the memo document. This approach is especially useful if you've created several macros and want to copy them to a different template or document.

When you create one or more macros for the Normal template, Visual Basic stores them as a macro project item. You can't copy individual macros, but you can copy a macro project item. When you copy a macro project item, all the macros within the macro project item are copied to a specified document or template.

Here's another important reason why you might want to copy a macro project item. The Table macro that you created earlier in this lesson is stored in the NewMacros macro project item in *your* Normal template. However, NewMacros isn't stored in anybody else's Normal template. Suppose that you want to send the LMR Promotion Memo 07 to other people, and you want them to be able to use the Table macro that you created. Because the macro isn't stored in the LMR Promotion Memo 07 document, you would need to copy NewMacros from your Normal template to the LMR Promotion Memo 07 document. When you send this document to other people, they will be able to use the Table macro and any other macros that might be stored in the NewMacros project item.

In this exercise, you copy the NewMacros macro project item to your original document, LMR Promotion Memo 07, so that other people who don't have access to your Normal template can use the Table macro that you've created.

> The default name for a macro project item is *New Macros*.

Open

1   On the Standard toolbar, click the Open button. Navigate to the Lesson07 folder in the Word Expert Practice folder, and double-click the file LMR Promotion Memo 07.

2   On the Tools menu, point to Macro, and click Macros.

The Macros dialog box appears.

3 Click the Organizer button.

The Organizer dialog box appears.

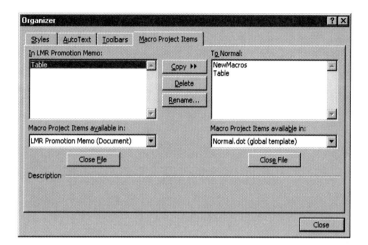

If you want to copy a macro project
item to a different file or template,
click the Close File button under the
current target file or template, click
the Open button (and then click All
Files, if desired, in the Files Of Type
list) and navigate to and double-click
the name of the document or
template that you want to copy a
macro to.

4 Verify that the Macro Project Items tab is selected.

The macro projects items available in the Normal template appear in
the list on the right.

5 In the list on the right, verify that NewMacros is selected, and click
the Copy button.

The NewMacro macro project item is copied to the LMR Promotion
Memo 07 document and appears in the list on the left.

6 Click the Close button.

7 Save the document with the name **LMR Promotion Memo 07
Updated**, and close the document.

tip
You can also copy the macro project to the template that this document uses
by clicking the Macro Project Items Available In down arrow on the left,
clicking Elegant Memo, clicking the Macro Project Items Available In down
arrow on the right, selecting the Normal template, in the To Normal list on
the right, selecting NewMacros, and then clicking the Copy button.

W2000E.6.3

Renaming a Macro

When you assign a macro to a toolbar or a menu, the name for the toolbar button or menu command contains the complete name of the macro. The macro name begins with the name of the template or document that the macro is stored in, the name of the macro project item, and the name of the macro itself. For example, now that you have assigned the Table macro to the Standard toolbar, the toolbar button contains the following name.

```
Normal.NewMacros.Table
```

Normal is the name of the template where the macro project item is stored, *NewMacros* is the name of the macro project item, and *Table* is the name of the macro. This button label is quite lengthy and occupies more space on the toolbar than it needs to. You can easily change the name of the macro button so that it is shorter and more descriptive. To do so, right-click any toolbar, and then on the shortcut menu that appears, click Customize to display the Customize dialog box. Right-click the macro button on the toolbar (or on the menu if you added the macro to a menu rather than to a toolbar), and then type a new name in the Name box.

Renaming a macro toolbar button or a macro menu command does not change the name of the macro itself; it changes only the name on the button or menu. However, there will be times when you want to change the name of a macro. For instance, suppose that you decide to record additional macros that create tables of different dimensions. You recognize that the name of your current macro, *Table*, will not be very descriptive when you view a list of macros after creating the other table macros. So you might decide to change the name of the macro to *Table5x2* to better describe what the macro does.

To rename a macro, you must use the Visual Basic Editor. To display the Visual Basic Editor, point to Macro on the Tools menu, and click Macros. Click the name of the macro that you want to rename, and click Edit. Each macro within the macro project item begins with the Visual Basic keyword *Sub*. Locate the Sub command that starts the macro that you want to rename. Select the name of the macro, type a different name, save the macro project, and then return to the Word document.

For example, the name of your Table macro will appear this way in the Visual Basic Editor:

```
Sub Table()
```

Remember that a macro name cannot contain spaces.

To change the name of the macro, select the word *Table*, type *Table5x2*, and on the File menu in the Visual Basic Editor, click Close And Return to Word.

You can also change the name of a macro project item (rather than the name of an individual macro). You might want to do this to make the macro project name more descriptive. To rename a macro project item, point to Macro on the Tools menu, and click Macros. Click the Organizer button, and click the Macro Project Items tab, if necessary. In the list on the right, click the macro project item that you want to rename, and then click the Rename button. In the Rename dialog box that appears, type the new name for the macro project, and click OK.

In this exercise, you rename the Table macro, and then you rename the macro project item in the LMR Promotion Memo 07 Edited document. Finally you change the name of the macro button on the Standard toolbar.

Open

1   On the Standard toolbar, click the Open button. Navigate to the Lesson07 folder in the Word Expert Practice folder, and double-click the file LMR Promotion Memo 07 Edited.

On the Tools menu, point to Macro, and click Macros.

2   The Macros dialog box appears.

3   In the list of macros, click Table, and click the Edit button.

The Visual Basic Editor appears and displays all macros stored in the NewMacros project.

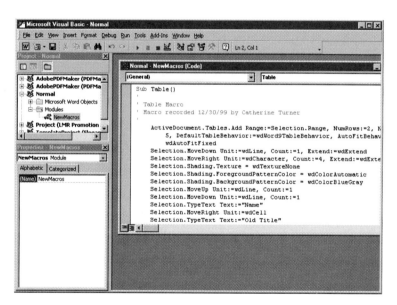

4   At the top of the Visual Basic Editor, locate the line *Sub Table( )*, and select the word *Table*.

5   Type **Table5x2**, and on the File menu, click Close And Return To Word.

The Visual Basic Editor closes.

6   On the Tools menu, point to Macro, and click Macros.

The Macros dialog box appears.

Notice that *Table* no longer appears in the list of macros, but the new macro name, *Table5x2*, does appear in the list.

7   Click the Organizer button.

The Organizer dialog box appears.

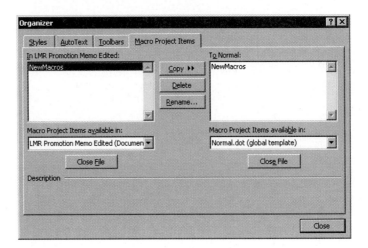

8   In the list on the left, click NewMacros, if necessary, and click the Rename button.

The Rename dialog box appears.

If you change the name of a macro project item, any macro buttons or menu items that open a macro within that macro project item will no longer work. At this point, the Normal.NewMacros.Table button on your Standard toolbar still works because you renamed the macro project item in the LMR Promotion Memo 07 Edited document, not the macro project item stored in the Normal template.

9   Type TableMacros, and click OK.

The new name for the macro project appears in the Macros dialog box.

10   In the Macros dialog box, click Close.

The Macros dialog box closes.

11   Right-click anywhere on the menu bar or on a toolbar, and click Customize.

The Customize dialog box appears.

12   On the Standard toolbar, right-click the Normal.NewMacros.Table button.

Word displays a menu that allows you to customize the button.

13 On the menu, select the contents of the Name box, type **Table5x2**, and then press Enter.

The menu closes, and the new name appears on the toolbar.

14 In the Customize dialog box, click Close.

The Customize dialog box closes.

15 Save the document.

Keep this file open for the next exercise.

W2000E.6.3

Deleting a Macro

Although you cannot copy or rename individual macros, you can delete them. You might want to delete a macro if it doesn't work correctly and you've decided to re-record it, or if you don't plan to use the macro again. After you delete a macro, you will also need to delete its toolbar button or menu command if you created one. You can delete a macro from the Normal template or from a different template, and you can delete a macro that's stored in a document.

In this exercise, you delete the Table macro from the Normal template and delete its button from the Standard toolbar.

1 On the Tools menu, point to Macro, and click Macros.

The Macros dialog box appears.

2 In the Macros In box, make sure that Normal.dot (Global Template) appears.

3 In the Macros dialog box, click Table5x2, and click the Delete button.

An alert box appears, asking if you want to delete the macro.

4 In the alert box, click Yes.

5 In the Macro dialog box, click the Close button.

The Macro dialog box closes.

6 Save the changes, and close the document.

Word closes the file.

7 On the Standard toolbar, click the More Buttons down arrow.

8 Point to Add Or Remove Buttons, and click Reset Toolbar.

An alert box appears, asking if you are sure that you want to reset changes made to the toolbar.

9 Click OK.

The macro button no longer appears on the Standard toolbar.

> If you don't see Reset Toolbar at the bottom of the menu, click the down arrow at the bottom of the menu to display additional menu commands.

tip

You can also delete a macro button from a toolbar by holding down the Alt key and dragging the macro button into the document.

Lesson Wrap-Up

In this lesson, you learned how to create a macro, assign a macro a toolbar or keyboard combination, run the macro in a Word document, edit and copy the macro, and rename and delete the macro you created.

If you are continuing to other lessons:

1   On the Tools menu, point to Macro, and click Macros.
2   Click the Organizer button.
3   In the left side of the dialog box, select TableMacros, if necessary, and click the Delete button.
4   Click Yes in the Alert box that appears.
5   In the Organizer dialog box, click the Close button.

If you are not continuing to other lessons:

1   On the Tools menu, point to Macro, and click Macros.
2   Click the Organizer button.
3   In the right side of the dialog box, select NewMacros, if necessary, and click the Delete button.
4   Click Yes in the alert box that appears.
5   In the Organizer dialog box, click the Close button.
6   On the File menu, click Exit.
    Word closes.

Lesson Glossary

global template A template that contains macros and styles that can be used by many other documents. In Word, Normal.dot is the global template.

macro A sequence of commands and entries that can be activated collectively by clicking a toolbar button, clicking a menu command, typing a key combination, or clicking the Run command in the Macros dialog box.

macro project item A collection of macros that have been stored in a document or template. The default name for a macro project item is NewMacros.

module The term used in the Visual Basic Editor to describe a macro project item or other Visual Basic object.

Normal template A set of page, paragraph, and character formats that you can use to create and edit most documents. When you start Word or click the New Blank Document button, Word creates a new blank document based on the Normal template.

project A Visual Basic program that can be saved within a Word document or template. A project can contain multiple macro project items. In turn, each macro project item can include multiple macros.

record To press keystrokes or click menu and toolbar commands to create a macro.

Visual Basic The programming language used to create macros in Word and other Office applications.

Visual Basic Editor A tool that can be used to edit macros created in Word or other Office applications.

Visual Basic for Applications (VBA) The version of Visual Basic that is supplied with Word and Office.

Quick Quiz

1 What programming language is used to create a macro?

2 What do you need to do to assign a macro to a toolbar before you record the macro?

3 How do you delete a macro?

4 What is a macro?

5 Why would you want to create a macro?

6 How do you run a macro?

7 How do you access the Macros dialog box?

important

In the Putting It All Together section below, you must complete Exercise 1 to continue to Exercise 2.

Putting It All Together

Exercise 1: Create a macro in the Normal template named **MailMerge** that will make form letters ready for merging in the mail merge process. Use LMR Letter 07 as the main document and LMR Teacher Database 07.xls as the data source to record the macro. Insert merge fields. Place the macro button on the Standard toolbar to the left of the More Buttons arrow. Close LMR Letter 07 without saving changes, open it again, and then run the macro.

Exercise 2: Delete the macro that you created in the previous exercise. Then delete the macro button from the toolbar.

LESSON 8

Creating Forms

After completing this lesson, you will be able to:

✔ *Add text form fields.*

✔ *Add drop-down form fields.*

✔ *Add check box form fields.*

✔ *Modify and protect a form field.*

✔ *Test and password-protect a form.*

You've probably been asked to complete questionnaires several times in your life, perhaps after staying at a hotel or dining in a restaurant. The management wants your opinion of the services that you received, so you are given a card with questions. The **form** has specific instructions and questions for you to answer and provides a location on the form where you can write down a response or check off one of several possible responses. If you've spent time browsing the Web, you've probably visited Web sites that ask you to complete a form in which you answer questions about yourself and about your interests.

You can use Microsoft Word 2000 to create both of these kinds of forms as well as other forms, such as invoices, purchase orders, employment applications, and employee time sheets. To make a document a form, start with your document, create the questions and instructions, and insert form fields. In Word, a form is a document that has instructions, questions, and spaces reserved for answers. A space reserved for an answer is called a **form field**. For example, you can create fields in which users can type their responses in text boxes. Word lets you create text boxes that accept letters, numbers, dates, times, and calculations from users.

You can also create a list of choices, or a set of check boxes. The user can use the mouse to click the desired choice, or the user can click in the box that represents his or her answer. Word then inserts an *X* in the box. Although a form you create in Word can be printed so that users can respond on paper, Word's form-creation capabilities are especially tailored so that a form can be filled out using a computer. If users will fill out the form on a computer, Word lets you protect your form so that users can enter text in form fields and use the mouse to make selections in other fields, but they cannot alter the layout of the form.

You can also create a form for users to fill out on the Web. Create a form as you normally would (as explained in this lesson), and then save the form as a Web page. If you use any field formatting or properties that have no HTML equivalent, Word will display a dialog box explaining how the form will be modified when you save it as a Web page.

You can also access the Forms toolbar by clicking the View menu, pointing to Toolbars, and then clicking Forms.

You use the Forms toolbar to insert form fields. Display the Forms toolbar by right-clicking any toolbar or menu, and on the shortcut menu that is displayed, clicking Forms.

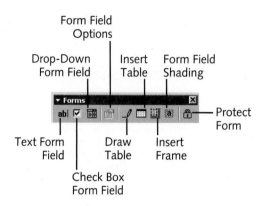

In this lesson, you will learn how to insert text fields, drop-down fields, and check box fields into a form. You'll also learn how to modify and protect a form by using a password. After you create the form, you'll test the form fields.

Sample files for the lesson

To complete the procedures in this lesson, you will need to use the practice file LMR Survey 08 in the Lesson08 folder in the Word Expert Practice folder on your hard disk.

W2000E.6.4

Adding Text Form Fields

When you want the user to type information in the response area, such as a room number (alphanumeric characters), dates, or times, you can create a **text form field**. For example, a toy company might create a customer warranty form that contains text form fields so that the consumer can fill in the name of the toy that he or she purchased, the date of purchase, and the model number of the toy. Suppose the model number of a new action figure is MW2458. The toy company can use a **default** entry when they create the customer warranty and enter the model number for the toy, so the consumer does not have a choice of what numbers to insert on the warranty.

A default is an action or approach used by a program when the user does not specify an alternative action. For example, if you opened Word on a computer on which Word 2000 was just installed, the Standard and Formatting toolbars are placed on the same row. This is one example of a default setting found in Word.

In the following exercises, the Standard and Formatting toolbars have been separated. For additional information on how to separate the toolbars, see the "Using the CD-ROM" section at the beginning of this book.

Text form fields can be divided into six categories, based on the field type that you specify when you insert the field. The field types and their uses are listed in the table on the following page.

Field Type	Used For
Regular text	A field that can contain any type of characters, including numbers, symbols, and letters. You specify a default entry to appear in the form by typing it in the Default Text box in the Text Form Field Options dialog box.
Number	A field that requires a numeric entry. You specify a default entry to appear in the form by typing it in the Default Number box in the Text Form Field Options dialog box.
Date	A field that requires a date entry. Users can enter the date in any valid date format *(October 8, 2000, 10/08/2000, Oct. 8, 00,* and so on). The date users enter will be converted to the date format that you specify in the Text Form Field Options dialog box. For example, if you format a date field as *M/d/yy,* the date entry *October 8, 2000* is automatically converted to *10/8/00.*
Current date	A field that always displays the current date. Word supplies this field when the form is opened, and the current date is inserted using the date format that you specify.
Current time	A field that always displays the current time. Word supplies this field when the form is opened, and the current time is inserted in the time format that you specify. For example, if you choose HH:mm, the time is displayed as 10:46, not 10:46:34. (If you want seconds to show, select the time format HH:mm:ss.)
Calculation	A field that contains a formula you can use to enter a calculation, such as a calculation to display a total order amount by multiplying a price by quantity ordered.

The marketing manager at Lakewood Mountains Resort is in the process of creating a form that will be used to ask visitors about their stay. In this exercise, you help her by displaying the Forms toolbar, and insert text form fields.

Open

1   On the Standard toolbar, click the Open button. Navigate to the Lesson08 folder in the Word Expert Practice folder, and double-click the file LMR Survey 08.

2   On the View menu, point to Toolbars, and click Forms.

The Forms toolbar appears.

> Remember that you can dock the Forms toolbar to move it out of the way by dragging the toolbar's title bar to any edge of the Word window. For more information on docking and undocking toolbars, see Lesson 5, "Customizing Word."

3   Click to position the insertion point at the beginning of the blank line below the text *Please enter the starting and ending dates of your stay,* and press Tab.

The insertion point is indented about .5 inch.

Text Form Field

4   On the Forms toolbar, click the Text Form Field button.

A text form field is inserted.

Form Field Options

5   On the Forms toolbar, click the Form Field Options button.

The Text Form Field Options dialog box appears.

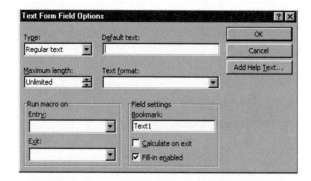

6   In the Text Form Field Options dialog box, click the Type down arrow, and click Date.

The text form field will hold the date response of the user.

7   Click the Date Format down arrow, click M/d/yy, and click OK.

The dialog box closes, and the date format is applied to the text form field.

8   Click to the right of the text form field, and press the Spacebar.

9   Type **to**, and press the Spacebar.

10 Click the text form field to select it.

11 Right-click the text form field.

A shortcut menu appears.

You use Copy and Paste on the shortcut menu to save time by copying a text form field so that you don't have to go through the steps of reselecting all the options for another text form field.

12 On the shortcut menu, click Copy.

13 Click to the right of the space after the word *to*, and right-click.

A shortcut menu appears.

14 On the shortcut menu, click Paste.

The date text form field is copied to the right of the word *to*.

15 Click the beginning of the blank line under *Please enter your room number*, and press Tab.

The text is indented about .5 inch.

Text Form Field

16 On the Forms toolbar, click the Text Form Field button.

A text form field is inserted.

17 On the Forms toolbar, click the Form Field Options button.

The Text Form Field Options dialog box appears.

Form Field Options

18 In the Text Form Field Options dialog box, click the Type down arrow, and click Number.

By default, all form fields are shaded for easy identification, so the user can tell what items need answers. You can remove the shading by clicking the Form Field Shading button on the Forms toolbar.

19 Click the Number Format down arrow, click 0, and then click OK.

The Text Form Field Options dialog box closes, and the number format is applied to the text form field.

Keep this file open for the next exercise.

Form Field Shading

W2000E.6.5

When you use a drop-down field, users can only select one choice from the list of options they are given.

After you create a drop-down form field and make other entries on the form, and then protect the form (which you will learn in the next exercise), the drop-down form field is considered a *drop-down list*.

Adding Drop-Down Form Fields

A **drop-down form field** is useful if you want users to select from a set of specific, descriptive choices. A drop-down form field displays all available choices in a list so that users can click their choice in the list. For instance, a ski lodge near Lakewood Mountains Resort uses a drop-down form field on a guest survey to ask visitors to select their favorite ski run. The ski lodge has about 10 different ski runs and recognizes that guests might not remember the names of the different ski runs on their own. A drop-down form field is useful in this case because all the ski runs are listed in the form. The lodge's guest survey uses another drop-down form field to ask skiers to identify their level of experience: beginner, intermediate, expert, or pro.

Drop-down form fields also enforce accuracy because you can specify the choices for the users. The users do not have to come up with their own answers (or remember certain names). Finally, the users don't type their entries, which in turn eliminates the risk of typos on the form.

In this exercise, you create a drop-down form field in the LMR Survey 08 form.

1. Scroll down and click to the left of the word *friendly*.

Drop-Down Form Field

2. On the Forms toolbar, click the Drop-Down Form Field button.

   A drop-down form field is inserted to the left of the word *friendly*.

Form Field Options

3. On the Forms toolbar, click the Form Field Options button.

   The Drop-Down Form Field Options dialog box appears.

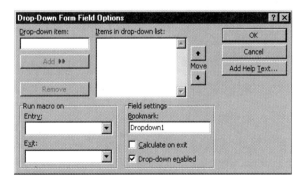

4. In the Drop-Down Item box, type **always**, and click the Add button.

   The word *always* is shown in the Items In Drop-Down List. Notice that the word *always*, which is the first selection in the list, will be displayed when users open the form.

Instead of pressing the Add button after each entry, you can also press Enter to insert the text into the drop-down list.

5. Type **usually**, and click the Add button.

   The entry appears in the Items In Drop-Down List.

6. Type **occasionally**, and click the Add button.

   The entry is added to the Items In Drop-Down List.

7. Type **never**, and click the Add button.

   The entry is added to the Items In Drop-Down List.

8   Click OK.

The items for the drop-down list are added, and all entries appear in the drop-down form field.

9   Click between the words *always* and *friendly*, and press the Spacebar.

A space is inserted between the drop-down list and the word *friendly*.

10   Select the drop-down form field, and right-click it.

A shortcut menu appears.

> When you are using the same form field for multiple questions, you can save time by using the shortcut menu to copy and paste the form field.

11   On the shortcut menu, click Copy.

12   In the next line, right-click to the left of the word *high*.

A shortcut menu appears.

13   On the shortcut menu, click Paste.

The drop-down form field is shown to the left of the word *high*.

14   Press the Spacebar.

A space is inserted between the drop-down list and the word *high*.

15   In the next line, right-click to the left of the word *reasonable*.

A shortcut menu appears.

16   On the shortcut menu, click Paste.

The drop-down form field appears to the left of the word *reasonable*.

17   Press the Spacebar.

A space is inserted between the drop-down list and the word *reasonable*.

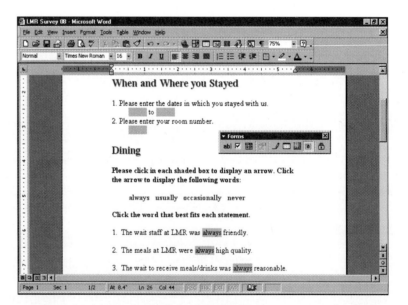

Keep this file open for the next exercise.

W2000E.6.5

In a Word form, multiple check boxes in a set are not mutually exclusive. For instance, if you type a survey question, provide two check boxes for a Yes or No response, and then place a default X in the Yes box, the user must uncheck the Yes and then check the No box to provide a No response. The Yes check box will not be cleared automatically.

Adding Check Box Form Fields

You can use a **check box form field** when you want to provide multiple options and then have users click an option. For example, you might ask the question, "Did you enjoy your stay?" and then create two check boxes for *Yes* and *No*. Or you might create several check boxes for the method of payment (Visa, MasterCard, or American Express) so that users can check the box that corresponds to their method of payment. Check boxes are also useful if you want users to be able to complete the form in a matter of minutes. Unlike the drop-down form field, where users can select only one answer, users can select multiple answers when check box form fields are inserted into the form. For example, a catering company recently hosted a holiday party for LMR employees and their spouses. The caterer who was in charge of the event later sent the LMR employees a ten-question survey in a Yes/No check box format. The LMR employees were able to answer the survey quickly since they didn't have to write out answers or additional comments.

When you use Word to add check box fields to your form, you can modify the size the of the check box and specify a default entry for the most likely response. For instance, you might create Yes/No check boxes in which each *Yes* box is already marked with an X. Users then only have to check items for which they want to answer No.

In the next exercise, you add check box form fields to the LMR Survey 08 form.

1 Scroll to the second page, and click to the left of the text *My room was clean upon receiving it, and cleaned each morning*.

Check Box Form Field

2 On the Forms toolbar, click the Check Box Form Field button.

A check box is added to the left of the word *My*.

Form Field Options

3 On the Forms toolbar, click the Form Field Options button.

The Check Box Form Field Options dialog box appears.

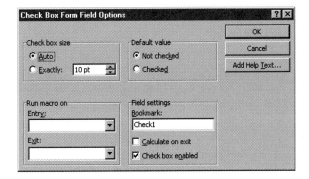

4 In the Check Box Size section, click the Exactly option.

You can also use the arrow buttons to the right of the text box to scroll through the size options and then click 16.

5 In the box to the right of the Exactly option, type **16**, and click OK.

The check box is resized to be 16 points and is selected.

6 Click between the check box form field and the word *My*, and press the Spacebar.

The text is moved one space to the right of the check box form field.

7   Select the check box form field, and right-click it.

A shortcut menu appears.

8   On the shortcut menu, click Copy.

9   Right-click to the left of the next line of text.

A shortcut menu appears.

10   On the shortcut menu, click Paste.

A check box form field appears at the beginning of the line of text.

11   Press the Spacebar.

The text is moved one space to the right of the check box form field.

12   Using steps 9 through 11, paste a check box form field in front of the next four lines of text, adding a space after the check box each time.

13   Click the blank line below the *Your Comments* heading.

14   On the Forms toolbar, click the Text Form Field button.

The text form field is inserted. Your document should look similar to the following illustration.

If you have trouble clicking below the heading, click the insertion point at the end of the heading, and press Enter.

Text Form Field

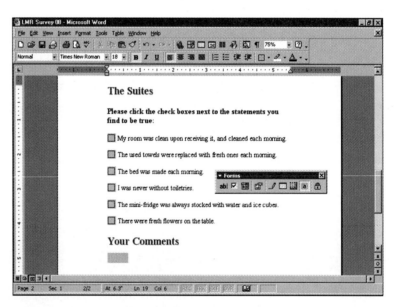

15   On the File menu, click Save As.

The Save As dialog box appears.

16   In the File Name box, type **LMR Survey 08 Edited**.

17   Click the Save button.

Word saves the document.

Keep this file open for the next exercise.

Modifying and Protecting Form Fields

You can modify a form just as you modify any document. You can add a page border, change text formatting, add graphics and tables, and so on. The TailSpin Toys company puts a questionnaire in every boxed toy it sells. The questionnaire includes the company logo and a balloon border around the questionnaire to make it more inviting for the consumer.

The only difference between modifying a form and modifying a document is that you can also modify form fields within a form. You can add frames or borders to form fields, remove the default shading for each field, and you can specify new options (called **properties**) in the form field options dialog boxes.

After you've modified all form fields and you feel that the form is complete, you can protect it. To protect a form field, click the Protect Form button on the Forms toolbar. Protecting a form prevents users from modifying the layout of the form, but still allows them to make entries in the form fields. Responses cannot be entered into a form until the form has been protected. If you protect a form and then decide you want to make additional changes to the layout of the form, you can unprotect the form by clicking the Protect Form button again.

Just as easily, users can also unprotect a form and modify the layout on their own. You can prevent users from unprotecting a form by password-protecting the document. When the document is password-protected, the form can't be unprotected unless the correct password is supplied.

In this exercise, you remove and redisplay the shading for all form fields, change an item in the drop-down list form field, insert a frame and border, and then protect the form.

Properties change the way the form field behaves and accepts entries (such as the date format in a text form field or a default entry in a text form field or check box form field). Or for a list form field, the properties change the entries that appear in the list.

Protect Form

Form Field Shading

You don't have to select the fields to remove or apply shading.

1   On the Forms toolbar, click the Form Field Shading button.

   The shading is removed from all form fields.

2   Click the Form Field Shading button again.

   All the shading reappears for the form fields.

3   Scroll to the first page, and below the heading *Dining,* double-click the first drop-down form field.

   The Drop-Down Form Field Options dialog box appears.

4   In the Items In Drop-Down List, click *occasionally,* and click the Remove button.

   Occasionally is removed from the Items In Drop-Down List.

5   In the Drop-Down Item box, type **sometimes**.

6   Click the Add button.

   The word *sometimes* appears at the bottom of the Items In Drop-Down List.

7   Use the Move Up and Move Down arrows to the right of the box to move *sometimes* above *never* and below *usually*.

If you want to remove an item from a drop-down list, in the Drop-Down Form Field Options dialog box, click the item in the Items In Drop-Down List box, and click the Remove button.

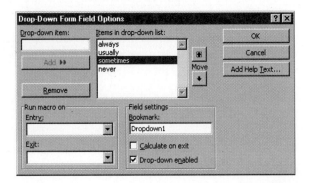

8   Click OK.

The drop-down list is modified with the new option *sometimes*.

Protect Form

9   On the Forms toolbar, click the Protect Form button.

The form is protected and the form fields are ready to be filled out.

10   Under the *Dining* heading, on the first page, click the drop-down list arrow.

The list includes *sometimes* as one of its items, replacing *occasionally*.

Protect Form

11   On the Forms toolbar, click the Protect Form button again to unprotect the form.

The form is unprotected and ready for further modifications.

12   On page 2, select the text form field below the heading *Your Comments*.

Insert Frame

13   On the Forms toolbar, click the Insert Frame button.

A frame is inserted around the text box, and black selection handles appear around the frame.

You can also move frames to any location on a page. Double-click the Frame border to display the Frame dialog box. In the Text Wrapping section, click None, and click OK. You can now drag the border of the frame to any location on the page.

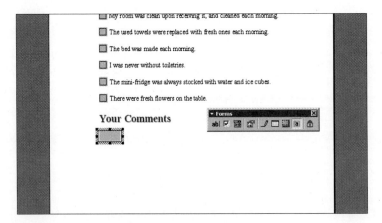

14   Drag the bottom-right selection handle down and to the right until the box is about five inches wide and two inches high.

15   Double-click the text form field inside the frame.

The Text Form Field Options dialog box appears.

16 In the Maximum Length box, select the text *Unlimited*, and type **150**.

Click the Add Help Text button if you want to assist the user by displaying help text when the user clicks in the field. You can specify that the help text should appear automatically in the status bar or when the user presses F1.

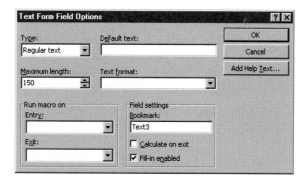

17 Click OK.

The framed text form field is limited to a maximum of 150 characters, and the dialog box closes.

18 Scroll up to the first page of the document, and select the room number text form field.

Draw Table

19 On the Forms toolbar, click the Draw Table button.

The Tables And Borders toolbar appears.

Outside Border

20 On the Tables And Borders toolbar, click the Border down arrow, click the Outside Border button, and then click outside the text form field to deselect it.

A border surrounds the text form field.

Keep this file open for the next exercise.

Because Word can only insert outside borders around a selected block of text, an outside border is added to the form field. If you had clicked the Border down arrow and chosen a different border button on the Tables And Borders toolbar (except for the No Border button), Word would still surround the text field with an outside border.

Testing and Password-Protecting a Form

The LMR Survey 08 form is now complete. The next step is to test the form. In the previous exercise, you briefly protected a form, tested one field, and then protected the form again. Responses cannot be entered into a form until the form has been protected. To test a form completely, you should protect the form and then test all form fields. If you determine that any changes are necessary, you can unprotect the form, make the necessary changes, and then protect the form again. Protecting a form is important because doing so ensures that users cannot change its body or alter the layout of form fields. Participants can only type answers or make selections in the form fields.

You can protect a form with or without assigning a password to the form. Protecting a form with a password involves more steps, so it is a good idea to protect a form without a password first, so that you can test the form fields. After you are certain that the fields work as you want them to, you can unprotect the form and protect the form again, assigning a password.

In this exercise, you protect the LMR Survey 08 Edited form without assigning a password, view and test the activated form fields, and then unprotect the form and protect the form again using a password.

Protect Form

If the Tables And Borders toolbar is in your way, click the Close button in the top-right corner of the toolbar. Don't close the Forms toolbar, because you will need it for this exercise.

Do not press Enter after each entry, or the fields in each form field won't be activated. You can press Tab, click the next form field where you want to enter a response, or click outside the form field to deselect the form field.

After you make your selection, you can also click at the end of the statement to display an arrow to the right of the next field. You can then click the arrow to display the drop-down list.

To eliminate the 150-character limitation that you set in an earlier exercise, on the Forms toolbar, click the Protect Form button to unprotect the document, double-click the text form field inside the frame, and then in the Maximum Length box, type Unlimited.

1   On the Forms toolbar, click the Protect Form button.

   Word protects the form, and users can now make entries in the form fields. The first date text form field is selected.

2   In the first date text form field, type **April 2, 2001**.

3   Click the date text form field to the right.

   April 2, 2001, in the first field, is converted to the M/d/yy (04/2/01) format that you specified earlier.

4   Type **4-09-01**.

5   Click the number text form field in the next question.

   Again, Word converts the date that you entered in the second date text form field to the M/d/yy format that you specified earlier.

6   In the number text form field in question 2, type **105**.

7   Click anywhere outside the number text form field.

   An arrow appears to the right of the next field.

8   Click the arrow, and click the word *usually* in the list.

   The new item appears in the drop-down form field.

9   Click the next field.

   An arrow and the drop-down list appear.

10   In the drop-down list, click *occasionally*.

   The new item appears in the drop-down field.

11   In the drop-down list of the next field, click *usually*.

12   Scroll to the second page of LMR Survey 08 Edited, and click the check box form field to the left of the first statement.

   An *X* appears in the field.

13   Click the check form field to the left of the first statement again.

   The *X* no longer appears.

14   Click the first, second, fourth, and sixth check boxes.

   The first, second, fourth, and sixth check boxes contain an *X*.

15   Click the text form field below the *Your Comments* heading, and type **I loved my stay at Lakewood Mountains Resort. I can't believe how beautiful it is here. The staff made me feel right at home. I have absolutely no complaints, and I plan to come back soon.**

   The text field lets you type up to 150 characters.

16   On the Forms toolbar, click the Protect Form button.

   The form is unprotected.

17   On the Tools menu, click Protect Document.

   The Protect Document dialog box appears.

Protect Form

18 In the Protect Document dialog box, click the Forms option, if necessary.

19 In the Password box, type the password **LMR**, and click OK.

The Confirm Password dialog box appears.

There are some passwords that you should avoid, such as your name or a number sequence such as *1234*. These are the most obvious and common passwords. When you choose a password, think of a word or name that is familiar only to you, but don't make your password so difficult that you won't remember it.

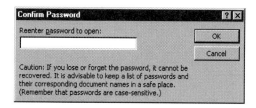

20 Retype the password **LMR** to confirm it, and click OK.

Word protects the form, and both dialog boxes close.

Notice that Word does not keep a list of passwords, so it is advisable to write down your password so that you don't forget it.

Lesson Wrap-Up

In this lesson, you learned how to insert form fields in a form; how to format fields and modify form field properties; how to protect, test, and unprotect a form; and how to password-protect a form.

If you are continuing to other lessons:

● On the File menu, click Close. If you are prompted to save the changes, click Yes.

Word saves and closes the file.

If you are not continuing to other lessons:

● On the File menu, click Exit. If you are prompted to save the changes, click Yes.

Word saves and closes the file.

Word closes.

Lesson Glossary

check box form field A field that allows users to select from among multiple options by clicking a check box.

default A choice made by a program when the user does not specify an alternate answer or option.

drop-down form field A field that allows users to display a list of descriptive choices from which they can select a response.

form A document with instructions, questions, and fields reserved for users to enter responses.

form field A location in a form where users can respond to a question or specify an appropriate response.

properties The ability to change the way a form field behaves and accepts entries (such as the date format in a text form field, or a default entry in a text form field or check box form field) or for a list form field, the ability to change the entries that appear in the list.

text form field On a form, a box in which users can type a text response to a question or instruction. Depending on the format specified for a text form field, the field can contain alphanumeric characters, numbers only, dates, or times.

Quick Quiz

1   Should you password-protect a form before or after you test the form? Explain your answer.

2   What are the three kinds of form fields that Word provides?

3   What toolbar do you use when you create a form, and how do you display this toolbar?

4   What form field would you use if you want respondents to choose from a list of responses?

5   How can you quickly protect a form to test the form fields?

6   What is a form?

important:

In the Putting It All Together section below, you must complete Exercise 1 before continuing to Exercise 2.

Putting It All Together

Exercise 1: If necessary, start Word. In the Lesson08 folder, open SkillCheck 08, and add the following form fields to the registration card:

Section	Form Field
Date	current date form field
Last name	text form field
First name	text form field
MI	text form field
Address	text form field
City	text form field
State/Province	text form field
Postal/ZIP code	number form field
Country	text form field
Home phone	number form field
Work phone	number form field
Credit card	check box form field (provide options for Visa, MasterCard, and American Express)
Check	check box form field
Cash	check box form field
Traveler's checks	check box form field
How long will you be staying?	number form field/ drop-down form field with the following information: Day(s), Week(s), Month(s)

Save the registration card as **SkillCheck 08 Edited**.

Exercise 2: Protect SkillCheck 08 Edited without a password, and test all form fields to make sure that they work properly. Unprotect the form, and remove the shading from the fields. Protect the form with a password. Save the form again with the same name.

Working Collaboratively

After completing this lesson, you will be able to:

✔ *Track changes.*

✔ *Accept and reject changes.*

✔ *Add comments.*

✔ *Protect a document.*

✔ *Create multiple document versions.*

If you are creating a letter or a memo in Microsoft Word 2000, you're probably the only person who will work on the document. You might ask a coworker to proofread the document before you send it, but you probably won't need others to make major contributions or suggestions to the document. On the other hand, if you are working on a document such as a major report or proposal, you might want to receive input from other people in your organization. Each individual will bring his or her own expertise to the document, ensuring that the document will be as accurate, complete, and professional as possible. Some people might want to make changes to the text, while others might want to just make comments and offer suggestions.

Suppose that you are preparing your company's annual report. You will be the last person to review the document before it is printed. Consequently, you are responsible for evaluating everyone's edits and comments and determining which edits should be made and which comments need to be addressed.

New!

If your computer is connected to a network server that uses the Microsoft Office Server Extensions, you can also create a **discussion**. A discussion is similar to a series of comments; however, in a discussion, multiple users can reply to each comment, other users can reply to previous responses, and so on. Word keeps track of who made which comments, who replied to comments, and which comments different replies are directed to.

If you were to give each person a printed copy of the annual report to mark up, you would have to go through every copy to review edits, comments, and suggestions. This editorial review process could be time consuming and inefficient, especially if different people make the same changes or corrections. Fortunately, Word provides a better way. The **change tracking** feature in Word allows you to identify and review changes made by different people to the same document.

If different people will be reviewing the same Word document, you could request that everybody use Word's **Versions** feature so that you can keep track of each person's changes separately. For instance, you could instruct each contributor to save a separate document version after he or she makes changes. If a particular contributor's changes are deemed to be incorrect or not useful, you can return to the document version that was saved prior to that contributor's changes.

The difference between change tracking and saving multiple document versions is subtle but important. With change tracking, all contributors' changes appear together in the document. With this approach, you can select, accept, or reject each change, regardless of who made the change. With multiple versions, Word stores each new version as part of the document—and only one version can be viewed at a time. In this way, you only have one copy of the document, but you can review the edits made by a particular contributor separately from other contributors.

In this lesson, you will learn how to track changes, accept and reject changes, and add comments. You'll also learn how to protect a document and create multiple document versions.

Sample files for the lesson

To complete the procedures in this lesson, you will use the practice files LMR Welcome Pamphlet 09 and LMR Sales Brochure 09 in the Lesson09 folder in the Word Expert Practice folder located on your hard disk. You'll use these files to track changes, add comments, protect a document, and create multiple versions of a document.

W2000E.7.4

> In the following exercises, the Standard and Formatting toolbars have been separated. For additional information on how to separate the toolbars, see the "Using the CD-ROM" section at the beginning of this book.

Tracking Changes

When you turn on change tracking, Word internally keeps track of any changes made by different people to a document. This kind of tracking is useful so that the final reviewer can identify changes made to the original document, determine which changes should be accepted and which ones should be rejected, and identify who made which changes. When you turn on change tracking, you can also elect to view **revision marks** for changes that different people have made. When you display revisions, any text that has been deleted appears crossed-out, with one line through the text. Text that has been inserted appears underlined. If several people make edits to a document, the strikeout and underlined text can make the document difficult to read. To help you read the edited document, you can temporarily hide the revision marks so that underlined text appears normally and strikeout text does not display at all. The editing changes remain in the document and can be displayed again with a few clicks. You can also hide or show revisions when you print a document that has been tracked.

If you've turned on change tracking for a document and view the revisions that different people have made, you'll notice that Word uses a different text color for each contributor's deletions and additions. Text that hasn't been changed remains in black. Word also displays a vertical bar in the margin for any lines that have been changed. The vertical bars help you locate revisions more quickly.

> The names that you see in the ScreenTips are those that the other users entered when they first installed Word on their computer.

The following screen shows how revision marks appear in a document. When you position the mouse pointer over a particular revision, Word displays a ScreenTip that indicates which contributor made the change.

> **Ron, 1/20/2000 3:27 PM:**
> Inserted

| We hope you ~~like~~ enjoy your stay at Lakewood Mountains Resort. Our staff ~~tries~~ strives to make sure your visit is as pleasurable and relaxing as possible. If you have any
| questions about resort activities or any of our ~~numerous~~ services, feel free to call the desk at any time of the day or night.

The marketing assistant at Lakewood Mountains Resort finished his draft of a pamphlet that welcomes guests to the resort and explains resort amenities. He has asked the marketing manager to review the document and turn on change tracking so he can identify which changes she has made.

In this exercise, you turn on change tracking in a document and you display revision marks for changes that have been or will be made to the document by others.

Open

1   On the Standard toolbar, click the Open button. Navigate to the Lesson09 folder in the Word Expert Practice folder, and double-click the file LMR Welcome Pamphlet 09.

2   On the Tools menu, point to Track Changes, and click Highlight Changes.

    The Highlight Changes dialog box appears.

3   Select all three check boxes in the dialog box, and click OK.

    Revisions to the document will now be tracked, displayed on the screen using revision marks, and printed with these same revision marks.

4   Select the word *congratulate* in the second sentence in the first paragraph.

5   Type **thank**.

    A line is placed through the word *congratulate*, and the word *thank* is underlined.

> You can also turn on change tracking by clicking the Track Changes button on the Reviewing toolbar, double-clicking the TRK button on the status bar, or by pressing Ctrl+Shift+E. When change tracking is turned on, the letters *TRK* on the status bar appear darker to indicate that this feature is active. To turn tracking off, click the Track Changes button again on the Reviewing toolbar, press Ctrl+Shift+E, or double-click the letters *TRK* on the status bar. If you activate tracking by using the Reviewing toolbar or the status bar, the revision marks won't be shown on screen unless you first select the Highlight Changes On Screen check box in the Highlight Changes dialog box.

Track Changes

> Notice that both words are shown in a different color than the original text, and a vertical bar appears in the left margin next to the line of text where the revision was made. Word uses a different revision color for each user. The color that Word selects can be different on different computers; however, all changes for a particular person appear in the same color.

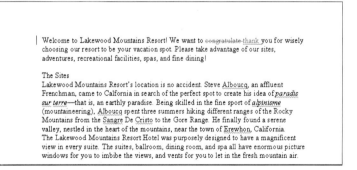

6   In the next line, select the word *sites*.

Notice that all your revision marks are displayed in the same color. Each reviewer's changes will appear in a different color so that it is clear who made the changes. You can move the mouse pointer over a revision to display a ScreenTip that shows the name of the person who entered the change and the date and time of the change.

7 Type **beautiful scenery**.

A line is placed through the word *sites,* and the words *beautiful scenery* are underlined. The changes appear in a different color than the original text, and the vertical bar in the left margin is extended for both of the edited lines.

8 Click before the words *Lakewood Mountains Resort's location* at the beginning of the second paragraph below the *The Sites* heading, and press Enter.

The paragraph is moved down, and a vertical bar appears in the margin to the left of the new blank line.

9 In the first sentence under the heading *Spa,* select the phrase *skiing or hiking,* and type **activities**.

A line is placed through the phrase *skiing or hiking,* and the word *activities* is underlined. The changes appear in a different color than the original text, and the vertical bar in the left margin is extended.

10 Scroll down and click after the exclamation point in the last line of the last paragraph, press the Spacebar, and type **If there is anything we can do to make your stay more enjoyable, please don't hesitate to ask.**

The new sentence is underlined and appears in a different color than the original text, and the vertical bar in the left column appears for both of the edited lines.

Notice that even adding a new line is considered a revision, and a vertical bar is added to the left margin after this step.

> Join us for breakfast, lunch, and dinner. Experience our dinning room's unadulterated view of Mineral Mountain as you enjoy your meal. Our head master chef, Suki White, has created all of the entrees by mixing French fare with cowboy cuisine. Who would have guessed that such a marriage would have brought rave reviews from food critics all over the world?
>
> If you like, you can have a private waitperson serve you in the comfort of your suite. Don't forget to request the violinist for romantic dinners! If there is anything we can do to make your stay more enjoyable, please don't hesitate to ask.

11 Save the document using the name **LMR Welcome Pamphlet 09 Edited**.

Keep this file open for the next exercise.

Accepting and Rejecting Changes

Now that the marketing manager has edited the pamphlet, the marketing assistant wants to review her changes. You can use Word to accept or reject changes made to the document. If the marketing assistant agrees with the changes, he can accept them selectively (that is, he can accept some changes but reject others). Those accepted changes become part of the document. If he disagrees with any changes, he can reject them. When a revision is rejected, the original text in the edited document appears, and the revision is deleted.

You can accept or reject changes in two ways: you can click buttons on the Reviewing toolbar, or you can click options in the Accept Or Reject Changes dialog box. In both techniques, you can review each change one at a time, or you can accept or reject all the changes at once. You might want to accept and reject changes one at a time if you know that some changes are valid, but also recognize that you might not agree with other changes. If you review an entire document and agree with every change that has been made, you can instruct Word to accept all changes. If you review a document and do not agree with any changes that have been made, you can instruct Word to reject all changes.

In this exercise, you use the Reviewing toolbar and the Accept Or Reject Changes dialog box to accept or reject revisions made in the previous exercise.

1 Press Ctrl+Home.

   The insertion point is positioned at the beginning of the document.

2 On the View menu, point to Toolbars, and click Reviewing.

   The Reviewing toolbar appears.

Next Change

3 On the Reviewing toolbar, click the Next Change button.

   The crossed-out word *congratulate* is selected.

4 On the Reviewing toolbar, click the Accept Change button.

   The word *congratulate* is deleted from the document.

Accept Change

5 On the Reviewing toolbar, click the Next Change button.

   The word *thank* is selected.

6 On the Reviewing toolbar, click the Accept Change button.

   The word *thank* becomes part of the document.

7 On the Reviewing toolbar, click the Next Change button.

   The word *sites* is selected.

Reject Change

8 On the Reviewing toolbar, click the Reject Change button.

   The word *sites* is incorporated into the document, and the strikeout line is removed from the word.

Notice that when the change becomes part of the document, it is no longer colored, but is changed to black.

9 Click within the word *sites* to deselect it.

10 On the Tools menu, point to Track Changes, and click Accept Or Reject Changes.

   The Accept Or Reject Changes dialog box appears.

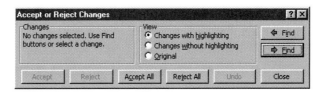

11 Click the Find button with the right-pointing arrow.

   The words *beautiful scenery* are selected.

A quick way to accept or reject a change is to right-click the changed text. On the shortcut menu that appears, click either Accept Change or Reject Change.

You can choose to accept or reject all remaining changes in a document without viewing them, but if you haven't reviewed the suggested changes, you'll lose this information when you accept or reject all the changes. If you track the changes made in your document, reviewing each change is the safest guarantee that all the changes will be made as you desire.

Keep the Reviewing toolbar open. You'll use the toolbar in the next exercise.

Save

12   Click the Reject button.

The words *beautiful scenery* are deleted from the document.

13   Click the Find button with the right-pointing arrow.

The words *skiing or hiking* are selected.

14   Click the Accept All button.

An alert box appears, asking if you want to accept all remaining changes without viewing them.

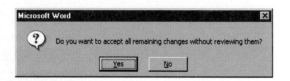

15   Click Yes.

The remaining changes are accepted.

16   In the Accept Or Reject Changes dialog box, click the Close button.

17   On the Tools menu, point to Track Changes, and click Highlight Changes.

The Highlight Changes dialog box appears.

18   Clear all check boxes, and click OK.

All check boxes are cleared, and the change tracking feature is no longer active. All future changes made to the document are immediately made without revision marks.

19   On the Standard toolbar, click the Save button to save the document.

Word saves the document.

Keep this file open for the next exercise.

W2000E.7.1

Adding Comments

The marketing assistant wants to send the same pamphlet to the general manager for review. The general manager wants to include notes explaining why he has suggested certain changes. But he doesn't want his explanations to be part of the document, only his changes. He can use Word to add explanatory notes, called **comments**, without making changes to the body of the document. He uses change tracking so that the marketing assistant can see what he added and deleted, but he inserts comments when he wants to explain a particular change that he has made.

When you insert a comment, the text that you comment on is highlighted in yellow and the comment is displayed when you or another reader positions the mouse pointer over the highlighted text. Each comment is labeled with the initials or name of the reviewer and a sequential comment number. The sequential comment numbers help other readers to keep track of how many comments exist as well as which reviewer added a certain comment.

To insert comments, you can display the Reviewing toolbar and click the Insert Comment button, or you can use the Insert menu and click Comment. It's a good idea to display and use the Reviewing toolbar if you think you'll want to make several comments in a document. Use the Comment command on the Insert menu if you expect to add only a few comments to a document.

In this exercise, you add comments to LMR Welcome Pamphlet 09 Edited, and then you view them.

1   Press Ctrl+Home.

The insertion point is positioned at the beginning of the document.

Insert Comment

2   In the third sentence in the paragraph, under the heading *Sites,* select the text *Alboucq spent three summers hiking different ranges of the Rocky Mountains from the Sangre De Cristo to the Gore Range.*, and on the Reviewing toolbar, click the Insert Comment button.

Word highlights the selected text, the comment appears, the insertion point moves to the comment pane, and the comment pane appears at the bottom of the window.

> If the Reviewing toolbar is not displayed, on the View menu, point to Toolbars, and click Reviewing.

> Your initials will probably be different than the initials shown in the illustration. You enter your user name and initials when you install Microsoft Office 2000 or Microsoft Word 2000. You can change the user name and initials in the Options dialog box. On the Tools menu, click Options, and then click the User Information tab.

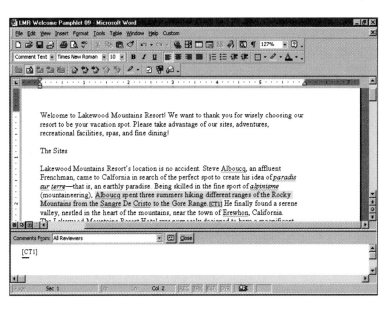

3   In the comment pane, type **Add specific mountain names.**

Word adds the comment to the document.

4   Click the Close button in the comment pane.

5   Hold the mouse pointer over any highlighted word.

A ScreenTip appears with the name of the reviewer and the comment.

Welcome to Lakewood Mountains Resort! We want to thank you for wisely choosing our resort to be your vacation spot. Please take advantage of our sites, adventures, recreational facilities, spas, and fine dining!

The Sites

Lakewood Mountains Resort's location is no accident. Steve Alboucq, an affluent Frenchman, came t **Catherine Turner:** the perfect spot to create his idea of *paradis sur terre*—that is, Add specific mountain names. g skilled in the fine sport of *alpinisme* (mountaineering). Alboucq spent three summers hiking different ranges of the Rocky Mountains from the Sangre De Cristo to the Gore Range. [CT1] He finally found a serene valley, nestled in the heart of the mountains, near the town of Erewhon, California. The Lakewood Mountains Resort Hotel was purposely designed to have a magnificent view in every suite. The suites, ballroom, dining room, and spa all have enormous picture windows for you to imbibe the views, and vents for you to let in the fresh mountain air.

The Adventures

Let Lakewood Mountains Resort take you on a wild venture. Hike the Indian Peaks

6   Move the mouse pointer away from the highlighted word.

The ScreenTip no longer appears.

Insert Comment

7   Below the *Spa* heading, in the first sentence, click anywhere within the word *activities*, and on the Reviewing toolbar, click the Insert Comment button.

The entire word *activities* is highlighted, the comment pane appears at the bottom of the screen, and the second comment is ready to be entered.

> You can resize the comment pane by dragging the gray bar between the document pane and the comment pane.

8   In the comment pane, type **What about listing the various activities the Resort provides?**

The comment is inserted in the document.

9   Click the mouse pointer in the document, scroll down, and then select the word *ask* in the last sentence of the last paragraph.

10   On the Insert menu, click Comment.

The word *ask* is highlighted, and in the comment pane the third comment is ready to be entered.

11   In the comment pane, type **Add another sentence to tell guests where they can be helped—at the Front Desk, for example.**

The text appears in the comment pane and is added to the document.

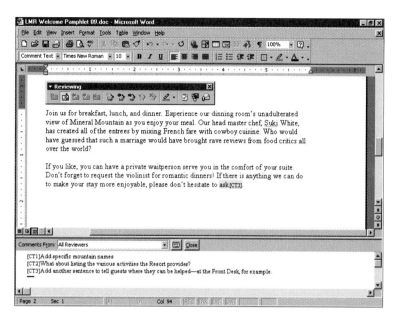

12   In the comment pane, click the Close button.

The comment pane closes.

Edit Comment

13   Scroll up in the main document, and click anywhere in the first high-lighted comment, and on the Reviewing toolbar, click the Edit Comment button.

The insertion point in the comment pane is inserted before the comment numbered 1.

14   In the comment pane, select the text *Add specific mountain names,* and type **Include the years he did this.**

The previous comment is deleted and replaced with the new comment.

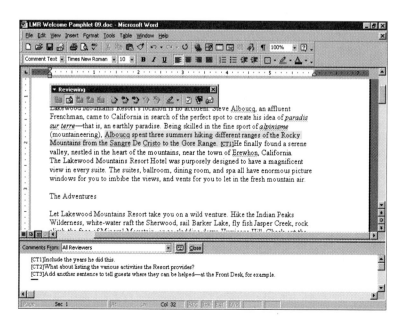

Delete Comment

15   Scroll through the main document, click the second comment, and then on the Reviewing toolbar, click the Delete Comment button.

The comment is deleted from the text, and the remaining comments are renumbered.

16   In the comment pane, click the Close button.

17   On the Standard toolbar, click the Save button.

Save

Word saves the document.

Keep this file open for the next exercise.

tip

Word provides multiple ways to edit or delete a comment. You can edit a comment by double-clicking the highlighted text that denotes the comment that you want to modify. Double-clicking the highlighted text opens the comment pane so that you can make the necessary changes. You can also right-click the highlighted text to display the shortcut menu and then click Edit Comment. Likewise, to delete a comment, right-click, and click Delete Comment. You can also click the Edit Comment or Delete Comment buttons on the Reviewing toolbar.

W2000E.7.2

Protecting a Document

If you've created a document and want others to view it, but you want to limit the ability of others to make changes, you can protect the document. When you protect a document, you can specify that other users can insert comments and that all of their changes will be tracked. Or you can specify that other users can insert comments, but cannot alter the document in any other ways. If you protect a document and then decide you don't want to restrict the changes that can be made to the document, you can easily unprotect the document. For added security, you can specify a password for a document. When you assign a password to a document, users can only open or change the document if they know the password.

To apply protection to a document, you click Protect Document on the Tools menu to display a dialog box of protection options. The following table details what a reviewer can and cannot do after you specify certain protection options.

If you choose	The reviewer can	The reviewer cannot
Tracked Changes	Make tracked changes; add comments. Unprotect the document.	Turn off tracking; accept or reject changes.
Comments	Create comments; edit and delete existing comments. Unprotect the document.	Make changes; accept or reject changes.
Tracked Changes with a password	Make tracked changes; add comments.	Turn off tracking; accept or reject changes; unprotect the document, unless he or she knows the password.
Comments with a password	Create comments; Edit and delete existing comments.	Make edits to text; accept or reject changes. Unprotect the document unless he or she knows the password.

If a reviewer unprotects the document, he or she is able to both turn off change tracking and accept or reject changes.

If a reviewer unprotects the document, he or she can make changes to the text and accept or reject the changes. If the reviewer edits or deletes existing comments, those changes are tracked.

If a reviewer modifies or deletes existing comments, those changes will be tracked.

In this exercise, you protect LMR Welcome Pamphlet 09 Edited using the Comments option. You insert a comment, try to make an unauthorized change, and then unprotect the document.

1   On the Tools menu, click Protect Document.

The Protect Document dialog box appears.

2   In the Protect Document dialog box, click the Comments option.

3   Click the Password (Optional) box, type **mountain**, and then click OK.

The Confirm Password dialog box appears.

Word does not keep a list of pass-words, so you should write down your passwords. If you use a separate password for each document, you should also write down the name of the document each password protects.

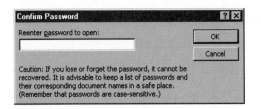

4   Type **mountain**, and click OK.

The password is confirmed, and the dialog boxes close.

5   In the second line of the first paragraph, select the word *adventures.*

6   On the Reviewing toolbar, click the Insert Comment button.

The word *adventures* is highlighted, and the comment pane appears.

Notice how Word renumbers sub-sequent comments after you add or delete a comment so that the comment numbers always stay in numeric order.

7   Type **What adventures are we talking about here?**

The comment is added to the document.

8   In the comment pane, click the Close button.

9   Select the first sentence in the first paragraph, and press the Back-space key.

You cannot delete the text because the document is protected so that the reviewer can only add comments or make changes to com-ments. The reviewer cannot make changes to any other part of the document.

Notice that when you try to make an unauthorized change, the text *This command is not available because the document is locked for edit* is displayed on the status bar.

10   On the Tools menu, click Unprotect Document.

The Unprotect Document dialog box appears.

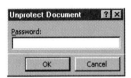

11   In the Password box, type **mountain**, and click OK.

The Unprotect Document dialog box closes.

12   Press Backspace.

The first sentence in the document is deleted because the document is no longer protected.

Undo

13   On the Standard toolbar, click the Undo button.

The first sentence reappears in the document.

14   On the View menu, click Toolbars and clear the Reviewing toolbar checkbox.

Save

15   On the Standard toolbar, click the Save button, and close the document.

Word saves and closes the document.

W2000E.7.5

For more information about creating templates and using Word's wizards, see Lesson 3, "Using Templates and Wizards."

Setting the Default Location for Workgroup Templates

In previous lessons, you learned how to customize toolbars and menus, create macros, and change styles and formats in a document. Changes such as these can be saved as a **template**. A template is a document that contains built-in text, styles, and other formatting that can be used to create other documents that will share the same basic formatting.

If you want to use specific formatting for all office memos, you can create a **workgroup template**. A workgroup template can be shared on a network. Any employee in the office can access the workgroup template on the network and use this template to create their memos. Because everybody in the office uses the same template, all memos have the same format and appearance.

You can store all workgroup templates in their own folder so that others can locate and open the templates from a common location on a server or other networked computer, but Word does not set a default location for the templates. However, Word does provides a default location for any ready-made templates and templates that you create by using a Word wizard. The default location is in a Templates folder on your hard disk (usually drive C). To set a default location for workgroup templates, on the Tools menu, click Options to display the Options dialog box. In the Options dialog box, click the File Locations tab.

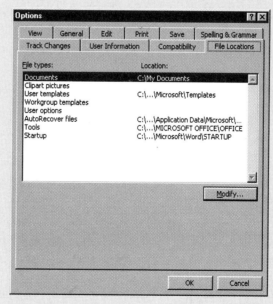

(continued)

continued

Select Workgroup templates and click the Modify button to display the Modify Location dialog box.

Depending on your computer settings, the illustration shown might not match your screen.

If you want to save the template in an existing folder, navigate to the existing folder so that the name is shown in the Folder Name box, and click OK. Or click the Create New Folder button to create a new folder, and click OK.

Create New Folder

W2000E.7.3

Creating Multiple Document Versions

If you plan to open, edit, and close a particular document several times, you might want to create a different document version for each editing session so that you can revert to a previous version if you or somebody else decides that the most current version is not usable. You could rename the document each time you save it (such as Annual Report 1, Annual Report 2, Annual Report 3, and so on), but this would result in multiple files on your hard disk, which can be confusing when you try to determine which version contains which changes. With Word's Versions feature, you can save each set of changes as a different document version *within* the same file. When you save a version of a document, you can add comments to help you remember which version contains which changes.

At times, it makes more sense to have different people make changes to the same document and save their changes as a different version rather than use the change tracking feature of Word. For example, suppose the marketing manager wants to give the brochure document to three creative-minded employees at the resort to see how each employee might improve the formatting and overall layout of the document. For this situation, change tracking wouldn't be very useful because Word does not track most formatting changes. Instead, the marketing manager can instruct all three employees to use the Versions feature in Word to save their formatting suggestions. The marketing manager can then view each version and use the one he likes best.

To save a document as a version, you click Versions on the File menu. Word uses your user information (specified in the User Identification tab of the Options dialog box) to record your name as part of the version. Word also stores the date and time the version was saved. If you decide you want to delete a particular version, click the version name in the Versions dialog box, and click the Delete button.

In this exercise, you create multiple versions of a file and delete one of them.

Open

1   On the Standard toolbar, click the Open button. Navigate to the Lesson09 folder in the Word Expert Practice folder, and double-click the file LMR Sales Brochure 09.

2   On the File menu, click Versions.

The Versions In LMR Sales Brochure dialog box appears.

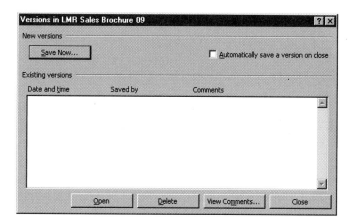

3   Click the Save Now button.

The Save Version dialog box appears.

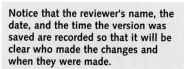

Notice that the reviewer's name, the date, and the time the version was saved are recorded so that it will be clear who made the changes and when they were made.

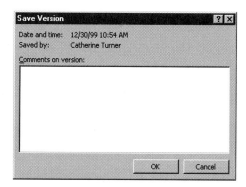

4   In the Comments On Version box, type **Edited text, original layout**, and click OK.

The dialog boxes close, the original version is saved, and the Versions icon now appears on the right side of the status bar.

5   Select the heading *Why Stay at LMR?*. On the Formatting toolbar, click the Font Size down arrow, and then click 28.

The selected text changes to 28 points in size.

6   On the File menu, click Versions.

The Versions In LMR Sales Brochure 09 dialog box appears.

Notice that the Existing Versions box shows a record of the original version, the comment that you typed earlier, the date and time that it was saved, and the name of the person who saved it.

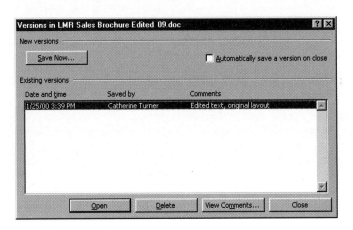

7   Click the Save Now button.

The Save Version dialog box appears.

8   In the Comments On Version box, type **New styles**, and click OK.

The dialog boxes close, and the new version is saved along with the original version.

9   Close the document.

Close

10   On the File menu, click LMR Sales Brochure 09.

The LMR Sales Brochure 09 opens.

The last saved version of a document opens each time you open the document.

11   On the File menu, click Versions.

The Versions In LMR Sales Brochure 09 dialog box appears.

Both versions are listed in the Existing Versions box, and as new versions are created, they, too, will be added to the Existing Versions box. The most recent versions will be listed first, and the newest version (the one that is open) will be selected.

12   In the Existing Versions box, click the oldest version of the file.

In this case, the oldest version of the file is the version that has the comment *Edited text, original layout.*

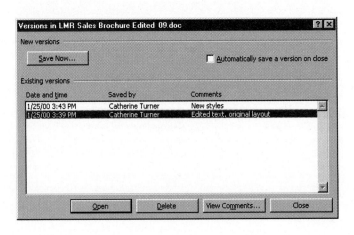

13 Click the Open button.

The original version opens in a separate window below the current version.

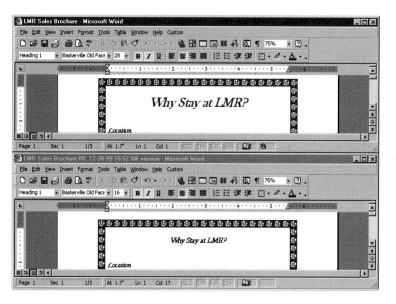

The original version is at the bottom of the screen and has the date and time on the title bar.

X

Close

14 Click the Close button in the top-right corner of the original version window.

The original version's window closes.

☐

Maximize

15 Click the Maximize button in the top-right corner of the LMR Sales Brochure 09 window.

The LMR Sales Brochure 09 window is maximized.

The original version has the comment *Edited text, original layout.*

16 On the File menu, click Versions, select the original version of the file, and then click the Delete button.

An alert box appears, asking if you are sure that you want to delete the file, and warning that the action is irreversible.

17 In the alert box, click the Yes button.

The alert box closes.

18 In the Versions In LMR Sales Brochure 09 dialog box, click the Close button.

The dialog box closes. The original version of the document is deleted, and the current version remains intact.

W2000E.7.6

XML tagging is new in Word 2000. Word also takes advantage of new HTML 4 capabilities to provide a better conversion of a Word document to an HTML document.

Converting Documents to and from HTML

Earlier versions of Microsoft Word allowed you to save Word documents in **HTML** (Hypertext Markup Language) format so that they could be viewed on a Web site. HTML is the format used to display documents on the Web. In previous versions of Word, however, the conversion to HTML often resulted in formatting that was different than the formatting in the original Word document. If you downloaded an HTML document from the Web and then opened it as a Word file so that you could edit it in Word, the document in Word often looked considerably different than it did on the Web.

Now you can create a document in Word and then display it as a Web page with much more uniform results. When the document is viewed in a Web browser, it will look much more like the original version than was possible with earlier versions of Word. Now Word saves all the pictures used in the original document as separate picture files so that they can be inserted and positioned in the HTML file correctly. That is, the HTML document contains references to the pictures so they can be displayed properly on a Web page.

Converting a Word document to HTML format, posting the HTML file to a Web site, and later downloading the HTML file for editing and conversion back into Word, is often called **round-tripping**. When a Word file is converted to Web format, published to the Web, and later saved as a file from within a Web browser, much of the original Word formatting is retained. This round-tripping approach is made possible because Word inserts formatting information in a Word document when it is converted to HTML. This formatting comes in the form of **XML** (eXtensible Markup Language) tags, which define the original formatting that was in the Word document. When the HTML file is later downloaded from the Web page and then opened in Word, Word uses the XML tags to reconstruct the original appearance of the Word document.

Another benefit of the XML formatting tags is that you can continue to work on a document in Word even after it has been saved in HTML format. Word uses the XML tags to format an HTML document so that it looks correct even when it is opened in Word. As you edit a document in Print Layout view, you can switch to Web Layout view to see how your changes will appear when the document appears in a Web browser.

(continued)

continued

Converting a document from Word to HTML and then back to Word is particularly useful if your organization uses an intranet (an internal Web site). After converting a Word document to HTML format, you can then save it to the intranet so that others can view the document by using their Web browser. If other users want to open the document in Word and make changes, they can easily do so. The document can then be saved again as an HTML file and saved back to the intranet so that the modified version can be viewed by others using their Web browser.

To use round-tripping, you create the document in Word and then save it as a Web page. To save a document as a Web Page, on the File menu, click Save As Web Page. The Save As dialog box appears, and you save the document as you would any Word file. The document is then displayed in Web Layout view.

After you have saved the document in HTML format, close it, and start Microsoft Internet Explorer or your default Web browser. On the File menu in Internet Explorer, click Open, and then click OK to display the Open dialog box. Click the Browse button to display the Microsoft Internet Explorer dialog box. Navigate to the desired file, click Open, and then in the Browse dialog box, click OK.

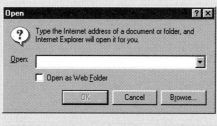

To save a Web page that you are viewing in Internet Explorer, on the File menu in Internet Explorer, click Save As, and provide a name for the Web document.

It is a good idea to also save the document as a Word document before you save it as a Web page. If the appearance of the document changes significantly after you convert it to HTML, you can discard the HTML file and use the saved Word document to make edits and design changes so that the document will then convert more reliably into HTML.

HTML files will have the Internet Explorer icon displayed next to the file name in Windows if Microsoft Internet Explorer is your default browser. If Netscape Navigator is your default Web browser, HTML files will show the Netscape icon when you view them in Windows.

Microsoft Internet Explorer

Lesson Wrap-Up

In this lesson, you learned how to track changes, accept and reject changes, add comments, protect a document, create multiple versions of a document, set the default location for workgroup templates, and convert documents to and from HTML.

If you are continuing to other lessons:

● On the File menu, click Close. If you are prompted to save the changes, click Yes.

If you are not continuing to other lessons:

● On the File menu, click Exit. If you are prompted to save the changes, click Yes.

Lesson Glossary

comments Text that is embedded in a file and is used for documentation purposes. Comments usually describe why changes were made and by whom.

change tracking A feature that identifies and keeps track of edits made to a document by different users. You can elect to view or hide edits when change tracking is turned on, and you can also selectively determine which changes will become part of the final document and which changes will be discarded.

discussion A reply to a comment from multiple users. For example, one user creates a comment, another user replies to the comment, other users reply to the reply, and so on, to create a threaded discussion from a single comment.

HTML (Hypertext Markup Language) The formatting language used to display documents on the Web.

revision marks Text that appears in a color other than black to show that the text has been added or deleted by a particular user. Deleted text also appears with a strikeout line through it and inserted text appears underlined.

round-tripping The Word Feature that allows you to convert a Word document into HTML format (retaining the formatting from the Word document), publish the corresponding HTML document to a Web site, and then save the HTML document from within Internet Explorer or your default Web browser, and open the document in Word so that it can be viewed and edited.

template A document containing built-in text, styles, and other formatting that can be used to create other documents that will share the same basic formatting. A template can contain text or formatting, macros, styles, menu and key assignments, and customized toolbars.

Versions A Word feature that allows you to save changes for different editing sessions of a document so that each editing session can be opened and reviewed independently. Multiple versions are stored in the same Word document.

workgroup template A template that is shared on a network.

XML (eXtensible Markup Language) Additional formatting tags that Word uses when a document is converted to HTML. XML tags define the original formatting that was in the Word document. When the HTML file is later downloaded from the Web page and then opened in Word, Word uses the XML formatting tags to reconstruct the original appearance of the Word document.

Quick Quiz

1   How can you view comments that have been inserted into a document?

2   How do you view all the versions of a document?

3   What is an advantage of tracking changes in a document?

4   How do you mark changes in a document?

5   What is a quick way to activate change tracking?

6   What is a workgroup template?

7   What happens when you accept a change that has been inserted into the document?

important:

In the Putting It All Together section below, you must complete Exercise 1 before continuing to Exercise 2.

Putting It All Together

Exercise 1: If necessary, start Word. Open the file named LMR Welcome Pamphlet 09. Turn on change tracking. Delete all but the first sentence of the first paragraph. Then after the first sentence, insert the following text:

> **You have selected one of the finest vacation spots in California. Please take advantage of our resort services and amenities. If there is anything that we can do to make your stay more enjoyable, please don't hesitate to ask.**

Protect the document for comments only, and then after the first paragraph, add the comment **I liked the original language better. Can we compromise?** Try to delete the first paragraph.

Exercise 2: Unprotect the document you protected in Exercise 1, and turn off change tracking. Accept all changes and delete the comment. Then create multiple versions of the document. Save the first version with the comment **unedited**. In the second version, make the entire first paragraph bold, and then save it with the comment **edited**. View both versions, and then delete the second version.

LESSON 10

Working with Tables of Contents and Indexes

After completing this lesson, you will be able to:

✔ *Format and compile a table of contents.*

✔ *Update a table of contents.*

✔ *Identify entries for an index.*

✔ *Create a cross-reference in an index.*

✔ *Format and compile an index.*

✔ *Edit and update an index.*

You encounter tables of contents and indexes just about every time you pick up a book, magazine, or other long document. If you need to find the start of Chapter 8 in a reference book, for example, you don't need to flip through the book to find the start of the chapter. Instead, you can turn to the beginning of the book and locate the starting page number for Chapter 8 in the table of contents. A **table of contents** lists the headings and subheadings in the order that they appear, along with the corresponding page numbers, as shown below.

Do-It-Yourself Bicycle Maintenance
  Table of Contents

Chapter 1: Understanding the Components of a Bicycle   3
          Frame   3
          Wheels   4
          Forks   6
          Cranks and Pedals   8
          Gears and Sprockets   11
Chapter 2: Keeping Your Bicycle Clean   13
Chapter 3: Repairing and Replacing a Tube   15
          Removing a Tube   16
          Finding a Leak   19
          Patching a Leak   21
          Replacing a Tube   24
Chapter 4: Repairing and Replacing a Chain   26
          Repairing a Broken Link   28
          Replacing a Chain   31

Indexes, found at the back of a book or other long document, are also helpful for finding information. An **index** is generally more thorough than a table of contents because it contains specific references to all topics, terms, dates, names, and places mentioned in a document, along with the page numbers where you can find each **entry** (topic).

Indexes are organized alphabetically by topic and by subtopic within a particular topic. A subtopic is often called a **subentry**. Most good indexes also contain **cross-references** for the same information to help you find the information more easily. For instance, if you're reading a book about bicycle maintenance and you want to find information about removing cranks and pedals, you would probably find an entry under *C (cranks)*, along with the entry *See also Pedals*, as shown below.

Bicycle
    cleanliness, 13–14
    components, 3–12
Chain
    broken link, 28–30
    repairing, 29–30
    replacing, 31–33
Cleanliness of your bicycle, 13–14
Components of your bicycle, 3–12
Cranks, 8–9. *See also* Pedals
Forks, 6
Frame, 3
Gears, 11–12. *See also* Cables, Sprockets
Leaks. *See* Tube
Pedals, 10–11
Repairing and replacing a chain. *See* Chain
Sprockets, 12
Tires, 5–6
Tubes
    repairing, 15–23
    replacing, 24–26
Wheels, 4–5

You can use Microsoft Word 2000 to create tables of contents, indexes, and cross-references when you create a long document. Word can generate a table of contents automatically by compiling text that has been formatted in any of the heading styles (Heading 1, Heading 2, and Heading 3 in the Normal template) and providing corresponding page numbers for the headings. Because Word can use heading styles to compile the table of contents for you, you don't need to retype the table of contents entries yourself. To create an index in a Word document, you select each entry and subentry that you want to include. Then you instruct Word to compile all of the selected entries into an alphabetic index at the end of the document. By selecting the entries rather than retyping them yourself in an index, you save time, and you reduce the chance of introducing typographical errors in the index.

To apply a style, on the Formatting toolbar, click the Style down arrow to display the list of styles, and click the style that you want to apply. You can find further explanations for creating and applying styles in Lesson 4, "Formatting Text," in the Microsoft Word 2000 Step by Step Courseware Core Skills Student Guide.

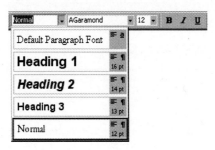

In this lesson, you will learn how to compile a table of contents, identify entries for an index, create a cross-reference, and edit and update an index.

Sample files for the lesson

To complete the procedures in this lesson, you will need to use the practice file LMR Pamphlet 10 in the Lesson10 folder in the Word Expert Practice folder located on your hard disk.

W2000E.2.10

Formatting and Compiling a Table of Contents

If you have applied heading styles to the headings in your document, you can later instruct Word to search for the heading styles and then compile the heading text into a table of contents. By default, Word uses the heading styles that are built into the Normal template, but you can specify other styles that Word should use to identify table of contents entries.

> You can preview different formats to see how each format would affect the appearance of your table of contents. When you select a format, Word displays a sample of the format in the Print Preview box of the Index And Tables dialog box.

When you instruct Word to create a table of contents, you can also define the format (the design) in which you want the table of contents to appear. Word provides several ready-made table of contents formats. The format that you choose is chiefly a matter of personal preference, although some of the formats suggest a particular target audience—formal, informal, elegant, academic, and so on.

> In the following exercises, the Standard and Formatting toolbars have been separated. For additional information on how to separate toolbars, see the "Using the CD-ROM" section at the beginning of this book.

The first time you use the Index And Tables dialog box, Word displays the format called From Template. This format applies all capital letters to main headings and mixed uppercase and lowercase letters for subheadings. The From Template format also separates each heading from its starting page number by inserting a **dot leader** tab. A dot leader tab is simply a line of dots that helps draw the eye from the heading to the correct page number in the table of contents, as shown below.

Chapter 1: UNDERSTANDING THE COMPONENTS OF A
BICYCLE... 3
Frame 3
Wheels 4
Forks 6
Cranks and Pedals 8
Gears and Sprockets 11

Other table of contents formats apply different capitalization, text formatting, and leader characters. Some of the formats do not apply any leader characters between each heading and its corresponding page number. If you select a particular format and then use the format to compile a table of contents, Word will remember the format the next time you create a table of contents for the same document or for a different document and will default to your previously selected format unless you change it again.

If you like a particular format but don't like the way leaders are used for the format, you can use the Index And Tables dialog box to change to a different leader character or to change the format so that it doesn't include leaders. The Index And Tables dialog box also includes options for selecting whether you want to include page numbers, whether you want to right-align the page numbers (against the right page margin), and the number of heading levels you want for your table of contents. If you change any of these options, Word will remember them the next time you display the Index And Tables dialog box.

The Lakewood Mountains Resort marketing manager is putting the finishing touches on a new pamphlet to advertise the resort. Even though the document is relatively short, the marketing manager wants to include a table of contents at the beginning of the pamphlet to show readers where they can locate information in the pamphlet.

In this exercise, you open a document in which Word's built-in styles have already been applied, and you format and compile a table of contents.

Open

1   On the Standard toolbar, click the Open button. Navigate to the Lesson10 folder in the Word Expert Practice folder, and double-click the file LMR Pamphlet 10.

2   Press Ctrl+Enter.

A new page is inserted at the beginning of the document.

3   Press the Up arrow key.

The insertion point moves to the top of the page 1, below the text *Welcome*.

4   On the Insert menu, click Index And Tables.

The Index And Tables dialog box appears.

5   In the Index And Tables dialog box, click the Table Of Contents tab.

The table of contents options appear. The selected format can vary, depending on the format that was used to create a table of contents previously in Word.

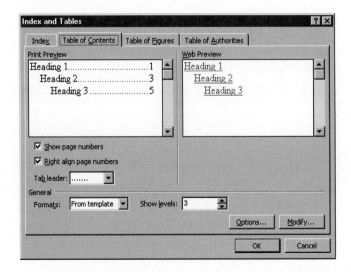

6 Click OK to accept the default table of contents settings.

The table of contents is created.

The default Heading 1 and Heading 2 styles are selected by default in the TOC level boxes. If your document does not use these styles, these defaults will have no effect on your table of contents. However, to be safe, you should remove the default styles if you plan to use only your own heading styles to create the table of contents.

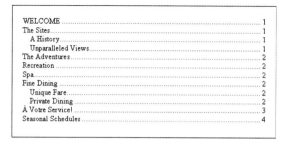

7 Save the document as **LMR Pamphlet 10 Edited**.

Keep this file open for the next exercise.

tip

You don't have to restrict your tables of contents entries to the ready-made heading styles (Heading 1, Heading 2, and Heading 3) provided in Word's Normal template. You can create and apply your own heading styles and then specify that Word use these headings to create the table of contents. To do so, on the Insert menu, click Index And Tables, and click the Table Of Contents tab. Click the Options button to display the Table Of Contents Options dialog box, which includes a list of all styles in your document. In the list of TOC Level boxes, type the table of contents level next to each heading style that you want to include in the table of contents. For instance, if you create two heading styles called A Head and B Head, you would probably specify A Head as a level 1 table of contents entry and B Head as a level 2 table of contents entry. Word will look for text that has the A Head and B Head styles applied and will use the text to compile two levels of entries for your table of contents.

W2000E.2.10

Updating a Table of Contents

Usually you create a table of contents after you complete your document because that's when the contents for all pages have been added and edited. But on occasion, you might edit one or more document headings after you've already used Word to compile the table of contents. Or you might add a significant amount of text, which changes the pagination of your document. If you make changes to your document, you can display the Index And Tables dialog box again, and click OK. Word will ask if you want to replace the existing table of contents. Click Yes if you want the headings and page numbers in your table of contents to reflect your most recent changes in the document.

You can also quickly update the table of contents to reflect your most recent changes by selecting the table of contents and pressing F9. A dialog box will appear, asking if you want to update the page numbers only or the page numbers and the entire table. Update only the page numbers if you're sure you haven't added or edited any headings. Update the entire table if you want to make sure that any modified, added, or deleted headings in the document are updated in the table of contents.

If you've compiled your table of contents at the start of a document, you can select the table of contents quickly by pressing Ctrl+Home.

If you compile a table of contents and then notice a misspelling or other typo in a heading, you might find it easier to simply correct the entry directly in the table of contents and then make the corresponding correction in the document without recompiling the table of contents. If you edit text in a table of contents, you must do so in a different manner than when you edit other text in a document. Word creates a hyperlink for each table of contents entry. If you click an entry, Word jumps to that heading and page in your document. To select the table of contents for editing, click anywhere in the right margin of the table of contents. You'll notice that all of the text for the table of contents appears shaded when you click anywhere in it. The shading indicates that the table of contents text is actually part of a TOC field code. You can then click and drag to select text and make your change as you normally would.

The marketing manager at Lakewood Mountains Resort wants to edit and reorganize some of the text in the pamphlet. In this exercise, you make changes to the document and then update the table of contents.

You can also insert a page break by clicking the location in the document where you want the break to occur and clicking Break on the Insert menu to display the Break dialog box. Click the Page Break option in the Break Types section of the dialog box, and click OK.

1   Scroll to the second page, and click to the left of the heading *The Sites*.

2   Press Ctrl+Enter.

A page break is inserted below the *Welcome* paragraph, and *The Sites* section moves to the third page.

3   Scroll down the page, and click to the left of the heading *The Adventures*.

4   Press Ctrl+Enter.

A page break is inserted below *The Sites* section, and *The Adventures* section is moved to the fourth page.

5   Press Ctrl+Home.

The insertion point moves to the beginning of the document, and the table of contents is selected. You can tell that the table of contents is selected because the entries appear shaded in gray.

6   Press F9.

The Update Table Of Contents dialog box appears, and the Update Page Numbers Only option is selected.

You can also update the table of contents by right-clicking it and clicking Update Field to display the Update Table Of Contents dialog box.

7   Click OK.

The page numbers in the table of contents are updated to reflect the changes that have been made to the document, shown on the following page.

Save

8   Save the document with the current name.

Keep this file open for the next exercise.

W2000E.2.12

You can view index entry field codes when formatting marks are displayed. By viewing index entry field codes, you can quickly identify the terms that you have already marked for your index. To display formatting marks on the Standard toolbar, click the Show/Hide ¶ button. Formatting marks are displayed by default when you begin marking index entries.

Show/Hide ¶

Identifying Entries for an Index

The first step in creating an index is to identify and mark the entries that you want included in the index. Select the text that you want to create an index entry for, and click Index And Tables on the Insert menu. Then on the Index tab, click the Mark Entry button to display the Mark Index Entry dialog box. You use this dialog box to insert an **index entry field code** (XE) for the text that you selected in the document. An index entry field code identifies the text and page that is to be inserted in the index. You can also use this dialog box to specify that you want the selected text to be a subentry under an existing main entry or to create a *See* or *See also* cross reference for the entry.

The procedure for marking index entries might seem a bit complex at first, but after you mark a few entries, you'll see how quick the process is and how much time you can save compared to typing the index manually. After you've displayed the Mark Index Entry dialog box and used it to mark your first index entry, you can leave the dialog box open so that you can quickly select and mark additional index entries.

important

Be careful and precise when you select text for index entries. For example, in the subheading *A History* you don't want to select *A* because the word *History* is all that should appear in the index entry. (You want the index entry to appear in the *H* section of the index, not as *A History* in the *A* section of the index.) Also, don't select special characters, such as quotation marks, at the start of an entry, unless you want the entry indexed separately from regular text. Special character entries are listed at the beginning of the index. For example, in a document that explains how to use Word, you might include the © and ™ characters at the start of the index with references to the pages where readers can find out how to insert these characters. However, if your document contains the text Lakewood Mountains Resort™, and you want to index Lakewood Mountains Resort along with the ™ symbol, you can include the symbol in your index entry. Because the index entry begins with an *L*, the entry will appear in the *L* section of the index, not in the special characters section at the start of the index.

In this exercise, you mark entries for an index.

1   On the third page of the document, in the subheading *A History*, select the word *History*.

2   On the Insert menu, click Index And Tables.

The Index And Tables dialog box appears.

3   In the Index And Tables dialog box, click the Index tab.

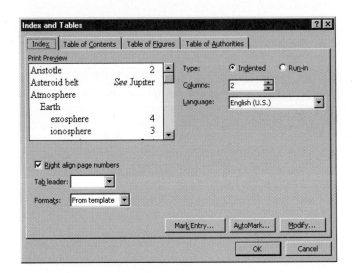

4   Click the Mark Entry button.

The Mark Index Entry dialog box appears, and the word *History* appears in the Main Entry box.

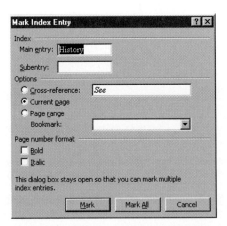

You can also display the Mark Index Entry dialog box by pressing Alt+Shift+X.

5   In the Mark Index Entry dialog box, click the Mark button.

Formatting marks appear by default, and the entry is marked with an index entry field code.

A·History{·XE·"History"·}¶

6   Move the Mark Index Entry dialog box to the top of your screen. Scroll down, if necessary, to the second paragraph on the page, and select the word *ballroom* in the second sentence.

7 Click the Mark Index Entry dialog box to activate it, and click the Mark button.

Word marks the entry with an index entry field code.

8 In the last line of the second paragraph, select the text *Mineral Mountain.*

9 Click the Mark Index Entry dialog box to activate it, and click the Mark All button.

Word marks all three occurrences of *Mineral Mountain* with an index entry field code.

10 Scroll down to the fourth page, and select the heading *Recreation.*

11 Click the Mark Index Entry dialog box, and click the Mark button.

Word marks the entry with an index entry field code.

12 Scroll to the fifth page, and select the word *Dining* in the heading *Private Dining.*

13 Click the Mark Index Entry dialog box, and click in the Subentry box.

14 In the Subentry box, type **Room Service**.

When you select a word or phrase that you want to include in the index, the Mark Index Entry dialog box will display the selected text in the Main Entry box and will use this text for the index entry. However, you can modify a main entry or subentry if you want it to be appear differently in the index. For example, suppose you select the word *Countries* but want the entry to be listed as *country* in the index. You simply edit the text in the Main Entry or Subentry box so that the text reads exactly as you want it to appear in the index.

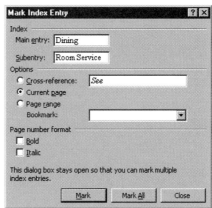

15 In the Mark Index Entry dialog box, click the Mark button.

Word marks *Dining* as a main entry with *Room Service* marked as a subentry under *Dining.*

Private·Dining{·XE·"Dining:Room·Service"·}¶

Keep this file open for the next exercise.

W2000E.2.11

Creating Cross-References in an Index

In a thorough index, it's commonplace to direct readers to a more appropriate place to find a topic in the index or to a different index entry that involves a similar topic. For example, if you were to look in the index of a computer book about Word, for example, below the term *data source,* you'll probably find a *See also* cross-reference for *mail merge* because you use data sources in a mail merge operation. A cross-reference encourages the reader to look at other terms in the index for additional or related information.

Indexes typically provide two kinds of cross-references: *See* and *See also*. A *See* cross-reference sends the reader to a different location in the index, where the desired topic and related page numbers can be found. For instance, suppose that you look in an index for *ISP*. The index entry you find is "ISP. *See* Internet service provider." You are redirected to this index entry to find the page numbers about ISPs. If you look in the index for *data source*, you might find page numbers related to data source information, but you might also find the entry "*See also* mail merge." A *See also* cross-reference directs you to additional index entries where you can find related information.

When you create an index cross-reference in Word, Word inserts the italicized word *See* before the cross-referenced term. You can delete the word *See*, if you want, or you can change the cross-reference to *See also* by typing the word *also* after *See*.

In this exercise, you create a cross-reference in the pamphlet index.

1   Scroll to the fourth page. In the second line under the heading *Recreation*, select the word *tennis*.

2   Click the title bar of the Mark Index Entry dialog box.

    The dialog box becomes active, and the selected word, *tennis*, appears in the Main Entry box.

3   In the Options section, click the Cross-Reference option.

    The insertion point moves to the space after *See* in the Cross-reference box.

4   Type **Recreation**, and click the Mark button.

    A cross-reference appears for the *tennis* index entry.

tennis{·XE·"tennis"·\t·"*See*·Recreation"·}

> The \t indicates that the entry that follows in quotation marks, "recreation," is a cross-reference that will be listed under the main entry, "tennis."

5   Close the Mark Index Entry dialog box.

    Keep this file open for the next exercise.

W2000E.2.12

Formatting and Compiling an Index

After you mark all the index entries that you want, you are ready to define the format for the index and compile the index. When you compile an index, Word searches for index entry field codes in the document. All of the marked index entries are then alphabetized and collected at the location of the insertion point, along with page numbers for each index entry. When you define the format prior to compiling the index, you choose the appearance or design (also called a format) for the index, how the numbers are aligned, and what tab leaders you want to use. In the exercise on creating a table of contents, you already saw the effects of one kind of **tab leader**, called a dot leader. A tab leader is a dashed, dotted, or solid line that fills the space between an entry and its page number. A tab leader draws the reader's eye across the space between the entry and the page number.

As is true for tables of contents, the Index And Tables dialog box provides different format designs that can be applied to an index. The format you choose is really a matter of taste, although some formats are less formal than others (such as the Bulleted format) and some formats provide a more stylized look (such as the Fancy format).

When you define the format for your index, you can specify whether you want to create an **indented index** or a **run-in index**. An indented index has subentries shown in an indented list below the main entry. The indented index is best for books whose indexes require many subentries because the indentation makes it easy to distinguish between main entries and subentries. A run-in index lists subentries in paragraph form after the main entry. Subentries in a run-in index are separated by a semicolon. A run-in index uses less space, and it is often used for books in which topics are more general.

After you mark the entries and format your index, you use Word's Index And Tables dialog box to compile the index.

In this exercise, you format and compile the index for the entries that you marked in the previous exercise.

1 Press Ctrl+End.

The insertion point moves to the end of the document.

The index will be inserted at the current location of the insertion point.

2 Press Ctrl+Enter.

Word inserts a page break after the *Seasonal Schedules* section, and the insertion point moves to the top of the next page.

3 On the Insert menu, click Index And Tables.

The Index And Tables dialog box appears.

4 In the Index And Tables dialog box, verify that the Index tab is selected.

5 Click the Formats down arrow, scroll down the list, and then click Simple.

A sample of the format appears in the Print Preview box.

6 In the Type section, verify that the Indented option is selected, and in the Columns section, verify that the number 1 appears in the box.

If the number 1 doesn't appear in the Columns box, use the Up and Down arrows to the right of the box to select the number 1.

The index format is defined. Subentries will be indented and the index will consist of one column per page. You are ready to compile the index.

7   Click OK.

Word compiles the index, which appears on the last page of the document.

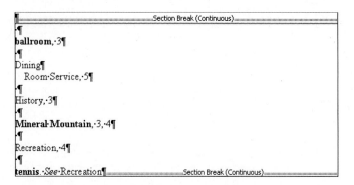

Save

8   Save the document with the current name.

Keep this file open for the next exercise.

Editing and Updating an Index

If you make changes to index entries in a document, or if you add or remove entries or repaginate the document, you'll need to update the index. Updating ensures your most recent changes to a document are reflected in the index. Word also allows you to make changes directly to the index, just as you can with a table of contents. For instance, in proof-reading your index, you might notice that a main index entry is plural instead of singular (for example, *ballrooms* instead of *ballroom*). You could locate the index entry field code for this entry, change the index entry to singular, and then update the index. However, it might be easier to simply make the change in the index itself.

The Lakewood Mountains Resort marketing manager isn't completely satisfied with the index because some of the entries are bold and some aren't. Also, she wants to delete the *ballroom* entry.

In this exercise, you delete an index entry, edit index entries, and then update the index. You also change the formatting of the index and update the index again.

1   Scroll up to the second paragraph on page 3, and in the second line, select the { XE "ballroom" } index entry field code, as shown below.

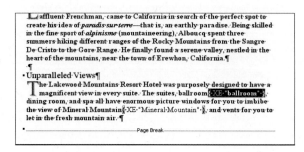

When you delete an entry, you select the entire index entry field code. When you edit an index entry, however, you select only the text between quotation marks in the index entry field code.

B

Bold

You can also update an index by right-clicking the index and clicking Update Field on the shortcut menu that appears.

2   Press Delete.

3   In the last sentence of the last paragraph on the same page, select the index entry *Mineral Mountain*, as shown below, and on the Formatting toolbar, click the Bold button.

The index entry is no longer bold, but the text in the document remains bold.

> in the fine sport of *alpinisme* (mountaineering), Alboucq spent three summers hiking different ranges of the Rocky Mountains from the Sangre De Cristo to the Gore Range. He finally found a serene valley, nestled in the heart of the mountains, near the town of Erewhon, California.¶
>
> • Unparalleled Views¶
>   The Lakewood Mountains Resort Hotel was purposely designed to have a magnificent view in every suite. The suites, ballroom, dining room, and spa all have enormous picture windows for you to imbibe the view of Mineral Mountain{XE·"Mineral·Mountain"·}, and vents for you to let in the fresh mountain air.¶
> •━━━━━━━━━━━━━━Page Break━━━━━━━━━━━━

4   Remove the bold formatting from the remaining *Mineral Mountain* index entries (in the first and last paragraphs on the fourth page).

5   Remove the bold formatting from the *tennis* index entry in the second line of the second paragraph on the fourth page.

6   Scroll to the end of the document, click anywhere in the index, and then press F9.

The index is updated. The *ballroom* entry is deleted from the index, and the bold formatting is removed from the *Mineral Mountain* and the *tennis* entries.

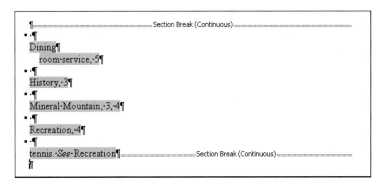

7   On the Insert menu, click Index And Tables.

The Index And Tables dialog box appears.

8   Click the Format down arrow, and click Fancy.

The new formatting appears in the Print Preview box.

9   Click the Tab Leader down arrow, and click the dotted line.

The new formatting appears in the Print Preview box.

10   Verify that the Index tab is selected, and select the Right Align Page Numbers check box.

The new formatting appears in the Print Preview box.

11   In the Type section, verify that the Indented option is selected.

12   In the Columns section, click the up arrow to select the number 2, and click OK.

An alert box appears, asking if you want to replace the selected index.

13   In the alert box, click Yes.

The index is updated to reflect the edits.

If you decide to change the format for an index after you've compiled it, you open the Index And Tables dialog box, select a different format, and click OK. Word will update the current index with the new formatting.

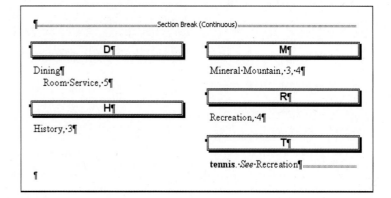

Save

14   Save and close the document.

Lesson Wrap-Up

In this lesson, you learned how to format, compile, and update a table of contents, and you learned how to mark index entries, specify the format for an index, compile the index, and update the index. You also learned how to create cross-references in an index.

If you are continuing to other lessons:

● On the File menu, click Close to close any open documents.
Word closes the files.

If you are not continuing to other lessons:

● On the File menu, click Exit.
Word closes.

Lesson Glossary

cross-references   Entries in an index that either refer the reader to an additional index entry where related information can be found (a *See also* cross-reference) or direct the reader to a different index entry where the desired information can be found (a *See* cross-reference).

dot leader   A line of dots in a table of contents entry that helps draw the eye from the heading to the given page number.

entry   A main topic in a table of contents that might also be referred to as topic or heading.

indented index   An index format in which subentries appear in an indented list below the main entry. An indented index is best for documents in which indexes require many subentries.

index   A reference section located at the end of a long document or book that the reader can use to find page numbers for specific information, such as concepts, important terms, names, dates, and places.

index entry field code (XE) A code used by Word to identify the text and page number for an entry that is to be inserted in an index.

run-in index An index format in which subentries are listed in paragraph form after the main entry. Subentries in a run-in index are separated by a semicolon. A run-in index uses less space than an indented index and is often used for documents in which there would be fewer index subentries.

subentry Part of an entry that represents aspects of that entry in greater detail.

tab leader A dashed, dotted, or solid line that fills the space between an entry and a page number in a table of contents or an index. A tab leader draws the reader's eye across the space between the entry and the page number.

table of contents A reference section at the beginning of a document that lists headings and subheadings in the order that they appear in the document, along with the corresponding page numbers where the topics can be found.

Quick Quiz

1   How do you update an index after you make changes to index entries?

2   How do you mark an entry for an index?

3   What is the difference between a table of contents and an index?

4   How do you create an index cross-reference?

5   What dialog box do you use to create a table of contents or an index?

important

In the Putting It All Together section below, you must complete Exercise 1 before continuing to Exercise 2.

Putting It All Together

Exercise 1: Open the file LMR Visitor Pamphlet 10, and create a table of contents. Edit the document so that each main heading is on its own page. Add a new subhead, *The Wild Outdoors,* below the *The Adventures* heading, apply the Heading 2 style to the new heading, and then update the table of contents. Save the document as **LMR Visitor Pamphlet 10 Updated**.

Exercise 2: In the file LMR Visitor Pamphlet 10 Updated, mark the following as main entries for the index: on the second page, the subheading *History;* and in the History paragraph, *Erewhon.* Insert the index into the document. Create a cross-reference for Steve Alboucq (in the first line of the first paragraph on the third page) so that readers will be directed to the *History* entry, modify the entries so they are all bold (except for the *History* cross-reference), and then update the index.

LESSON 11

Using Long Document Formats

After completing this lesson, you will be able to:

✔ *Understand footnotes and endnotes.*

✔ *Insert footnotes and endnotes.*

✔ *Locate notes in a document.*

✔ *Move and delete notes.*

✔ *Modify reference marks.*

✔ *Create and use bookmarks.*

✔ *Create and edit a master document and subdocuments.*

One of the most daunting tasks involved in preparing a long document, such as a research paper, has traditionally been adding footnotes to cite sources at the end of each page. With typewriters and older word processing programs, the only way you could add footnotes was to measure the space required at the bottom of each page for any footnotes to be placed on the page. You had to remember not to type any body text in the space that you reserved for footnotes. If you measured incorrectly or, as a result of additional writing or editing, you had to add or remove footnotes, you often had to retype the contents of the page. Fortunately, Microsoft Word 2000 automates the process of adding and removing footnotes and provides several other techniques that make it easy to work with long documents.

For example, you can choose to add your notes at the end of your document (endnotes) rather than at the bottom of pages (footnotes), and you can change the formatting for footnotes, endnotes, and the reference numbers or symbols that Word inserts for each note. You can also insert bookmarks at different places in a lengthy document to make each location easy to find for your readers or to make it easier to find your place in a document when you return to it. When you insert bookmarks, you can use the Go To dialog box to go directly to the text that you bookmarked. For instance, in a technical document, you might introduce several terms that are new to some readers. At the end of the document, you might create a glossary so that readers can find all definitions in a convenient location. When you introduce a term in the document, you might create a bookmark to its corresponding glossary entry. When the reader clicks the bookmark, the definition at the end of the document automatically appears.

In this lesson, you will learn several techniques for working effectively with long documents. Specifically, you'll learn how to insert, modify, and locate footnotes, endnotes, and bookmarks. You'll also learn how to link several subdocuments to a master document so that all subdocuments can be edited independently and then combined later into a single document.

**Sample files
for the lesson**

To complete the procedures in this lesson, you will use the practice files Instructional Principles 11 and Section I in the Lesson11 folder in the Word Expert Practice folder located on your hard disk. You'll use the Instructional Principles 11 file to create and modify footnotes and endnotes and to create and use bookmarks. You'll insert the Section I file as a subdocument to a master document.

Understanding Footnotes and Endnotes

Footnotes and endnotes are used to add more detailed information about a topic in a document, such as a definition, a specific date and its importance, or a citation's source. These notes appear at the bottom of a page or at the end of a document so that they don't interrupt the flow of text in the body of the document. The only difference between footnotes and endnotes is their placement in a document. A **footnote** typically appears at the bottom of a page, while an **endnote** appears at the end of a section, chapter, or document. In Word, both footnotes and endnotes are made up of two parts: the **reference mark** and the **note text**.

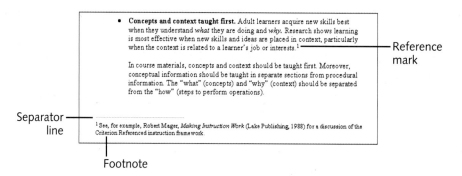

Reference mark — Separator line — Footnote

Reference marks are the symbols or numbers that appear after words or sentences in the body of the document. These reference marks are usually sequential numbers (although symbols can also be used) that help the reader determine which notes apply to which text and, of course, also indicate that there are corresponding notes for the reference marks. Corresponding symbols or numbers are placed at the bottom of the page or at the end of the document and are followed by the actual note text. Readers can choose to keep reading the body of a document and read the notes later, or they can stop reading when they see a reference mark and then read the corresponding note.

By default, Word automatically numbers reference marks. Word uses Arabic numerals (1, 2, 3, and so on) to number footnotes and lowercase Roman numerals to number endnotes (i, ii, iii, iv, and so on). However, you can change the numbering style if you prefer a different number format. A horizontal line separates the note text from the document text. In general, use numbered reference marks when you have several notes, especially several notes per page. The numbering helps the reader determine which note goes with which reference number in the text. Symbols might be preferable if your document will only contain one or a few informational notes (such as *All prices are guaranteed until August 31, 2002* or † *The park opens at 7:00 A.M. and closes at dusk*).

W2000E.2.8

In the following exercises, the Standard and Formatting toolbars have been separated. For additional information on how to separate the toolbars, see the "Using the CD-ROM" section at the beginning of this book.

Inserting Footnotes and Endnotes

Determining whether to use footnotes or endnotes is often a matter of preference, although some organizations and educational institutions provide standards that you must follow. Consider an example in which endnotes would be used. At Lakewood Mountains Resort, a vice president is preparing a paper for an upcoming convention on hotel and restaurant management. The convention's guidelines for submitting papers require that each paper cite sources and other reference information at the end of the document. So the vice president uses Word to add endnotes to her paper.

Now consider an example in which footnotes might be used. The concierge at Lakewood Mountains Resort is writing an article on customer service for a hotel and restaurant management trade journal. The journal requires that authors cite their sources and other reference information at the bottom of the page on which the reference material appears. She uses Word's footnoting capabilities to add these footnotes as she prepares the article.

The first step in inserting a footnote or endnote into a document is to decide where you want the reference mark to appear. You then click to position the insertion point at this location and insert a note. By default, Word numbers reference marks in sequence (starting with the number 1) as you add them and formats the notes either at the bottom of the page (if you are inserting footnotes) or at the end of the document (if you are inserting endnotes).

In this exercise, you insert footnotes and endnotes into a document.

Open

1   On the Standard toolbar, click the Open button. Navigate to the Lesson11 folder in the Word Expert Practice folder, and double-click the file Instructional Principles 11.

2   On page 1, in the paragraph that follows the first two bulleted items, click after the comma at the end of the phrase *Although researchers disagree about the specific characteristics of adult learners,*.

As mentioned earlier, you can also use a symbol as a reference mark. To select a symbol, in the Numbering section of the Footnote And Endnote dialog box, click Custom Mark, click the Symbol button to display all symbols, and then select a symbol.

3   On the Insert menu, click Footnote.

The Footnote And Endnote dialog box appears.

Footnote and Endnote	? ✕
Insert	
⦿ Footnote	Bottom of page
○ Endnote	End of document
Numbering	
⦿ AutoNumber	1, 2, 3, ...
○ Custom mark:	[ ]
	Symbol...
OK Cancel	Options...

4 In the Insert section, verify that the Footnote option is selected. In the Numbering section, verify that AutoNumber is selected, and click OK.

The insertion point moves to the bottom of the first page. A line and the number 1 are shown at the bottom of the page, where the text of the footnote will appear.

5 Type **See "Adult Learning: An Overview" by Stephen Brookfield, in** *The International Encyclopedia of Education.* **Pergamon Press, 1995.**

The footnote is entered.

> - Adults have a larger base of knowledge that can be used in learning new concepts and skills.
> - Adults have specific goals for learning.
> - Adults want to apply what they learn right away.
>
> There's no doubt that many adults have these characteristics. Anyone who has taught adults (as ActiveEducation courseware developers have done) knows that they are often less "passive" than child learners. Adults want to know what, and why, and how. If course material is not explained to their satisfaction, they feel justified in demanding further explanation. Moreover, they are proud of the knowledge they've already acquired; they enjoy using it to acquire new knowledge.
>
> But to assume that there is a "typical" adult learner is a mistake—particularly when it comes to computer instruction. Experienced computer instructors know that all adult learners are not alike. Three factors vary widely from one student to the next:
>
> ---
> [1] See "Adult Learning: An Overview" by Stephen Brookfield, in *The International Encyclopedia of Education.* Pergamon Press, 1995.

6 Scroll to the middle of the first page, and click at the end of the first sentence under the heading *Characteristics of Adult Learners*, after *...for the approach he recommended* (and after the period).

7 On the Insert menu, click Footnote.

The Footnote And Endnote dialog box appears.

8 In the Insert section, click Endnote, and click OK.

The insertion point moves to the end of the document. The lowercase numeral *i* appears.

> You combine footnotes and endnotes in the same document in this exercise for instructional purposes only. Normally, you would choose either footnotes or endnotes for a document, but not both.

9 Type **Knowles' most influential books were** *Self-Directed Learning* **(1975) and** *Andragogy in Action* **(1984).**

The endnote is entered.

> To that end, many training organizations provide customized Web-based training for a variety of software and technology areas. Because Web-based courses are more individualized by comparison with classroom instruction, a Web-based course should begin with a pre-test to measure what a student already knows. Based on the results, the Web-training engine can dynamically generate a curriculum focused on what the student needs to learn. This is not only consistent with the best principles of instructional design: it also helps students learn faster and with no wasted effort.
>
> Web-based training should not be perceived as a replacement for instructor-led, classroom training. It is simply an alternative. Although Web-based training does not fit all learning styles (some adults prefer to have a "live" instructor present and want to interact with other students), it is a sound instructional delivery alternative for those who cannot afford the time or expense to travel to a classroom location or who only have time for training at unusual hours.
>
> ---
> [i] Knowles' most influential books were *Self-Directed Learning* and *Andragogy in Action* (1985).

10 Scroll to the top of page 3, and click to position the insertion point after the period at the end of the first bulleted item, which ends *...confirmed by subsequent learning research.*

11 On the Insert menu, click Footnote.

The Footnote And Endnote dialog box appears.

If you change any settings in the Footnote And Endnote dialog box and then close and reopen the current document, you'll notice that your options are retained in the Footnote And Endnote dialog box. However, Word retains these settings for the current document only—they will not be reflected in other documents that you create or open.

12   In the Insert section, click Footnote, and click OK.

The reference mark (2) is inserted in the text, the number 2 is shown below the first footnote, and the insertion point moves to the bottom of the first page.

13   Type **George Miller, "The Magic Number Seven, Plus or Minus Two,"** *Psychological Review, issue 63*.

The footnote is entered.

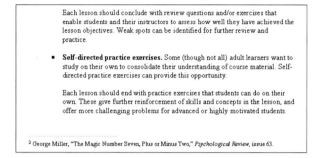

14   Click anywhere inside the document.

15   Save the document as **Instructional Principles 11 Edited**.

Word saves the document.

Keep this file open for the next exercise.

Locating Notes in a Document

Print Layout is the preferred view when you create footnotes or endnotes because this is the only view in which you can see footnotes and endnotes as they appear in the document. In Web Layout view, you can see only the endnotes as they appear in the document, but not the footnotes. In Normal and Outline views, you cannot see the footnotes or the endnotes. However, if you use Normal view or Outline view, you can double-click a reference mark to display the Notes pane, as shown below. Web Layout view doesn't open the Notes pane; instead, the end of the document appears so that you can view the endnotes.

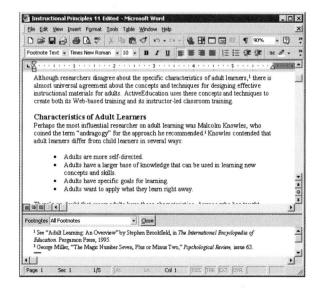

You can also view footnotes and endnotes by placing the mouse pointer over a reference mark to display the footnote or endnote in a ScreenTip. This approach works in all views and provides a quick way to read a particular endnote or footnote without having to scroll to the location of the note.

When you are working with a long document, the reference marks for footnotes and endnotes might be scattered throughout the document, but you can use Word to find a specific footnote or endnote quickly. For example, if you know you want to view a footnote for a particular reference mark number, you can use the Go To tab of the Find And Replace dialog box to go directly to this note. If you've created footnotes and want to quickly read them or review them in sequence, you can use Word to browse through the notes.

In this exercise, you go to a specific footnote, browse for footnotes and endnotes, and then view an endnote.

1   Press Ctrl+Home to move the insertion point to the beginning of the document.

2   On the Edit menu, click Go To.

> You can also access the Find And Replace dialog box by clicking Find or Replace on the Edit menu or by pressing F5 or Ctrl+G.

The Find And Replace dialog box appears with the Go To tab displayed.

3   In the Go To What list, click Footnote.

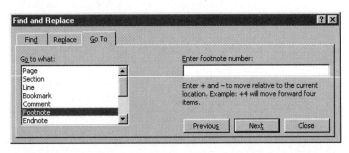

4   In the Enter Footnote Number box, type **1**, and click the Go To button.

The insertion point moves to the left of the first footnote reference mark.

5   In the Find And Replace dialog box, click the Close button.

6   At the bottom of the vertical scroll bar, click the Select Browse Object button.

Select Browse Object

The Select Browse Object menu appears.

7   On the Select Browse Object menu, click the Browse By footnote icon.

Browse By Footnote.

The insertion point moves to the left of the second footnote reference mark.

Previous Footnote

8 At the bottom of the vertical scroll bar, click the Previous Footnote button.

The insertion point moves back to the left of the first footnote reference mark.

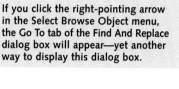

Select Browse Object

9 At the bottom of the vertical scroll bar, click the Select Browse Object button.

The Select Browse Object menu appears.

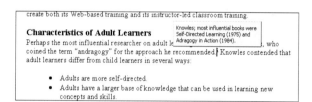

Browse By Endnote

10 In the Select Browse Object menu, click the Browse By Endnote icon.

The insertion point moves to the left of the first endnote reference mark.

> If you click the right-pointing arrow in the Select Browse Object menu, the Go To tab of the Find And Replace dialog box will appear—yet another way to display this dialog box.

11 Position the mouse pointer over the reference mark.

The endnote appears in a ScreenTip.

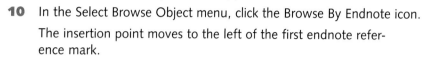

> If you are not in Normal view, the insertion point will move to the endnote at the end of the document.

12 On the View menu, click Normal.

The document is displayed in Normal view.

13 Double-click the reference mark for the endnote.

The Notes pane appears.

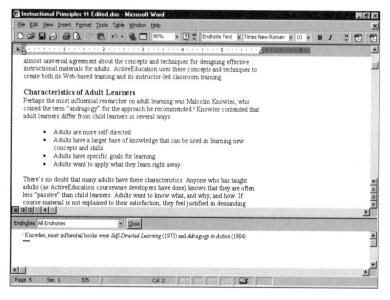

14 In the Notes pane, click the Close button.

The Notes pane closes.

15 On the View menu, click Print Layout.

The document appears in Print Layout view.

Save

16 Save the document with the current name.

Keep this file open for the next exercise.

Moving and Deleting Notes in a Document

When you edit text in a long document that contains footnotes or endnotes, your edits often affect the placement and numbering of the notes. Suppose that you decide to add a quotation in the body of your document, and then you decide to move a case study to a different page. Or, as you read through the document, you realize that you typed a footnote correctly but inserted the reference mark in the wrong location. As a result, you want to move the reference mark and its footnote to the correct location. Or suppose that the quotation that you added to the document uses the same source as an existing footnote. You can copy the footnote to the second location to save yourself the time required to type the text for the note again. When you move, copy, or delete notes in your document, Word renumbers the other notes for you.

To move a note, you simply select the reference mark for the note, click Cut on the Standard toolbar, position the insertion point at the desired location, and click the Paste button. The reference mark is renumbered, if necessary. You can tell if the reference mark is correctly selected because it will appear highlighted in black

To copy a note, you select the reference mark, click Copy on the Standard toolbar, position the insertion point at the new location, and then click the Paste button.

To delete a note, you select the reference mark, and press Delete or Backspace.

In this exercise, you move, copy, and delete notes.

1   Scroll to the botton of page 2 of the document.

2   At the end of the last paragraph, click after the period at the end of the text ...*(steps to perform operations).*

3   On the Insert menu, click Footnote.

   The Footnote And Endnote dialog box appears.

4   In the Insert section, verify that the Footnote option is selected, and click OK.

   The reference mark (2) is inserted in the text.

The previous footnote 2 is renumbered as footnote 3 because the footnote you are inserting now comes before it.

5   Type **See Robert Mager,** *Making Instruction Work* **(Lake Publishing, 1988) for a discussion of the Criterion Referenced Instruction framework.**

The footnote is entered; however, it is at an incorrect location. You will need to move it to the correct location.

> • **Learning assessments to measure student progress.** Measurement of student progress can identify areas where further work is needed. Review questions at the end of each lesson not only provide such measurement, but further reinforce each student's understanding of the lesson material.
>
> Each lesson should conclude with review questions and/or exercises that enable students and their instructors to assess how well they have achieved the lesson objectives. Weak spots can be identified for further review and practice.
>
> • **Self-directed practice exercises.** Some (though not all) adult learners want to study on their own to consolidate their understanding of course material. Self-directed practice exercises can provide this opportunity.
>
> ---
> [2] See Robert Mager, *Making Instruction Work* (Lake Publishing, 1988) for a discussion of the Criterion Referenced Instruction framework.
> [3] George Miller, "The Magic Number Seven, Plus or Minus Two," *Psychological Review*, issue 63.

6   Scroll to the top of page 3 and select the reference mark (2) for footnote 2.

7   Drag the reference mark (which appears with a dotted rectangle when you drag it) to the end of the paragraph above it (the bulleted item that ends with ...*a learner's job or interests.* on page 2 until the dotted rectangle is to the right of the period after the word *interests*.

The footnote moves to the new location.

> • **Concepts and context taught first.** Adult learners acquire new skills best when they understand *what* they are doing and *why*. Research shows learning is most effective when new skills and ideas are placed in context, particularly when the context is related to a learner's job or interests. [2]
>
> In course materials, concepts and context should be taught first. Moreover, conceptual information should be taught in separate sections from procedural
>
> ---
> [2] See Robert Mager, *Making Instruction Work* (Lake Publishing, 1988) for a discussion of the Criterion Referenced Instruction framework.

Copy

8   Scroll to the top half of page 1, select the reference mark for footnote 1 (after the words *characteristics of adult learners*), and on the Standard toolbar, click the Copy button.

The reference mark and corresponding footnote are copied to the Windows Clipboard.

Paste

9   Scroll to the top of page 2, and click at the end of the quotation by Stephen Brookfield, which ends with ...*a uniquely adult form of practice,* click after the ending quotation mark, and then on the Standard toolbar, click the Paste button.

The reference mark is copied to the new location and numbered. Subsequent footnotes are also renumbered.

> Course materials should state specific, measurable learning goals for the course itself, for each lesson, and for each section within lessons. Such goals not only make learning more efficient, but also make it possible to verify that the students have mastered the course content.
>
> • **Concepts and context taught first.** Adult learners acquire new skills best when they understand *what* they are doing and *why*. Research shows learning is most effective when new skills and ideas are placed in context, particularly when the context is related to a learner's job or interests.[3]
>
> ---
> [2] See "Adult Learning: An Overview" by Stephen Brookfield, in *The International Encyclopedia of Education*. Pergamon Press, 1995.
> [3] See Robert Mager, *Making Instruction Work* (Lake Publishing, 1988) for a discussion of the Criterion Referenced Instruction framework.

If you want to use drag and drop to copy a note, you must hold down the Ctrl key prior to dragging.

10 Scroll to the bottom of the page to see the copied footnote.

11 Scroll to the middle of page 1, select the reference mark (i) for the endnote, and press Delete.

The endnote is deleted from the text.

12 On the Standard toolbar, click the Undo button.

The endnote is returned to the document.

13 Save the document with the current name.

Keep this file open for the next exercise.

Changing the Placement of a Note

Although you normally place footnotes at the bottom of each page, you can change the location of notes so that they appear immediately below the text on each page (which can be useful if text on several pages does not reach the bottom of the page). And even though you normally place endnotes at the end of a document, you might want to change this so that notes appear at the end of each section in a document (such at the end of each report section rather than all notes at the end of the document). To change the placement of a note, on the Insert menu, click Footnote to display the Footnote And Endnote dialog box, and click the Options button to display the Note Options dialog box.

> You can also use the Note Options dialog box to change numbering of footnotes or endnotes to symbols. In the dialog box, click the Number Format down arrow, and click the set of symbols at the bottom of the list.

Click the All Endnotes tab or the All Footnotes tab, depending on the type of note that you want to change. Click the Place At down arrow, and then click the desired placement option. Click OK, and then close the Footnote And Endnote dialog box.

If you include footnotes in a document and later decide that you want to use endnotes instead, you don't have to redo all the notes. With Word, you can quickly convert all footnotes to endnotes, or all endnotes to footnotes. To change the note style, on the Insert Menu, click Footnote, and in the Footnote And Endnote dialog box, click the Options button. In the Note Options dialog box, click the Convert button to display the Convert Notes dialog box, click the desired option, and click OK.

> You can use the Note Options dialog box to make a variety of changes to footnotes and endnotes. You can change the format of reference marks and modify how the notes are numbered (by section, by page, and so on).

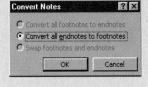

Modifying the Reference Mark Style

Word uses ready-made character and paragraph styles to format footnotes and endnotes. You can use these default styles for notes, or you can apply a different style to change the appearance of notes. You can modify the numbering format as well as the starting number for notes (for example, to accommodate notes in different files that will be compiled later into one document).

To change the appearance of footnote or endnote text and footnote or endnote reference marks, on the Format menu, click Style to display the Style dialog box, and click the Footnote (or Endnote) Text style or the Footnote (or Endnote) Reference style. Click the Modify button to display the Modify Style dialog box, and change any formatting for the endnote or footnote style as needed. (For more information on creating, editing, and applying styles, see Lesson 2, "Using Advanced Document Formatting.")

You can also use the Footnotes And Endnotes dialog box to change the appearance of notes. In the Footnotes And Endnotes dialog box, you can click the Options button to display the Note Options dialog box. Click the Number Format down arrow, and click the desired reference mark numbering approach. For example, you might want to specify that endnotes be numbered using Arabic numbers (instead of the default lowercase Roman numerals).

In this exercise, you modify the style of reference marks.

1   Scroll to the middle of page 1, and select the reference mark for footnote 1.

2   On the Formatting toolbar, click the Font down arrow, and click Arial Black.

The reference mark font changes to Arial Black.

> Much of this research has focused on the best ways to teach computer skills to adults. Although researchers disagree about the specific characteristics of adult learners,[1] there is almost universal agreement about the concepts and techniques for designing effective instructional materials for adults. ActiveEducation uses these concepts and techniques to create both its Web-based training and its instructor-led classroom training.

You can quickly modify the style of a reference mark by displaying the Footnote And Endnote dialog box and clicking the Symbol button. In the Symbol dialog box, select a custom symbol for each reference mark.

important

If you change the font for a character style (including a footnote or endnote reference mark style), Word applies the style change only to the currently selected character. If you want to automatically update a character style for all occurrences of the style, use the following approach: Select any reference mark, and change the formatting using the Formatting toolbar buttons. In the Style list, click the name of the reference mark style (Footnote Reference or Endnote Reference). In the Modify Style dialog box that appears, click Update The Style To Reflect Recent Changes?, and then click Automatically Update The Style From Now On. All instances of the style will be changed to reflect your formatting changes.

3   Scroll down, if necessary, and select the endnote number (i) and the space after it (at the end of the first sentence after the heading *Characteristics of Adult Learners*).

4   On the Insert menu, click Footnote.

The Footnote And Endnote dialog box appears.

5   Click the Endnote option.

6   In the Footnote And Endnote dialog box, click the Symbol button.

The Symbol dialog box appears.

7   Click the diamond symbol, and click OK.

> You can also insert symbols from a specific font. Click the Font down arrow and click the name of a font. The Symbol dialog box will then show available symbols for the selected font.

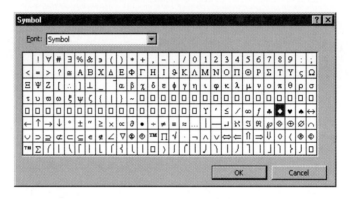

8   In the Footnote And Endnote dialog box, click OK.

Word replaces the endnote number reference mark with the symbol and also changes the number to the symbol at the end of the document.

> You might need to delete the previous reference number in the endnote at the end of the document.

> To that end, many training organizations provide customized Web-based training for a variety of software and technology areas. Because Web-based courses are more individualized by comparison with classroom instruction, a Web-based course should begin with a pre-test to measure what a student already knows. Based on the results, the Web-training engine can dynamically generate a curriculum focused on what the student needs to learn. This is not only consistent with the best principles of instructional design: it also helps students learn faster and with no wasted effort.
>
> Web-based training should not be perceived as a replacement for instructor-led, classroom training. It is simply an alternative. Although Web-based training does not fit all learning styles (some adults prefer to have a "live" instructor present and want to interact with other students), it is a sound instructional delivery alternative for those who cannot afford the time or expense to travel to a classroom location or who only have time for training at unusual hours.
>
> ---
> ♦ [i] Knowles; most influential books were *Self-Directed Learning* (1975) and *Adragogy in Action* (1984).

9   Scroll to footnote number 2 in the middle of page 2, select the footnote number, and on the Insert menu, click Footnote.

The Footnote And Endnote dialog box appears.

10   In the Insert section, click Footnote.

11   Click the Footnote option.

12   Click the Options button.

The Note Options dialog box appears.

13 In the Note Options dialog box, click the Number Format down arrow, click the lowercase *a,b,c* option, and then click OK.

The Footnote and Endnote dialog box shows that footnotes are autonumbered in the *a,b,c* format.

> If a message box appears asking you to type some text for a footnote or endnote mark, click OK, and click Close in the Footnote And Endnote dialog box.

14 Click the OK button to close the dialog box.

Word changes the footnotes to letters and lists them in alphabetical order.

15 Save the document using the current name.

Keep this file open for the next exercise.

Modifying the Note Separator Line

Word uses a horizontal line called a **separator** to separate footnotes and endnotes from the text in a document. The separator line creates an "academic" or formal look for the document. Most textbooks and journals use separator lines to differentiate body text from notes.

You can modify the separator line by inserting text to the left or right of the line (for example, you might want to insert the word *Footnotes* or *Notes*), or by adding a border around the line. For a more informal document, you can also delete the separator line.

To modify the separator line:

1 On the View menu, click Normal to switch to Normal view.

2 On the View menu, click Footnotes.

The View Footnotes dialog box appears.

> If you work through these steps, you'll notice that the note text is not displayed with the separator line.

3 Make sure View Footnote Area is selected (or View Endnote Area if you are modifying the endnote separator), and click OK.

The Notes pane appears.

(continued)

continued

> **4** Click the Footnotes down arrow, and click Footnote Separator or Endnote Separator (depending on whether you are editing the footnote or endnote separator line).
>
> **5** Edit or format the separator as you desire.
>
>   ■ To delete the separator line, select the line, and press Delete.
>
>   ■ To restore the default separator line, click the Reset button.
>
> **6** After you make the desired changes in the Notes pane, click the Close button, and switch to Print Layout view to see the modified separator line.

W2000E.2.3

Creating and Using Bookmarks

If you use a bookmark with a book or novel, it's easy enough to insert the bookmark between the pages that you are currently reading so that you can return to that location later. But what do you do when you are editing a long document in Word and the phone rings, your coworker stops by to chat, or your boss calls an emergency meeting? If you save and close the document and then reopen it later, you might have to spend several minutes searching for where you left off.

With Word, you can insert an electronic **bookmark** that you can use to quickly and easily return to a specific, predefined point in the document. If you've inserted bookmarks into a document, you can also create hyperlinks at other locations and then specify that Word will go to a particular bookmark when a reader clicks the hyperlink. For example, early in a long document, perhaps in Section I, you might type *Section V explains our current financial picture in more depth*. You could then create a bookmark at the start of Section V in the document. Then in the *Section V explains...* reference, you could insert a hyperlink for the phrase *Section V* so that when readers click the hyperlink, Word immediately displays the start of Section V of the document.

In this exercise, you insert and use a bookmark, and then you delete it.

1 Scroll to the top of page 4, and click at the beginning of the heading *How Instructional Concepts Can Apply to Computer Training*.

> If you convert a Word document to the Adobe Acrobat PDF format, any bookmarks and hyperlinks are retained in the PDF file.

2 On the Insert menu, click Bookmark.

The Bookmark dialog box appears.

You cannot use spaces in Bookmark names. Include an underscore (_) if you want to represent a space.

To view bookmarks in a document, click Options on the Tools menu to display the Options dialog box. Click the View tab, and in the Show section, click Bookmarks, and then click OK.

3 In the Bookmark name box, type **Reference1**, and click the Add button.

The bookmark named Reference1 is added to the document, and the Bookmark dialog box closes.

4 Press Ctrl+Home to position the insertion point at the beginning of the document, and on the Insert menu, click Bookmark.

The Bookmark dialog box appears, and Reference1 is selected in the Bookmark Name list.

5 In the Bookmark dialog box, click the Go To button.

The insertion point moves to the location of the bookmark.

6 In the Bookmark dialog box, verify that Reference1 is selected, and click the Delete button.

The Reference1 bookmark is deleted.

7 Click the Close button to close the Bookmark dialog box.

8 Save the document with the current name, and then close the document.

Word saves and closes the document.

tip

If you've created bookmarks, you can insert hyperlinks at other locations in the document that readers can use to quickly jump to the bookmarked locations. You can even create hyperlinks to other documents on the same network or to Web pages on the Internet. First create a bookmark for a location in your document. Then create a link to this bookmark elsewhere in your document, to a path and document on your network, or to a Web page. Select the reference text, and on the Insert menu, click Hyperlink. Click the Place In This Document button, click the plus symbol to the left of Bookmarks in the list, and click the name of the bookmark to which you want to link.

W2000E.2.9

Creating Master Documents and Subdocuments

A **master document** is a file that stores links to other Word documents, called **subdocuments**, that will ultimately be joined with the master document to create a single finished product. When one user is working on a subdocument, it is locked for editing and cannot be accessed by other users until the subdocument is closed.

For example, suppose your organization is creating an annual report for shareholders. The report will contain a brief introduction highlighting the general accomplishments of the company for the past year. The remainder of the report will be divided into sections, and a different departmental manager will be responsible for writing each section. To facilitate the creation of the annual report, you might designate the introduction as the master document and then specify that each file (for each additional section of the report) be a subdocument. After all of the subdocuments have been finalized, the links in the master document are used to collect the subdocuments into one large document—the annual report.

> One of the values of subdocuments is that their content is stored in seperate files on your hard disk, thus reducing the amount of memory (RAM) required to display the master document.

When you create subdocuments, you can use an existing document as the master document and then insert subdocuments from existing files. Or you can create the master document and the subdocument headings and file names. When you save the master document, each heading that you've specified as a subdocument becomes its own document, with the heading used as the file name. Users can then open these subdocuments and create and edit the content.

Create Subdocument

To create a subdocument, you must first construct an outline (in Outline view) in the master document. When you create an outline heading, you can then click the Create Subdocument button on the Outlining toolbar to make that heading the name of a subdocument. You can use the ready-made heading styles in the Normal.dot template (Heading 1, Heading 2, and Heading 3) to determine the hierarchy of the subdocuments, or you can create and apply your own styles and use them as subdocument names.

In a master document, you can either **expand** or **collapse** the subdocuments that are part of the master document. When a master document is expanded in Outline view, all of the contents for each subdocument appear in a gray box. The illustration on the next page shows an expanded master document and two subdocuments. The first subdocument is named *Section I*, and the second subdocument is named *Section II*. In the Section I subdocument, text has been added under the first heading, but no text has been added under the second heading. In the Section II subdocument, two headings have been created, but no text has yet been added under the headings. You can click the Subdocument icon near the top-right corner of a subdocument box to open the document in a separate window and add or edit content.

Subdocument

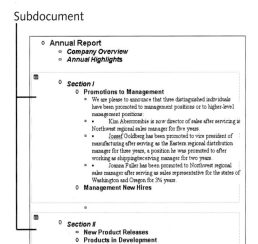

If you collapse the subdocuments in a master document, each subdocument appears as a hyperlink. You can click a hyperlink to open the subdocument and edit it directly, or you can click the Subdocument icon in the top-right corner of the subdocument box to open the subdocument. The following illustration shows a master document with five subdocuments that have been collapsed into hyperlinks.

Subdocument Icons   Hyperlinks

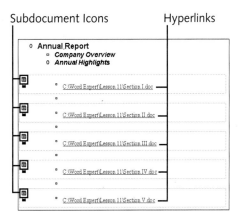

You can also switch to Page Layout or Normal view to view the subdocuments as hyperlinks; however, Outline view is the only way to create or insert new subdocuments and to view the content of a subdocument without actually opening the subdocument itself. In Outline view, you can also use the Outlining toolbar to lock one or more subdocuments so that they can't be edited. The following illustration shows the buttons on the Outlining toolbar that you can use to create and work with master documents in Outline view.

> On the Outlining toolbar, you can click the Promote and Demote buttons to change the level of a heading.

Promote

Demote

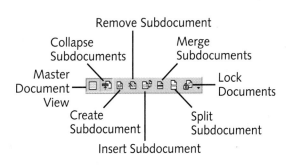

In this exercise, you create a master document, create a heading for a subdocument, and insert an existing document into the master document for use as a subdocument. Then you change the views of the master document and open a subdocument by clicking its hyperlink.

New Blank Document

The Outlining toolbar includes the buttons that you need to insert subdocuments and modify their order.

Insert Subdocument

1   On the Standard toolbar, click the New Blank Document button.

2   On the View menu, click Outline.

Word switches to Outline view and displays the Outlining toolbar.

3   Type **Annual Report**, and press Enter twice.

Word creates the heading for your master document and inserts a blank line. The heading is formatted with the Heading 1 style.

4   On the Outlining toolbar, click the Insert Subdocument button.

The Insert Subdocument dialog box appears.

5   Use the Look In list to navigate to the Lesson11 folder in the Word Expert Practice folder located on your hard disk. In the Lesson11 folder, double-click the Section I document.

The Section I document appears as a subdocument within the master document, as shown below.

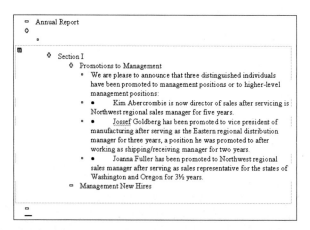

Demote

6   Type **Section II**, and on the Outlining toolbar, click the Demote button.

The heading changes to the Heading 2 style to match the level of the subdocument you inserted.

Create Subdocument

7   On the Outlining toolbar, click the Create Subdocument button.

The heading becomes a second subdocument within the master document.

8   On the File menu, click Save As.

The Save As dialog box appears.

9   Click Save to accept the suggested name *Annual Report*, which is the heading for the master document.

Collapse Subdocuments

10 On the Outlining toolbar, click the Collapse Subdocuments button.

The subdocuments appear as hyperlinks. Each hyperlink displays the path to the subdocument.

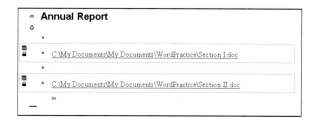

11 Click the first hyperlink (for the Section 1 subdocument).

The subdocument opens so that you can edit the subdocument directly.

> If you edit the contents of a subdocument from the master document in Outline view and then save the master document, Word will save your changes in the subdocument as well.

12 In the first bullet item for Kim Abercrombie, select the words *servicing is* and type **serving as**.

13 Save and close the subdocument.

The correction is saved to the subdocument, and the master document reappears.

Expand Subdocuments

14 On the Outlining toolbar, click the Expand Subdocuments button.

In the Section I outline, notice that your correction is reflected in the master document.

> To insert and create subdocuments, the subdocuments must be expanded.

important

When you attempt to print a master document, Word will ask you if you want to first open the subdocuments. If you click No, the master document will print links for the subdocuments in the master document—not the contents of the subdocuments. If you click Yes, Word will print the master document contents followed by the contents of all subdocuments.

Lesson Wrap-Up

In this lesson, you learned how to create, modify, and locate footnotes and endnotes; how to create and use bookmarks; and how to create a master document. You also learned how to create and insert subdocuments, how to expand and collapse subdocuments, and how to open a subdocument for editing.

If you are continuing to other lessons:

Save

1 On the Standard toolbar, click the Save button.

Word saves the document.

2 On the File menu, click Close.

Word closes the file.

If you are not continuing to other lessons:

Save

1   On the Standard toolbar, click the Save button.
Word saves the file.

2   On the File menu, click Exit.
Word closes.

Lesson Glossary

bookmark   A location or selection of text that is marked so that you can use the Go To tab of the Find And Replace dialog box to return to the bookmark quickly. You can also create a hyperlink to a bookmark.

collapse   To conceal data in a document. If you collapse subdocuments in a master document, each subdocument appears as a hyperlink.

endnote   A note located at the end of a document or at the end of a section in a document that provides more information about text in the body of the document.

expand   To show all data in a document. When a master document is expanded in Outline View, all the contents each subdocument appear in a gray box.

footnote   A note located at the bottom of a page (or after all text on a page) that provides more information about text in the body of the document.

master document   A file that stores links to other documents and serves as a container for related documents that will be combined to create a single finished product.

note text   The information supplied by the footnote or endnote. Note text appears at the end of the document (or section) for an endnote, and at the bottom of the page (or after all text on a page) for a footnote.

reference mark   A number or symbol displayed in a document that directs the reader to a corresponding footnote or endnote.

separator   A horizontal line that separates footnotes and endnotes from the text in a document.

subdocuments   Documents that are linked to a master document so that the subdocuments can be printed in sequence.

Quick Quiz

1   When would you use footnotes or endnotes?

2   What is the difference between a footnote and an endnote?

3   How do you display the Footnote And Endnote dialog box?

4   How can you easily find footnotes and endnotes in a document?

5   How do you insert a bookmark into a Word document?

important

In the Putting It All Together section below, you must complete Exercise 1 to continue to Exercise 2.

Putting It All Together

Exercise 1: Open the file Adult Learners 11, and add the following footnote at the end of the quotation at the bottom of page 4:

Malcolm S. Knowles, *Andragogy in Action.* Jossey-Bass, 1984.

On page 3, at the end of the bulleted paragraph that begins *Hands-on exercises to reinforce learning*, add the following endnote.

Miller, Galanter, & Pribram, *Plans and the Structure of Behavior.* Holt, Rinehart, & Winston, 1960.

View the notes using the Select Browse Object button, display the notes in a ScreenTip, and delete the endnote. Save the document as **Adult Learners 11 Edited**.

Exercise 2: On page 2 of Adult Learners 11 Edited, add a bookmark called **Design** at the beginning of the heading *Instructional Design for Adult Learners*. Use the bookmark, display it in the document, and then delete it. Save and close the document.

Quick Reference

Core Skills

Lesson 1: Getting Started with Word

To start Microsoft Word 2000

1   Click the Start button on the Windows taskbar.
2   On the Start menu, point to Programs.
3   On the Programs submenu, click Microsoft Word.

To display a ScreenTip

●   Position the mouse pointer over a button or a screen element for a few seconds.

To display a menu

●   On the menu bar, click the name of the menu.

To view an expanded menu

1   On the menu bar, click the name of the menu.
2   Click the double arrow at the bottom of the menu.
     Or
     Wait a few seconds for the expanded menu to appear on its own.

To enter text

1   Click to position the insertion point where you want to insert text.
2   Type the text.

To use Click And Type

1   In Print Layout view, position the mouse pointer where you want to insert text.
2   Double-click, and begin typing.

To save a document for the first time

Save

1   On the Standard toolbar, click the Save button.
2   Type the file name in the File Name box.
3   Click the Save In down arrow, and select a location for the file.
4   Click the Save button.

To save a document after making changes

Save

● Click the Save button.

To close a document

● On the File menu, click Close.

To create a new blank document

New Blank Document

● On the Standard toolbar, click the New Blank Document button.

To quit Word

● On the File menu, click Exit.

To display the Office Assistant

● On the Help menu, click Show The Office Assistant.

To use the Office Assistant to get help

1   On the Help menu, click Show The Office Assistant if the Office Assistant isn't already displayed.
2   Click the Office Assistant.
3   Type a question in the box.
4   Click the Search button.
5   Click one of the topics to read about it.

To hide the Office Assistant

● On the Help menu, click Hide The Office Assistant.

To turn off the Office Assistant

1   Right-click the Office Assistant, and click Options.
2   Click the Options tab.
3   Clear the Use The Office Assistant check box.
4   Click OK.

Lesson 2: Editing a Document

To open a file

Open

1   On the Standard toolbar, click the Open button.
2   Navigate to the folder where the file is stored.
3   Click the file's name.
4   Click the Open button.

To navigate through a document

● Use the mouse pointer.

      Or

Use the arrow keys.

Or

Use the scroll bars.

Or

Use the key combinations.

To scroll through text

● Use the vertical scroll bar, scroll arrows, and scroll box to move up and down.

Or

Use the horizontal scroll bar, scroll arrows, and a scroll box to move left to right.

Or

Previous Page

Use the Previous Page button to move to the beginning of the previous page.

Or

Next Page

Use the Next Page button to move to the beginning of the next page.

To insert text

1 Click to position the insertion point in the document where you want to insert the text.

2 Begin typing.

To select text

● Drag the mouse pointer over the text.

Or

Use the selection area to the left of the document.

To undo an action

Undo

● On the Standard toolbar, click the Undo button.

To restore an action

Redo

● On the Standard toolbar, click the Redo button.

To create a folder

Create New Folder

1 On the File menu, click Save As.

2 Click the Create New Folder button.

3 Type a name for the folder in the Name box.

4 Click OK.

To save a file with a different name

1 On the File menu, click Save As.

2 If necessary, navigate to the folder in which you want to store the file.

3 In the File Name box, type a name for the new copy of the file.

4 Click the Save button.

To save a file with a different format

1 On the File menu, click Save As.

2 If necessary, in the File Name box, type a new name for the document.

3 Click the Save As Type down arrow.

4 Click the file format in which you want to save the document.

5 Click Save.

Lesson 3: Using Templates and Wizards

To use the Normal template

New Blank Document

● On the Standard toolbar, click the New Blank Document button.

To use a template other than the Normal template

1 On the File menu, click New to display the New dialog box.

2 Click the desired category tab.

3 Double-click the desired template icon.

4 Update the document as desired, and save the file.

To create a template from an existing document

1 Create or open the document on which you want to base the template.

2 On the File menu, click Save As.

3 Type a name for the template in the File Name box.

4 Click the Save As Type down arrow, and click Document Template.

5 Leave the document in the default location (the folder called Templates).

Or

Click the Save In down arrow, and navigate to the folder in which you want to store the template.

6 Click the Save button.

7 Modify the template as desired.

8 Save the template.

To create a template from a template

1 On the File menu, click New to display the New dialog box.

2 Click the desired category tab.

3 Double-click the template icon on which you want to base the new template.

4 Update the current template with changes that you want for the new template, and click the Save button.

5   In the File Name box, type the name of the new template.

6   Click the Save As Type down arrow, and click Document Template.

7   Click the Save button.

To start a wizard

1   On the File menu, click New.

2   Click the desired category tab.

3   Double-click the wizard icon that you want to use.

4   Follow the screen prompts, clicking Next to move from one dialog box to the next.

Or

Click the flowchart on the left side of the dialog box to skip to a specific step.

5   Click the Finish button.

6   Modify the document as desired, and save it.

Lesson 4: Formatting Text

To apply a bold attribute

1   Select the text.

Bold

2   On the Formatting toolbar, click the Bold button.

Or

Press Ctrl+B.

To apply the italics attribute

1   Select the text.

Italic

2   On the Formatting toolbar, click the Italic button.

Or

Press Ctrl+I.

To apply the underline attribute

1   Select the text.

Underline

2   On the Formatting toolbar, click the Underline button.

Or

Press Ctrl+U.

To format text

1   Select the text.

2   On the Formatting toolbar, click the Style down arrow.

Or

Click the Font down arrow.

Or

Click the Font Size down arrow.

To format text using the Font dialog box

1 Select the text.

2 On the Format menu, click Font.

3 Make selections as desired.

To align text

1 Click the paragraph that you want to align.

Or

Select all or part of the multiple paragraphs that you want to align.

2 On the Formatting toolbar, click the appropriate alignment button.

To cut or copy text

1 Select the text that you want to move or copy.

2 On the Standard toolbar, click the Cut or Copy button.

3 Click the insertion point in the location in which the text is to appear or be duplicated.

4 On the Standard toolbar, click the Paste button.

Cut   Copy

Paste

To paste from a file created in another program

1 Open the file and select the text or object that you want to paste into Word.

2 On the Edit menu, click Paste Special.

3 On the Paste Special dialog box, select the format that you want to insert the text or object.

4 Select Paste.

Or

Select Paste Link.

5 Click OK.

To move text using the mouse pointer

1 Select the text that you want to move or copy.

2 Position the mouse pointer over the selected text and hold down the left mouse button.

3 Drag the mouse pointer to the new location.

To paste from among multiple selections in the Office Clipboard

1 Select the text that you want to move or copy.

2 On the Standard toolbar click the Cut or Copy button.

3 Repeat steps 1 and 2 for every selection that you want to move or copy.

4 Click where the item is to appear.

5 On the View menu, point to Toolbars, and click Clipboard.

Cut   Copy

6 On the Clipboard toolbar, click the item that you want to paste.

7 Repeat step 6 for every item that you want to paste.

To apply a style to text

1 Select the text to be formatted.

2 On the Formatting toolbar, click the Style down arrow.

3 Click the style that you want to apply.

To create a paragraph border

1 Click in the paragraph to be formatted.

Tables And Borders

2 On the Standard toolbar, click the Tables And Borders button.

3 On the Tables And Borders toolbar, click the Line Style down arrow, and click a border style.

4 Click the Border down arrow, and click the Border button to apply the border.

To add shading to a paragraph

1 Click in the paragraph to be shaded.

Tables And Borders

2 On the Standard toolbar, click the Tables And Borders button.

3 Click the Shading Color down arrow, and click a color.

To preview a document

Print Preview

● On the Standard toolbar, click the Print Preview button.

To print a document

Print

● On the Standard toolbar, click the Print button.

To print a document using special print settings

1 On the File menu, click Print.

2 In the Copies section, type the desired number of copies in the Number Of Copies box.

3 In the Page Range section, click Current Page to print the current page; click All to print all the pages; click Pages to print specific pages, and then type the desired page numbers in the Pages box.

4 Click OK.

To print selected text

1 Select the text that you want to print.

2 On the File menu, click Print.

3 In the Page Range section, click Selection.

4 Click OK.

Lesson 5:
Changing the Layout of a Document

To change the page margins using the Page Setup dialog box

1   On the File menu, click Page Setup.
2   If necessary, click the Page Margins tab.
3   Type the new page margin settings in the appropriate boxes.
4   Click OK.

To change page margins using the ruler

1   On the View menu, click Print Layout.
2   Position the insertion point over the page margin marker until the insertion point becomes a double-headed arrow.
3   Drag the marker to the new location.

To insert a hard page break:

1   Click to position the insertion point at the location where you want to add the break.
2   Press Ctrl+Enter.

To apply paragraph formatting:

1   Select the appropriate paragraph(s).
2   On the Format menu, click Paragraph.
3   Change the settings as necessary.
4   Click OK.

To indent a paragraph using the ruler

1   Select the paragraph.
2   Drag the First Line Indent, Hanging Indent, and the Left Indent markers to fully indent the paragraph.
    Or
    Drag only the First Line Indent marker only to indent the first line.
    Or
    Drag only the Hanging Indent marker only to create a hanging indent.
    Or
    Click and drag the Left Indent marker.
3   Deselect the text.

To set one tab stop:

1   On the Format menu, click Tabs.
2   Type the new tab stop in the Tab Stop Position box.
3   If desired, in the Alignment or Leader section, select the desired option.

4   Click the Set button.

5   Click OK.

To set multiple tab stops

1   On the Format menu, click Tabs.

2   In the Tab Stop Position box, type the position for the first tab stop.

3   In the Alignment section, select the desired tab alignment.

4   If desired, in the Leader section, select the desired leader option.

5   Click the Set button.

6   In the Tab Stop Position box, type the position for the second tab stop.

7   If necessary, in the Alignment or Leader sections, select the desired option.

8   Click the Set button.

9   Repeat the process for additional tab stops you want to set.

10 Click OK.

To set a tab stop using the ruler

1   Select the paragraph(s) for which you want to set the tabs.

2   Click the Tab Align button at the far left side of the ruler to specify tab alignment type.

3   Click the ruler at the location where you want the new tab.

4   Deselect the text.

To clear a tab stop

●   Drag the tab stop marker off the ruler.

To add page numbers

1   On the Insert menu, click Page Numbers.

2   Click the Position down arrow, and then select the page number position.

3   Click the Alignment down arrow, and then select the desired alignment.

4   Click OK.

To open a header or footer box

1   On the View menu, click Header And Footer.

2   Scroll to the top of a page for the header or to the bottom of a page for the footer.

To edit a header or footer

1   On the View menu, click Header And Footer.

2   Scroll to the header or footer that you want to change.

3   Click the toolbar buttons that you want to use.

4   Type or edit the text as necessary.

To change page orientation

1 On the File menu, click Page Setup.
2 If necessary, click the Paper Size tab.
3 In the Orientation section, click the Portrait or Landscape option.
4 Click OK.

Lesson 6: Using Automated Formatting

To set AutoFormat options

1 On the Tools menu, click AutoCorrect.
2 Click the AutoFormat As You Type tab.
3 In the Apply As You Type section, click the Desired settings.
4 Click OK.

To create an automatic border

1 Position the insertion point where you want to insert the border.
2 Type three dashes (—) to create a single-line border the width of the margins.

   Or

   Type three equal signs (===) to create a double-line border the width of the margins.
3 Press Enter.

To create an automatic bulleted list

1 Position the insertion point in the desired location.
2 Type * and press the Spacebar for a bulleted list.
3 Type the list data, pressing Enter after each new list item (except the last list item).
4 Press Enter twice after the last list item is entered.

To create an automatic numbered list

1 Position the insertion point in the desired location.
2 Type 1. and press the Spacebar for a numbered list.
3 Type the list data, pressing Enter after each new list item (except the last list item).
4 Press Enter twice after the last list item is entered.

To modify bulleted and numbered lists

1 Click the first item in a numbered list, or select all the items in a bulleted list.
2 On the Format menu, click Bullets And Numbering.
3 Click either the Bulleted tab or the Numbered tab on the Bullets And Numbering dialog box.

4   Click a bullet or number style.

5   If desired, click the Customize button, make changes, and then click OK.

6   Click OK.

To copy formatting using the Format Painter

1   Select the text that has the formatting you want to copy.

Or

On the Formatting toolbar (or in the Font dialog box or the Paragraph dialog box, whichever is most appropriate), click the format attributes or styles you wish to apply.

Format Painter

2   On the Standard toolbar, click the Format Painter button.

3   Select the text to be formatted and release the mouse button.

To create an AutoText entry

1   Type the text and/or insert the picture that is to be included in the AutoText entry, and then select the text and/or picture.

2   Press Alt+F3.

3   Type a name (up to 32 characters) in the Please Name Your AutoText Entry box.

4   Click OK.

To insert an AutoText entry

1   Position the insertion point where you want to insert the entry.

2   On the Insert menu, hold the mouse pointer on AutoText to open the submenu, and then click AutoText.

3   Click the desired entry in the Enter AutoText Entries Here box.

4   Click the Insert button.

Or

1   Position the insertion point where you want to insert the entry.

2   Type the name of the AutoText entry.

3   Press F3.

To create and print an envelope

1   On the Tools menu, click Envelopes And Labels, and click the Envelopes tab.

2   Enter or edit the Delivery Address.

3   Enter or edit the Return Address.

4   Insert an envelope in the printer as shown in the Feed box.

5   Click the Print button.

To create and print a label

1   On the Tools menu, click Envelopes And Labels, and click the Labels tab.

2   Enter or edit the label address.

3   To select the label type, click the Options button, click a label type in the Product Number box, and then click OK.

4   To print a full page of labels, on the Envelopes And Labels dialog box, click Full Page Of Same Label.

5   To print a single label, click the Single Label option, and type or select the row and column where you want the label to print.

6   Insert a label page in the printer.

7   Click the Print button.

Lesson 7: Using Editing and Proofing Tools

To check the spelling of an entire document

Spelling And Grammar

1   On the Standard toolbar, click the Spelling And Grammar button.

2   Click an option in the Suggestions box, and click the Change button.

Or

To ignore the word through the document, click Ignore All.

Or

To add the word to the dictionary, click Add.

3   Click OK.

To customize the spell check operations

1   On the Tools menu, click Options.

2   Click the Spelling & Grammar tab, and make selections as desired.

3   Click OK.

To turn on grammar check for a document

1   On the Tools menu, click Options.

2   Click the Spelling & Grammar tab, if necessary.

3   Click the Check Grammar With Spelling check box to turn this feature on, and click OK.

To check the grammar of a document

Spelling And Grammar

1   On the Standard toolbar, click the Spelling And Grammar button.

2   Click the Change button to make the suggested replacement displayed in the Suggestions text box.

Or

Click the Ignore button to ignore an error; click the Ignore All button to ignore the error throughout the document.

To change grammar options

1   On the Tools menu, click Options.

2   Click the Spelling & Grammar tab, if necessary.

3 Click the Writing Style down arrow and select the desired rule guidelines.

4 Click the Settings button for more control over the writing style.

5 Click OK.

To use the thesaurus

1 Right-click the word in question.

2 Point to Synonyms on the Short-cut menu.

3 Click the synonym you want to replace.

Or

1 On the Tools menu, click language and point to Thesarus.

To perform a Find operation

1 On the Edit menu, click Find.

2 To increase Find criteria and narrow the search, click the More button to display the search options.

3 In the Find What box, type the find search string.

4 Click the Find Next button until you're finished searching, or there are no more occurrences.

5 Click the Cancel button to return to the document window.

To use Go To style

1 On the Edit menu, click Go To.

2 Select Page in the Go To What list.

3 Type the desired page number in the Enter Page Number box.

4 Click the Go To button.

To perform a Replace operation

1 On the Edit menu, click Replace.

2 To increase the Find criteria and narrow the seach, click the More button to display the search options.

3 Type the search string in the Find What box.

4 Type the replacement string in the Replace With box.

5 Click the Replace button to make the replacement; click the Replace All button to make all replacements throughout the document without confirmation.

6 Click OK.

To view AutoCorrect entries

1 On the Tools menu, click AutoCorrect.

2 Click the AutoCorrect tab, if necessary.

3 Scroll through the list at the bottom of the dialog box.

To add an exception to AutoCorrect

1 On the Tools menu, click AutoCorrect.

2 Click the AutoCorrect tab, if necessary.

3 Click the Exceptions button.

4 Click the desired tab, and type the exception.

5 Click the Add button.

6 Click OK.

To highlight text

1 Select the text you want highlighted.

2 On the Formatting toolbar, click the Highlight down arrow.

3 Click a color.

Highlight

To remove highlighted text

1 Select the highlighted text.

2 On the Formatting toolbar, click the Highlight down arrow.

3 Click None.

Highlight

To insert the date and/or time

1 On the Insert menu, click Date And Time.

2 Click the desired format.

3 Click OK.

To Insert a date as a field

1 On the Insert menu, click Field.

2 Select the desired category.

3 Select the desired field name.

4 Click OK.

To insert a special character

1 On the Insert menu, click Symbol.

2 Click the Special Characters tab.

3 Select the desired character.

4 Click the Insert button.

5 Click Close.

Lesson 8: Working with Graphics

To insert a picture into a document

1 If necessary, click the Print Layout View button on the status bar.

Print Layout View

2 Click to position the insertion point where you want to insert the picture.

3 On the Insert menu, point to Picture, and click From File.

4 In the Insert Picture dialog box, click the Look In down arrow, and select the appropriate drive and folder.

5 In the file list, click the file that you want to insert.

6 Click the Insert button.

To insert a Clip Art picture into a document

Print Layout View

1 If necessary, click the Print Layout View button on the status bar.

2 Click to position the insertion point where you want to insert the picture.

3 On the Insert menu, point to Picture, and click Clip Art.

4 If necessary, in the Insert Clip Art window, click the Picture tab.

5 Click the picture category, and click the picture that you want to insert.

6 Click the Insert Clip button on the menu that appears.

To size a picture using the sizing handles

1 Select the picture.

2 Drag the left or right sizing handles to change the horizontal width of the picture.

Or

Drag the top or bottom sizing handles to change the vertical height of the picture.

Or

Drag a corner handle to simultaneously change both the horizontal and vertical dimensions.

To change the text wrap style

Text Wrapping

1 On the Picture toolbar, click the Text Wrapping button.

2 Click to position the insertion point where you want to change the text wrap.

3 Select the desired style, and click anywhere outside the picture to deselect it.

To create WordArt

Insert WordArt

1 If necessary, on the View menu, point to Toolbars, and click Drawing.

2 On the Drawing toolbar, click the Insert WordArt button.

3 Click the desired style.

4 Type the desired text, select font and size and then click Ok.

To create an AutoShape

1 On the Drawing toolbar, click the AutoShapes button to display the AutoShapes menu.

2 On the AutoShapes menu, point to the category of shape that you want to create, and click the desired shape.

3   In the area where you want to insert the AutoShape, drag to draw the AutoShape.

To fill a shape with color

1   Click the shape.

Fill Color

2   On the Drawing toolbar, click the Fill Color button's down arrow.

3   Click the desired fill color.

Lesson 9: Working with Columns

To create columns of equal width

Columns

1   Select the text that is to be formatted into columns. (Skip this step if you want the entire document formatted into columns.)

2   On the Standard toolbar, click the Columns button.

3   Click the number of columns that you want, or drag the Columns menu to the right to create more than four columns.

To create columns of unequal width using the Columns dialog box

1   Select the text to be formatted into columns.

2   On the Format menu, click Columns.

3   To create two columns of unequal width, in the Presets section, click Left to make the left column narrower, or click Right to make the right column narrower.

Or

To create customized columns, in the Number Of Columns box, type the desired number of columns, clear the Equal Column Width option, and then type the desired measurements in the Width boxes.

4   Click OK.

To adjust column widths using the Columns dialog box

1   Click the column text to be modified.

2   On the Format menu, click Columns.

3   To convert the text to two columns of unequal width, in the Presets section, click Left to make the left column narrower, or click Right to make the right column narrower.

Or

To customize the column widths, clear the Equal Column Width box, and type the desired measurements in the Width boxes.

4   Click OK.

To adjust column widths using the ruler

1   Click or select the column(s) to be modified to display the ruler.

2   Position the mouse pointer on the Move Column marker.

3   Hold down the Alt key and drag the marker to adjust the column widths.

4   When the columns are adjusted to the desired measurements, release the Alt key.

To change the spacing between columns using the Columns dialog box

1   Click the column text to be modified.

2   On the Format menu, click Columns.

3   If necessary, in the Columns dialog box, clear the Equal Column Width check box.

4   In the Spacing boxes, type the desired measurement.

5   Make adjustments to the Width boxes as desired.

6   Click OK.

To change the spacing between columns using the ruler

1   Click or select the column(s) to be modified to display the ruler.

2   On the ruler, drag the desired column marker to adjust the column spacing as desired.

To insert a manual column break using a keystroke combination

1   Move the insertion point to the location where you want to insert the break.

2   Press Ctrl+Shift+Enter.

To insert a manual column break

1   Move the insertion point to the location where you want to insert the break.

2   On the Insert menu, click Break.

3   In the Break dialog box, click the Column Break option.

4   Click OK.

To delete a manual column break

Show/Hide ¶

1   Click the Show/Hide ¶ button.

2   Position the insertion point on or to the right of the column break marker.

3   Press Delete or Backspace.

To insert a vertical line between columns

1   Click anywhere in the section that contains the columns that you want to separate with a vertical line.

2   On the Format menu, click Columns.

3   Select the Line Between check box, and click OK.

Lesson 10: Working with Tables

To insert a table using the Insert Table button

Insert Table

1   Click to position the insertion point where you want to insert the table.
2   On the Standard toolbar, click the Insert Table button.
3   On the Insert Table menu, drag the mouse pointer over the boxes and click the desired number of rows and columns.

To draw a table using the Tables And Borders button

Tables And Borders

1   On the Standard toolbar, click the Tables And Borders button.
2   Drag the mouse pointer diagonally to create the table boundaries.
3   Drag the pointer to create vertical and horizontal lines, which create the columns and rows.
4   Click the Tables And Borders button again to stop drawing.

To insert a table using the Insert Table dialog box

1   Click to position the insertion point where you want to insert the table.
2   On the Table menu, point to Insert, and click Table.
3   In the Number Of Columns box, type the number of columns that you want in the table.
4   In the Number Of Rows box, type the number of rows.
5   Click OK.

To navigate within a table

1   Click the desired cell.
2   Type the cell information
3   Press Tab to move to the next cell.
    Or
    Press a key combination to move to the desired location.

To select cells in a table

●   Press a key combination.
    Or
    Click the selection area to the left of a row.
    Or
    Click the top of a column.
    Or
    Click the bottom left corner of the cell.

To merge cells

1   Select the cells that you want to join.
2   On the Table menu, click Merge Cells.

To insert columns or rows into a table

1 Click in a cell next to where you want to insert the row or column.

2 On the Table menu, point to Insert, and click Columns To The Left, Columns To The Right, Rows Above, or Rows Below, as desired.

To delete columns or rows from a table

1 Click in the column or row that you want to delete, or select multiple rows or columns.

2 On the Table menu, point to Delete, and click Columns or Rows, depending on whether you want to delete rows or columns.

To resize an entire table

1 Position the insertion point over the table resize handle until a double-headed arrow appears.

2 Drag the handle in any direction to resize the table as desired.

To resize a column or row

1 Position the insertion point over a horizontal or vertical border anywhere in the table until a double-arrow resizing pointer appears.

2 Drag the resizing pointer in the desired direction.

To change borders in a table

Tables And Borders

1 Click anywhere in the table, and on the Standard toolbar, click the Tables And Borders button.

2 Use the toolbar buttons to select a border size and type, to draw borders, or to erase borders.

To add shading to a table

1 Select the table cells to be shaded.

Tables And Borders

2 On the Standard toolbar, click the Tables And Borders button.

3 Click the Shading Color down arrow, and click a color.

Lesson 11: Word and the Web

To create a hyperlink to a Web address

1 Type a Web address.

2 Press the Spacebar or Enter.

To create a hyperlink for a string of text

Insert Hyperlink

1 Type and select the text that you want to use as a hyperlink.

2 On the Standard toolbar, click the Insert Hyperlink button.

3 In the Type The File Or Web Page Name box, type the Web address.

4 Click OK.

To send a Word document as an attachment to an e-mail message

1   Open the document that you want to send, and then, if necessary, connect to the Internet.

2   On the File menu, point to Send To, and click Mail Recipient (As Attachment).

3   In the e-mail message window, in the To box, type the e-mail address of the recipient.

4   In the message area, type a message.

5   Click Send.

To send a Word document as the body of an e-mail message

1   Open the document that you want to send, and then, if necessary, connect to the Internet.

2   On the Standard toolbar, click the E-mail button.

E-mail

3   On the e-mail header in the To box, type the recipient's e-mail address.

4   Click Send.

To preview a Web page in the Web browser

1   Open the document that you want to preview.

2   On the File menu, click Web Page Preview.

To preview a Web page in Word

1   Open the document that you want to preview.

2   Click the Web Layout View button to the left of the horizontal scroll bar.

To save a document as a Web page

1   Save the document as a Word file.

2   On the File menu, click Save As Web Page.

3   Click Save.

Expert Skills

Lesson 1: Using Advanced Paragraph and Picture Formatting

To turn widow/orphan control on and off

1   On the Format menu, click Paragraph.

2   If necessary, click the Line And Page Breaks Tab.

3   Clear or select the Widow/Orphan Control check box.

To insert a field

1   Click to position the mouse pointer in the location where you want to insert the field.

2   On the Insert menu, click Field.

3   In the Categories list, click a category.

4   In the Field Names list, click a field.

5   Click OK.

To move a picture

●   Drag the picture to a new location using the four-headed pointer.

To resize a picture

1   Click the picture to display its sizing handles.

2   Drag a corner sizing handle to resize the entire picture.

Or

Drag a side sizing handle to make the picture taller or wider.

To delete a picture

1   Click the picture.

2   Press Delete.

To apply a text-wrapping style to a picture

1   Select the Picture.

2   Display the Picture toolbar.

3   Click the Text Wrapping button.

4   Click an option on the Text Wrapping menu.

Lesson 2:
Using Advanced Document Formats

To create a style

1   On the Format menu, click Style.

2   Click the New button.

3   Type a name for the style in the Name box.

4   Click the Style Type down arrow, and click either Paragraph or Character.

5   Click the Format button to select a formatting characteristic.

6   Select formatting attributes as desired.

7   Click OK twice.

8   Click the Close button.

To use an existing style to create a style

1   On the Format menu, click Style.
2   Click the New button.
3   Type a name for the style in the Name box.
4   Click the Based On down arrow, and click a style to base the new style upon.
5   Click the Format button to select a formatting characteristic.
6   Select formatting attributes as desired.
7   Click OK twice.
8   Click the Close button.

To use sample text to create a paragraph style

1   Select the formatted text.
2   On the Formatting toolbar, click in the Style box.
3   Type a name for the style, and press Enter.

To use sample text to create a character style

1   Select the formatted text.
2   On the Format menu, click Style.
3   Click the New button.
4   In the Name box, type a name for the style.
5   Click the Style Type down arrow, and click Character.
6   Click OK.
7   Click the Close button.

To apply a style

1   Select or click the text.
2   On the Formatting toolbar, click the Style down arrow.
3   Click the style.

To update a style

1   Modify the formatting of text that has a style applied to it.
2   On the Formatting toolbar, click in the Style box, and press Enter.
3   Click OK.

To delete a style

1   On the Format menu, click Style.
2   If necessary, click the style in the Styles list.
3   Click the Delete button.
4   Click Yes in the alert box.
5   Click the Close button.

To find and replace a style with another style

1   On the Edit menu, click Replace.

2   If necessary, click the More button.

3   If necessary, click in the Find What box.

4   Click the Format button, and click Style.

5   Click the style to find, and click OK.

6   Click in the Replace With box.

7   Click the Format button, and click style.

8   Click Style.

9   Click a style that will replace the other style.

10   Click OK.

11   Click the Replace All button to replace all occurrences of the style.

12   Click OK, and click the Close button.

       Or

       Click the Find Next button and click the Replace button only when Word selects a style that you want to change.

13   Click the Close button.

To find and replace a format with another format

1   On the Edit menu, click Replace.

2   If necessary, click the More button.

3   If necessary, click in the Find What box.

4   Click the Format button, and select a format.

5   Make desired changes, and click OK.

6   Click in the Replace With box.

7   Click the Format button, and select a format.

8   Click a format.

9   Make desired changes.

10   Click OK.

11   Click the Replace All button to replace all occurrences of the format.

12   Click OK, and click the Close button.

       Or

       Click the Find Next button and click the Replace button only when Word selects a format that you want to change.

13   Click the Close button.

To find and replace a special character

1   On the Edit menu, click Replace.

2   If necessary, click the More button.

3   If necessary, click in the Find What box.

4   Click the Special button, and select a special character.

5   Click in the Replace With box.

6   Click Replace All button to replace all occurrences of the special character.

7   Click OK, and click the Close button.

Or

Click the Close button.

To find and replace a non-printing character

1   On the Edit menu, click Replace.

2   If necessary, click the More button.

3   If necessary, click in the Find What box.

4   Click the Special button, and click a non-printing character.

5   Click in the Replace With box.

6   Type the text that you want to replace the non-printing character with, or use the Special button to select a different character.

7   Click the Replace All button to replace all occurrences of the non-printing character.

8   Click OK, and click the Close button.

Or

Click the Find Next button and click the Replace button only when Word selects a non-printing character that you want to change.

9   Click the Close button.

To create alternating footers

1   On the View menu, click Header And Footer.

2   Click in the footer.

Insert Page Number

3   On the Header And Footer toolbar, click the Insert Page Number button.

4   Click the Page Setup button.

5   Select the Different Odd And Even check box, and click OK.

6   Type text in an odd footer and format the text as desired.

7   Scroll to an even footer, and click in the footer.

8   Click the Insert Page Number button.

9   Type text in the even footer and format as desired.

10   Close the Header And Footer toolbar.

To create a first-page footer

1   On the View menu, click Header And Footer.

2   Click in the footer.

Insert Page Number

3   On the Header And Footer toolbar, click the Insert Page Number button.

4   Click the Page Set Up button.

5   Select the Different First Page check box, and click OK.

6   Format the footer as desired.

7   Close the Header And Footer toolbar.

To create a watermark

1   Double-click the header or footer.

2   Insert a graphic, a text box (to type text into), or WordArt into the header or footer.

3   Format the watermark as desired.

4   Close the Header And Footer toolbar.

To create column breaks

1   Position the insertion point in the document where you want to insert the column break.

2   On the menu, click Break.

3   In the Break dialog box, click the column break option.

4   Click OK.

Lesson 3: Working with Tables and Lists

To embed a worksheet in a Word document

1   Open the Word document and click where you want the table to appear.

2   On the Insert menu, click Object.

3   Scroll down in the Object Type list, and click Microsoft Excel Worksheet.

4   Click OK.

To modify an embedded Excel worksheet

1   Double-click the embedded worksheet to activate it and access all the Excel tools.

2   Modify the worksheet as desired.

3   Click outside the worksheet to deactivate it and to display it as a table.

To perform calculations in a table

1   Click the cell that will contain the formula.

2   On the Table menu, click Formula.

3   In the Formula box, type the desired formula.

Or

To use a Word function, click the Paste Function down arrow, click the function that you want, and then type the cells to be used in the Formula box.

4   Click the Number Format down arrow, and click the desired number format.

To link Excel data as a table

1   Open the Word document to which you want to link the object.

2   Click where you want the link to appear.

3   On the Insert menu, click Object.

4   Click the Create From File tab.

5   Click Browse, and navigate to the desired file.

6   Click the file, and click Insert.

7   Select the Link To File check box, and click OK.

To sort data in a table

1   Click in the table that you want to sort.

2   On the Table menu, click Sort.

3   Click the Sort By down arrow and choose the column that you want to sort.

4   Click the Type down arrow and change other options as desired.

5   Click OK.

To sort lists

1   Select the list that you want to sort.

2   On the Table menu, click Sort.

3   Change options as desired.

4   Click OK.

To sort paragraphs

1   Select the paragraphs that you want to sort.

2   On the Table menu, click Sort.

3   Change options as desired.

4   Click OK.

Lesson 4: Using Charts

To create a chart using Microsoft Graph 2000

1   Click the mouse pointer in the Word document where you want the chart to appear.

2   On the Insert menu, click Object to display the Object dialog box.

3   Scroll down the Object Type list, and click Microsoft Graph 2000 Chart.

4   Click OK

5   Click the Select All button in the data sheet and press Delete to remove the sample data.

6   In the datasheet, click the cell where you want to begin typing data.

7   When you have finished entering data in the datasheet, click a blank area of the document to close the datasheet. The chart will still be displayed in the Word document.

To modify the chart type

Chart Type

1   Double-click the chart to activate it.
2   On the Standard toolbar, click the Chart Type down arrow.
3   Click the desired Chart Type button.
4   Drag the sizing handles of the chart to make sure the numbers and text fit into the chart.

To change the background color of a chart

Fill Color

1   Double-click the chart to activate it.
2   Click the background that you want to modify.
3   On the Standard toolbar, click the Fill Color down arrow.
4   Click the square with the desired color.

To change the bar colors in a bar chart

Fill Color

1   Double-click the chart to activate the chart.
2   Click the bar that you want to modify.
3   On the Standard toolbar, click the Fill Color down arrow.
4   Click the square with the desired color.

To import an Excel worksheet into a chart

Import File

1   Create a chart.
2   On the Standard toolbar, click the Import File button.
3   In the Import File dialog box, click the Look-in down arrow.
4   Navigate to the desired file, and double-click the file.
5   If the Excel workbook contains more than one worksheet, click the name of the desired worksheet, and click OK.

Lesson 5: Customizing Word

To move a docked toolbar

1   Position the mouse pointer over the move handle at the left end of the toolbar.
2   Once the move pointer appears, drag the toolbar to the desired location.

To move a floating toolbar

●   Drag the toolbar by its title bar to the desired location.

To open the Customize dialog box

1   On the Tools menu, click Customize.
    Or
    Right-click a toolbar or menu.

2   On the shortcut menu, click Customize.

Or

On the View menu, point to Toolbars, and click Customize

To add a button to a toolbar

1   Open the Customize dialog box.
2   Click the Commands tab.
3   In the Categories list, click a category.
4   Drag the desired command from the Commands list to the desired
     location on the toolbar.
5   Close the Customize dialog box.

To remove a button from a toolbar

1   Open the Customize dialog box.
2   Drag the button from the toolbar into the document window.
3   Close the Customize dialog box.

To move a button on a toolbar

1   Open the Customize dialog box.
2   Select the button that you want to move.
3   Drag the button to the desired location.
4   Close the Customize dialog box.

To create a custom toolbar

1   In the Customize dialog box, click the New Toolbar button
2   Type the name for your toolbar in the Toolbar Name box, and
     click OK.
3   In the Customize dialog box, click the Commands tab.
4   Drag the buttons that you want from the Commands list to the toolbar.
5   Close the Customize dialog box.

To delete a toolbar

1   Open the Customize dialog box.
2   Click the Toolbars tab.
3   In the Toolbars list, click the name of the toolbar that you want to
     delete.
4   Click the Delete button.
5   Click OK to confirm the deletion.
6   Close the Customize dialog box.

To add a command to a menu

1   If the menu is on a toolbar, display the toolbar.
2   Open the Customize dialog box.

3   Click the Commands tab.

4   In the Categories list, click a category.

5   Drag the desired command to the menu.

6   When the menu is displayed, point to the location on the menu where you want the new command to appear, and then release the mouse button.

7   Close the Customize dialog box.

To delete a command from a menu

1   If the menu is on a toolbar, display the toolbar.

2   Open the Customize dialog box.

3   Click the menu, and when the list is displayed, select the command that you want to delete.

4   Drag the command onto the document window.

5   Close the Customize dialog box.

To create a custom menu

1   Display the toolbar to which you want to add the menu.

2   Open the Customize dialog box.

3   In the Customize dialog box, click the Commands tab.

4   In the Categories list, click New Menu.

5   Drag New Menu from the Commands list to the toolbar where you want the menu to appear.

6   Right-click the new menu, type a name in the Name box on the shortcut menu, and then press Enter.

7   Click the New Menu button to display a blank menu.

8   In the Categories list, click a category.

9   Drag the command that you want to add to the menu from the Commands list to the custom menu.

10   When you are finished adding commands, close the Customize dialog box.

To customize a shortcut key

1   Open the Customize dialog box.

2   Click Keyboard to display the Customize Keyboard dialog box.

3   In the Categories list, click the desired category.

4   In the Commands list, click the desired command.

5   In the Press New Shortcut Key box, type the shortcut key combination that you want to assign.

6   When you have found a shortcut key combination that is available, click Assign.

7   Close the Customize dialog box.

To delete a shortcut key

1   Open the Customize dialog box.
2   Click Keyboard to display the Customize Keyboard dialog box.
3   In the Categories box, click the category that contains the command.
4   In the Current Keys box, click the shortcut key that you want to delete.
5   Click Remove.
6   Close the Customize dialog box.

To display shortcut keys in ScreenTips

1   Open the Customize dialog box.
2   Click the Options tab.
3   Select the Show Shortcut Keys In ScreenTips check box.
4   Close the Customize dialog box.

To modify a button on a toolbar

1   Open the Customize dialog box.
2   Select the button and right-click it or click the Modify Selection button in the Customize dialog box.
3   On the Shortcut menu, click Edit Button Image, and click the desired icon.
    Or
    Point to the Change Button Image, and click the desired icon.
4   Close the Customize dialog box.

To change the name of a menu

1   Open the Customize dialog box.
2   Right-click the menu that you want to change.
3   In the Name box, type the new name, and press Enter.
4   Close the Customize dialog box.

To change how commands appear on a menu

1   Open the Customize dialog box.
2   Click the menu that contains the command that you want to change.
3   Right-click the menu command.
4   On the shortcut menu, click the option that you want to change.
5   Close the Customize dialog box.

Lesson 6: Merging Documents for Mailing

To create a main document

1   On the Tools menu, click Mail Merge.
2   In the Mail Merge Helper dialog box, in the Main Document section, click the Create button.
3   In the Create list, click the type of main document that you want to create.
4   In the Alert box, click the Active Window button.

To create a data source

1   On the Tools menu, click Mail Merge .
2   In the Mail Merge Helper dialog box, click the Get Data button.
3   In the Get Data list, click Create Data Source.
4   To remove a field name from the Field Names In Header Row list, click the field name, and then click the Remove Field Name button.
5   To add a field name, type the field name in the Field Name box, and click the Add Field Name button.
6   In the Create Data Source dialog box, click OK.
7   In the File Name box, type a file name.
8   Click the Save button.
9   In the Alert box, click the Edit Data Source button.
10 Type the field data.
11 Click the Add New button or press Enter to add another record.
12 Click OK.

To insert merge fields into a main document

1   Click where the field information is to be inserted.
2   On the Mail Merge toolbar, click the Insert Merge Field button.
3   Click a field name in the list.
4   Repeat the above steps until all fields are entered.
5   Save the completed file.

To merge a main document with a data source

1   Click where the field information is to be inserted.
2   On the Mail Merge toolbar, click the Insert Merge Field button.
3   Click a field name in the list.
4   Repeat the above steps until all fields are entered.
5   Save the completed file.

Merge To New Document

6   On the Mail Merge toolbar, click the Merge To New Document button.
7   Save the new document with a new name.

To sort data records in a data source

1   Open the data source file.

Mail Merge Helper

2   On the Mail Merge toolbar, click the Mail Merge Helper button.

3   In the Merge Data With The Document section, click the Query Options button.

4   In the Query Options dialog box, click the Sort Records tab.

5   Click the Sort By down arrow, and click a data field by which you want to sort the records.

6   Click Ascending to sort the records from A to Z, or click Descending to sort the records from Z to A.

7   Click OK.

8   In the Merge The Data With The Document section, click the Merge button.

9   In the Merge dialog box, click the Merge button.

To filter data in a data source

1   Open the data source document.

Mail Merge Helper

2   On the Mail Merge toolbar, click the Mail Merge Helper button.

3   In the Merge The Data With The Document section, click the Query Options button.

4   If necessary, click the Filter Records tab.

5   In the Query Options dialog box, click the Field down arrow, and click a field to be checked.

6   Click the Comparison down arrow, and click the desired type of comparison.

7   In the Compare To box, type the text or value that is to be used for comparison.

8   Click OK.

9   In the Merge The Data With The Document section, click the Merge button.

10   In the Merge dialog box, click the Merge button.

To merge a document with a different data source

1   Open an existing document.

2   On the Tools menu, click Mail Merge.

3   In the Main Document section, click the Create button.

4   In the Create list, click an option.

5   In the Alert box, click the Active Window button.

6   In the Data Source section, click the Get Data button.

7   In the Get Data list, click Open Data Source.

8   Click the Files Of Type down arrow, and click a file type.

9   Navigate to the folder where the database is stored, and then double-click the database.

10   If a dialog box is displayed, click OK.

11   In the alert box, click the Edit Main Document button.

12   On the Mail Merge toolbar, click the Insert Merge Fields button to insert the fields into the document.

13   On the Mail Merge toolbar, click the Merge To New Document button.

Merge To New Document

To create mailing labels from a mailing list

1   On the Standard toolbar, click the New Blank Document button.

2   On the Tools menu, click Mail Merge.

New Blank Document

3   In the Mail Merge Helper dialog box, click the Create button.

4   In the Create list, click Mailing Labels.

5   In the alert box, click the Active Window button.

6   In the Mail Merge Helper dialog box, click the Get Data button.

7   In the Get Data list, click Open Data Source, and open the data file containing the address data.

8   If a dialog box is displayed, click OK.

9   In the alert box, click the Set Up Main Document button.

10   In the Label Options dialog box, select options as desired and then click OK.

11   In the Create Labels dialog box, click the Insert Merge Field button, and click the first field name for the label.

12   Repeat the previous step until all fields are entered, and click OK.

13   In the Mail Merge Helper dialog box, click the Merge button.

14   In the Merge dialog box, click the Merge button.

Lesson 7: Using Macros

To record a macro

1   On the Tools menu, point to Macro, and click Record New Macro.

2   In the Record Macro dialog box, type a macro name in the Macro Name box.

3   Type a description for the macro in the Description box, if you want.

4   Click OK, and perform the desired operations.

5   On the Macro toolbar, click the Stop Recording button.

Stop Recording

To assign a macro after it has been created

1   On the Tools menu, click Customize.

2   In the Customize dialog box, click the Commands tab.

3   In the Categories list, scroll to and click Macros.

4   In the Commands list, click the macro that you want to assign.

5   Drag the macro to the toolbar or menu where you want the macro positioned.

6   Close the Customize dialog box.

To assign a macro to a menu or toolbar

1   On the Tools menu, point to Macro and click Record New Macro.

2   In the Record Macro dialog box, type a macro name.

3   In the Assign Macro To section, click the Toolbars button to display the Customize dialog box.

4   Click the Commands tab.

5   In the Commands section, click the macro's name.

6   Drag the macro to the desired position on the menu or toolbar.

7   In the Customize dialog box, click the Close button.

8   Record the macro.

To run a macro

1   Position the insertion point where you want to insert the result of the macro.

2   Click the macro name on the toolbar or menu that you assigned it to.

    Or

    Press the key combination that you assigned to the macro.

To edit a macro

1   On the Tools menu, point to Macro and click Macros.

2   In the Macros dialog box, type or click the macro name in the Macro Name list.

3   Click the Edit button to display the Visual Basic Editor window.

4   In the Visual Basic Editor window, correct the appropriate instructions.

5   On the File menu, click Close And Return To Microsoft Word.

To copy a macro

1   On the Tools menu, point to Macro and click Macros.

2   In the Macros dialog box, click the Organizer button.

3   Verify that the Macro Project Items tab is selected.

4   Select the macro project that you want to copy, and click the Copy button.

5   Close the Organizer dialog box.

To rename a macro

1   On the Tools menu, point to Macro and click Macros.

2   In the Macros dialog box, click the macro you want to edit in the list of macros, and click the edit button.

3   At the top of the Visual Basic Editor window locate and select the title line.

4   Type the new macro name.

5   Click Close And Return to Word.

To rename a macro project

1   On the Tools menu, point to Macro and click Macros.
2   In the Macros dialog box, click the Organizer button.
3   In the Organizer dialog box, click the macro, and click the rename button.
4   In the Rename dialog box, type the new macro name.
5   Close the Macro dialog box.

To rename a macro button on a toolbar

1   Right-click a toolbar and click Customize and the shortcut menu that appears.
2   Right-click the macro.
3   In the Name box, type the new name.
4   In the Customize dialog box, click the Close button.

To delete a macro

1   On the Tools menu, point to Macro and click Macros.
2   Type or click the macro name in the Macro Name list.
3   Click the Delete button.
4   In the alert box, click Yes.
5   Click the Close button.

To delete a macro name from a toolbar

1   Click the More Buttons drop-down arrow at the far-right end of the toolbar where the macro is displayed.
2   Point to Add Or Remove Buttons.
3   Click Reset Toolbar.
4   Click OK in the alert box.

Lesson 8: Creating Forms

To display the Forms toolbar

1   Right-click a toolbar.
2   On the shortcut menu, click Forms.
    Or
1   On the View menu, click Toolbars.
2   Click Forms.

To insert a text form field and specify options

1   Display the Forms toolbar.

Text Form Field

2   Click in the desired location, and on the Forms toolbar, click the Text Form Field button.
3   On the Forms toolbar, click the Form Field Options button.

4   In the Text Field Options dialog box, click the Type drop-down arrow, and click a text type.

5   Type default text in the Default Text box, if desired.

6   Modify the length and format of text as needed.

7   Click OK.

To insert a drop-down form field and specify options

1   Display the Forms toolbar.

2   Click in the desired location, and on the Forms toolbar, click the Drop-Down Form Field button.

Drop-Down Form Field

3   On the Forms toolbar, click the Form Field Options button.

4   In the Drop-Down Form Field Options dialog box, type answer choices (items to be listed) in the Drop-down Item list, and click the Add button.

5   Click the Move Up or Move Down button to modify the item order, if necessary.

6   Click OK.

To insert a check box form field and specify options

1   Display the Forms toolbar.

2   Click in the desired location, and on the Forms toolbar, click the Check Box Form Field button.

Check Box Form Field

3   On the Forms toolbar, click the Form Field Options button.

4   In the Check Box Form Field Options dialog box, in the Check Box Size section, modify the size of the check box.

5   In the Default Value section, click Checked to display an X in the check box, or click Not Checked to display an empty check box.

6   Click OK.

To protect a form without using a password

1   Display the Forms toolbar.

2   On the Forms toolbar, click the Protect Form button.

Protect Form

To protect a form using a password

1   On the menu bar, click Tools.

2   On the Tools menu, click Protect Document.

3   In the Protect Document dialog box, verify that Forms is selected.

4   Type a password.

5   Click OK.

6   In the Confirm Password dialog box, retype your password.

7   Click OK.

To unprotect a form

Protect Form

1   Display the Forms toolbar.

2   On the Forms toolbar, click the Protect Form button.

3   If necessary, type a password, and click OK.

To modify a form field

1   Display the Forms toolbar.

2   Make sure the form is unprotected. If it isn't, unprotect the form.

3   If necessary, select the form field.

4   Click the desired button on the Forms toolbar to make changes.

Lesson 9: Working Collaboratively

To turn on change tracking feature by using the Tools menu

1   On the Tools menu, point to Track Changes, and click Highlight Changes.

2   In the Highlight Changes dialog box, select the Track Changes While Editing check box.

3   Select the Highlight Changes On Screen check box, if desired.

4   Select the Highlight Changes In Printed Document check box, if desired.

5   Click OK.

6   Edit the document as desired.

To view the Reviewing toolbar

●   On the View menu, point to Toolbars and click Reviewing.

To accept or reject an individual change in a document

1   On the Tools menu, point to Track Changes, and click Accept Or Reject Changes.

2   In the Accept Or Reject dialog box, click the Find button with the right-pointing arrow.

3   Review the proposed changes.

4   Ignore the change and move to the next change by clicking the Find button with the right-pointing arrow.

Or

Edit the selected text.

Or

Click the Accept button to accept the change.

Or

Click the Reject button to reject the change.

5   Repeat steps 4 and 5 until all changes have been accepted or rejected.

6   Close the Accept or Reject Changes dialog box.

To accept or reject changes using the Reviewing toolbar

Accept Change

Reject Change

Track Changes

1   Click the Next Change or Previous Change button to move to changes in the text.

2   Click the Accept Change button to accept changes.

3   Click the Reject Change button to reject changes.

4   Click the Track Changes button to turn on change tracking and edit the document.

To accept or reject all changes in a document

1   On the Tools menu, point to Track Changes, and click Accept Or Reject Changes.

2   In the Accept Or Reject Changes dialog box, lick the Accept All button.

Or

Click the Reject All button.

3   Click Yes to verify your decision.

4   Close the Accept Or Reject Changes dialog box.

To add a comment

1   Click to the right the word on which you want to comment.

Or

Select the text that relates to the comment that you want to create.

2   On the Reviewing toolbar, click the Insert Comment button.

Or

On the Insert menu, click Comment to select the word (or words) and display the comment window.

3   In the comment pane, type your comment.

4   In the comment pane, click the Close button.

To view one comment

●   Position the mouse pointer over a highlighted area of text to display the comment in a ScreenTip.

To view multiple comments

1   On the View menu, click Comments to display the comment pane.

2   Use the scroll bar to scroll through the comments.

To protect a document

1   On the Tools menu, click Protect Document.

2   In the Protect Document dialog box, in the Protect Document For section, click the desired option.

3   Type a password in the Password (Optional) box, if desired.

4   Click OK.

To unprotect a document that is not password-protected

●   On the Tools menu, click Unprotect Document.

To unprotect a document that is password-protected

1   On the Tools menu, click Unprotect Document.

2   Type the password.

3   Click OK.

To save a version of an existing file

1   On the File menu, click Versions.

2   Click Save Now.

3   In the Save Version dialog box, type an explanation of the version in the Comments On Version box.

4   Click OK.

To open an earlier version of an open file

1   On the File menu, click Versions.

2   In the Existing Versions box, select the desired version.

3   Click the Open button.

To delete a version

1   On the File menu, click Versions.

2   In the Existing Versions box, select the desired version.

3   Click the Delete button.

4   Click Yes to verify the deletion.

5   Close the Versions In dialog box.

To set the default location for workgroup templates

1   On the Tools menu, click Options. In the Options dialog box, click the File Locations tab.

2   Select Workgroup templates.

3   Click the Modify button.

4   In the Modify Location dialog box, navigate to the desired folder.
    Or
    Click the Create New Folder button to create a new folder.

5   Click OK.

To convert a document from Word to HTML and then back to Word

1   Create or edit a document in Word.

2   On the File menu, click Save As Web Page.

3   View the Web page document in a browser.

4   Save the Web page with a new name to a folder on your hard disk.

5   Open the saved Web page in Word.

6   Switch between Web Layout view and Print Layout view to view the differences in layout.

Lesson 10: Working with Tables of Contents and Indexes

To format and compile a table of contents

1   Click where you want the table of contents to appear

Or

Create a new first page for the document and click this page.

2   On the Insert menu, click Index And Tables.

3   Click the Table Of Contents tab.

4   Click the Tab Leader down arrow, and click a tab leader, if desired.

5   Click the Formats down arrow, and select the desired format.

6   In the Show Levels box, click the up or down arrow to choose the desired number of levels, and click OK.

To update a table of contents

1   Select the entire table of contents.

2   Press F9.

3   In the Update Table Of Contents dialog box, click the Update Page Numbers Only option to update only the page numbers.

Or

Click the Update Entire Table option to update the entire table.

4   Click OK.

To mark index entries

1   Select the desired text.

2   On the Insert menu, click Index And Tables.

3   Click the Index tab.

4   Click the Mark Entry button to display the Mark Index Entry dialog box.

5   If desired, edit the text in the Main Entry box, and type a subentry in the Subentry box.

6   Click the Mark button to mark one occurrence of an entry.

Or

Click the Mark All button to mark all occurrences of an entry.

To create an index cross-reference

1   Select the text that you want to index.

2   On the Insert menu, click Index And Tables.

3   Click the Index tab.

4   Click the Mark Entry button.

5   In the Options section, click the Cross-Reference option.

6   Type the reference, modifying the default text, if desired.

7   Click the Mark button.

To format and compile an index

1   Click at the end of the document.

2   On the Insert menu, click Index And Tables.

3   Click the Index tab.

4   In the Type section, click the desired option (Indented or Run-in).

5   In the Columns section, type the desired number of columns in the Columns box.

6   In the Formats section, click the Formats down arrow, and then click the desired format.

7   If desired, select the Right Align Page Numbers check box to align the page numbers on the right side of the page.

8   If the Right Align Page Numbers check box is selected, click the Tab Leader down arrow, and click a tab leader style, if desired.

9   Click OK.

To edit an index entry in a document

1   In the document, select the text between the quotation marks in the index entry.

2   Edit as desired.

To delete an index entry

1   In the document, select the entire index entry, including the field code.

2   Press Delete.

    Or

    Press Backspace.

To update an index

1   Click anywhere in the index.

2   Press F9.

To reformat and update an index

1   On the Insert menu, click Index And Tables.

2   Click the Index tab.

3   Redefine index settings.

4   Click OK.

5   In the alert box, click Yes.

Lesson 11: Using Long Document Formats

To insert footnotes and endnotes

1   Click to position the insertion point where you want the reference mark.

2   On the Insert menu, click Footnote.

3   In the Footnote And Endnote dialog box, in the Insert section, click Footnote or Endnote, and click OK.

4   Type the desired text.

To browse through notes in a long document

Select Browse Object

1   Click the Select Browse Object button.

2   On the Select Browse Object menu, click the Browse By Footnote icon or the Browse By Endnote icon.

3   Click the Next Footnote or Previous Footnote button (or the Next Endnote or Previous Endnote button) to move from note to note.

To go directly to a specific note

1   On the Edit menu, click Go To.

2   In the Go To What list, click Footnote or Endnote.

3   In the Enter Footnote/Endnote box, type the specific reference mark number.

4   Click the Go To button.

To view a note

●   Position the mouse pointer over the reference mark to view the note in a ScreenTip.
Or
Double-click the reference mark to open the Notes pane.

To move a note

1   Select the reference mark.

2   Drag the reference mark to the desired location.

To copy a note

1   Select the reference mark.

2   Hold down Ctrl as you drag the reference mark to the desired location.

To delete a note

1   Select the reference mark.

2   Press Delete

Or

Press Backspace.

To change the placement of a note

1   On the Insert menu, click Footnote.

2   In the Footnote And Endnote dialog box, click the Options button.

3   In the Note Options dialog box, click the All Endnotes tab or the All Footnotes tab, depending on the type of note that you want to change.

4   Click the Place At down arrow, and click the desired placement.

5   Click OK.

To modify the note separator line

1   On the View menu, click Footnotes.

2   In the View Footnotes dialog box, click View Footnote Area or View Endnote Area, and click OK

3   In the Notes pane, click the down arrow, and click Footnote Separator or Endnote Separator.

4   Edit the separator by inserting text before or after the line, by deleting the line, or by adding a border or graphic to the separator.

To modify a reference mark style

1   On the Format menu, click Style to display the Style dialog box.

2   Click Footnote or Endnote Reference Style.

3   Click the Modify button.

4   Modify the style as desired.

Or

1   Click the reference mark.

2   On the Formatting toolbar, click the Style down arrow.

3   Select the desired style.

To create a bookmark

1   Click to position the insertion point where you want to create a bookmark.

2   On the Insert menu, click Bookmark.

3   In the Bookmark Name box, type a name for the bookmark.

4   Click the Add button.

To use a bookmark

1   On the Insert menu, click Bookmark.
2   In the Bookmark Name list, click the bookmark representing the desired location.
3   Click the Go To button.

To delete a bookmark

1   On the Insert menu, click Bookmark.
2   Click the bookmark you want to delete.
3   Click Delete.

To create a master document

New Blank Document

1   On the Standard toolbar, click the New Blank Document button.
2   On the View menu, click Outline.
3   Type the document title.

To insert a subdocument

1   Click to position the insertion point in the desired location in the master document.
2   On the Outlining toolbar, click the Insert Subdocument button.
3   If necessary, click the Look In down arrow, navigate to the desired file, and double-click it.
    Or
    If the file is already displayed in the dialog box, double-click it.

To create a subdocument

Create Subdocument

1   Construct an outline in the master document.
2   On the Outlining toolbar, make sure the Expand Subdocuments button is pushed in, and click the Create Subdocument button.

Index

Special Characters

ActiveEducation and Microsoft Press

Microsoft Word 2000 Step by Step Courseware has been created by the professional trainers and writers at ActiveEducation, Inc., to the exacting standards you've come to expect from Microsoft Press. Together, we are pleased to present this training guide.

ActiveEducation creates top-quality information technology training content that teaches essential computer skills for today's workplace. ActiveEducation courses are designed to provide the most effective training available and to help people become more productive computer users. Each ActiveEducation course, including this book, undergoes rigorous quality control, instructional design, and technical review procedures to ensure that the course is instructionally and technically superior in content and approach.

ActiveEducation (*www.activeeducation.com*) courses are available in book form and on the Internet.

Microsoft Press is the book publishing division of Microsoft Corporation, the leading publisher of information about Microsoft products and services. Microsoft Press is dedicated to providing the highest quality computer books and multimedia training and reference tools that make using Microsoft software easier, more enjoyable, and more productive.

About the Authors

Expert Skills

Ron Pronk is the author of more than a dozen books on computers, including *Windows 3.1 Insider* (John Wiley & Sons) and *Digital Camera Companion* (Coriolis Group Books). He is a two-time recipient of the Award of Excellence and two-time recipient of the Award of Merit from the Society for Technical Communicators and has served as an instructional design consultant for such companies as Delmar Publishing, Mitchell Press, South-Western Publishing, West Publishing, Coriolis Group Books, and National Computer Systems. He is also a certified Microsoft Word Expert.

Holly Freeman is the author of *Microsoft Word 2000 Intermediate* and *Microsoft Outlook 2000 Intermediate*, published for ActiveEducation. She was the project editor for *Microsoft Internet Explorer 5 Step by Step*, published for Microsoft Press. Holly is currently a project editor and staff writer for ActiveEducation. She is also a certified Microsoft Word Expert.

Jennifer Mears is a former Associated Press reporter who spend seven years covering political and state government in Colorado. She is a 1990 graduate of Middlebury College in Middlebury, Vermont.

Stay in the *running* for maximum productivity.

These are *the* answer books for business users of Microsoft Office 2000. They are packed with everything from quick, clear instructions for new users to comprehensive answers for power users—the authoritative reference to keep by your computer and use every day. The RUNNING series—learning solutions made by Microsoft.

- RUNNING MICROSOFT® EXCEL 2000
- RUNNING MICROSOFT OFFICE 2000 PREMIUM
- RUNNING MICROSOFT OFFICE 2000 PROFESSIONAL
- RUNNING MICROSOFT OFFICE 2000 SMALL BUSINESS
- RUNNING MICROSOFT WORD 2000
- RUNNING MICROSOFT POWERPOINT® 2000
- RUNNING MICROSOFT ACCESS 2000
- RUNNING MICROSOFT FRONTPAGE® 2000
- RUNNING MICROSOFT OUTLOOK® 2000

mspress.microsoft.com

Maximize the potential of Microsoft Office 2000— on your PC and on the Web!

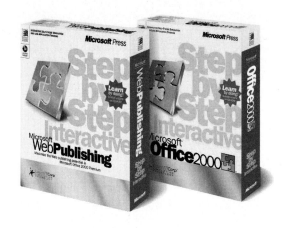

MICROSOFT OFFICE 2000 STEP BY STEP INTERACTIVE

U.S.A.   **$29.99**

U.K.   £20.99 [V.A.T. included]

Canada $44.99

[*Recommended*]

ISBN: 0-7356-0506-8

WEB PUBLISHING STEP BY STEP INTERACTIVE

U.S.A.   **$29.99**

U.K.   £20.99 [V.A.T. included]

Canada $44.99

[*Recommended*]

ISBN: 0-7356-0651-X

MICROSOFT® OFFICE 2000 STEP BY STEP INTERACTIVE and WEB PUBLISHING STEP BY STEP INTERACTIVE are the perfect multimedia learning solutions to help you get the most out of Microsoft Office 2000. MICROSOFT OFFICE 2000 STEP BY STEP INTERACTIVE shows you how to maximize the productivity potential of all the programs in the Office 2000 suite. And WEB PUBLISHING STEP BY STEP INTERACTIVE is the fast way to learn how to use all the Web publishing tools and features in Microsoft Office 2000 Premium. Build your skills quickly using real-life exercises, conceptual overviews, concrete examples, live practice, and built-in assessment tools. Get both learning systems to get productive and get on the Web fast!

Microsoft®

mspress.microsoft.com

MICROSOFT LICENSE AGREEMENT
Book Companion CD

IMPORTANT—READ CAREFULLY: This Microsoft End-User License Agreement ("EULA") is a legal agreement between you (either an individual or an entity) and Microsoft Corporation for the Microsoft product identified above, which includes computer software and may include associated media, printed materials, and "online" or electronic documentation ("SOFTWARE PRODUCT"). Any component included within the SOFTWARE PRODUCT that is accompanied by a separate End-User License Agreement shall be governed by such agreement and not the terms set forth below. By installing, copying, or otherwise using the SOFTWARE PRODUCT, you agree to be bound by the terms of this EULA. If you do not agree to the terms of this EULA, you are not authorized to install, copy, or otherwise use the SOFTWARE PRODUCT; you may, however, return the SOFTWARE PRODUCT, along with all printed materials and other items that form a part of the Microsoft product that includes the SOFTWARE PRODUCT, to the place you obtained them for a full refund.

SOFTWARE PRODUCT LICENSE

The SOFTWARE PRODUCT is protected by United States copyright laws and international copyright treaties, as well as other intellectual property laws and treaties. The SOFTWARE PRODUCT is licensed, not sold.

1. **GRANT OF LICENSE.** This EULA grants you the following rights:

   a. **Software Product.** You may install and use one copy of the SOFTWARE PRODUCT on a single computer. The primary user of the computer on which the SOFTWARE PRODUCT is installed may make a second copy for his or her exclusive use on a portable computer.

   b. **Storage/Network Use.** You may also store or install a copy of the SOFTWARE PRODUCT on a storage device, such as a network server, used only to install or run the SOFTWARE PRODUCT on your other computers over an internal network; however, you must acquire and dedicate a license for each separate computer on which the SOFTWARE PRODUCT is installed or run from the storage device. A license for the SOFTWARE PRODUCT may not be shared or used concurrently on different computers.

   c. **License Pak.** If you have acquired this EULA in a Microsoft License Pak, you may make the number of additional copies of the computer software portion of the SOFTWARE PRODUCT authorized on the printed copy of this EULA, and you may use each copy in the manner specified above. You are also entitled to make a corresponding number of secondary copies for portable computer use as specified above.

   d. **Sample Code.** Solely with respect to portions, if any, of the SOFTWARE PRODUCT that are identified within the SOFTWARE PRODUCT as sample code (the "SAMPLE CODE"):

      i. **Use and Modification.** Microsoft grants you the right to use and modify the source code version of the SAMPLE CODE, *provided* you comply with subsection (d)(iii) below. You may not distribute the SAMPLE CODE, or any modified version of the SAMPLE CODE, in source code form.

      ii. **Redistributable Files.** Provided you comply with subsection (d)(iii) below, Microsoft grants you a nonexclusive, royalty-free right to reproduce and distribute the object code version of the SAMPLE CODE and of any modified SAMPLE CODE, other than SAMPLE CODE, or any modified version thereof, designated as not redistributable in the Readme file that forms a part of the SOFTWARE PRODUCT (the "Non-Redistributable Sample Code"). All SAMPLE CODE other than the Non-Redistributable Sample Code is collectively referred to as the "REDISTRIBUTABLES."

      iii. **Redistribution Requirements.** If you redistribute the REDISTRIBUTABLES, you agree to: (i) distribute the REDISTRIBUTABLES in object code form only in conjunction with and as a part of your software application product; (ii) not use Microsoft's name, logo, or trademarks to market your software application product; (iii) include a valid copyright notice on your software application product; (iv) indemnify, hold harmless, and defend Microsoft from and against any claims or lawsuits, including attorney's fees, that arise or result from the use or distribution of your software application product; and (v) not permit further distribution of the REDISTRIBUTABLES by your end user. Contact Microsoft for the applicable royalties due and other licensing terms for all other uses and/or distribution of the REDISTRIBUTABLES.

2. **DESCRIPTION OF OTHER RIGHTS AND LIMITATIONS.**

   • **Limitations on Reverse Engineering, Decompilation, and Disassembly.** You may not reverse engineer, decompile, or disassemble the SOFTWARE PRODUCT, except and only to the extent that such activity is expressly permitted by applicable law notwithstanding this limitation.

   • **Separation of Components.** The SOFTWARE PRODUCT is licensed as a single product. Its component parts may not be separated for use on more than one computer.

   • **Rental.** You may not rent, lease, or lend the SOFTWARE PRODUCT.

   • **Support Services.** Microsoft may, but is not obligated to, provide you with support services related to the SOFTWARE PRODUCT ("Support Services"). Use of Support Services is governed by the Microsoft policies and programs described in the user manual, in "online" documentation, and/or in other Microsoft-provided materials. Any supplemental software code provided to you as part of the Support Services shall be considered part of the SOFTWARE PRODUCT and subject to the terms and conditions of this EULA. With respect to technical information you provide to Microsoft as part of the Support Services, Microsoft may use such information for its business purposes, including for product support and development. Microsoft will not utilize such technical information in a form that personally identifies you.

   • **Software Transfer.** You may permanently transfer all of your rights under this EULA, provided you retain no copies, you transfer all of the SOFTWARE PRODUCT (including all component parts, the media and printed materials, any upgrades, this EULA, and, if applicable, the Certificate of Authenticity), **and** the recipient agrees to the terms of this EULA.

   • **Termination.** Without prejudice to any other rights, Microsoft may terminate this EULA if you fail to comply with the terms and conditions of this EULA. In such event, you must destroy all copies of the SOFTWARE PRODUCT and all of its component parts.

3. **COPYRIGHT.** All title and copyrights in and to the SOFTWARE PRODUCT (including but not limited to any images, photographs, animations, video, audio, music, text, SAMPLE CODE, REDISTRIBUTABLES, and "applets" incorporated into the SOFTWARE PRODUCT) and any copies of the SOFTWARE PRODUCT are owned by Microsoft or its suppliers. The SOFTWARE PRODUCT is protected by copyright laws and international treaty provisions. Therefore, you must treat the SOFTWARE PRODUCT like any other copyrighted material **except** that you may install the SOFTWARE PRODUCT on a single computer provided you keep the original solely for backup or archival purposes. You may not copy the printed materials accompanying the SOFTWARE PRODUCT.

4. **U.S. GOVERNMENT RESTRICTED RIGHTS.** The SOFTWARE PRODUCT and documentation are provided with RESTRICTED RIGHTS. Use, duplication, or disclosure by the Government is subject to restrictions as set forth in subparagraph (c)(1)(ii) of the Rights in Technical Data and Computer Software clause at DFARS 252.227-7013 or subparagraphs (c)(1) and (2) of the Commercial Computer Software—Restricted Rights at 48 CFR 52.227-19, as applicable. Manufacturer is Microsoft Corporation/One Microsoft Way/Redmond, WA 98052-6399.

5. **EXPORT RESTRICTIONS.** You agree that you will not export or re-export the SOFTWARE PRODUCT, any part thereof, or any process or service that is the direct product of the SOFTWARE PRODUCT (the foregoing collectively referred to as the "Restricted Components"), to any country, person, entity, or end user subject to U.S. export restrictions. You specifically agree not to export or re-export any of the Restricted Components (i) to any country to which the U.S. has embargoed or restricted the export of goods or services, which currently include, but are not necessarily limited to, Cuba, Iran, Iraq, Libya, North Korea, Sudan, and Syria, or to any national of any such country, wherever located, who intends to transmit or transport the Restricted Components back to such country; (ii) to any end user who you know or have reason to know will utilize the Restricted Components in the design, development, or production of nuclear, chemical, or biological weapons; or (iii) to any end user who has been prohibited from participating in U.S. export transactions by any federal agency of the U.S. government. You warrant and represent that neither the BXA nor any other U.S. federal agency has suspended, revoked, or denied your export privileges.

DISCLAIMER OF WARRANTY

NO WARRANTIES OR CONDITIONS. MICROSOFT EXPRESSLY DISCLAIMS ANY WARRANTY OR CONDITION FOR THE SOFT-WARE PRODUCT. THE SOFTWARE PRODUCT AND ANY RELATED DOCUMENTATION ARE PROVIDED "AS IS" WITHOUT WARRANTY OR CONDITION OF ANY KIND, EITHER EXPRESS OR IMPLIED, INCLUDING, WITHOUT LIMITATION, THE IMPLIED WARRANTIES OF MERCHANTABILITY, FITNESS FOR A PARTICULAR PURPOSE, OR NONINFRINGEMENT. THE ENTIRE RISK ARISING OUT OF USE OR PERFORMANCE OF THE SOFTWARE PRODUCT REMAINS WITH YOU.

LIMITATION OF LIABILITY. TO THE MAXIMUM EXTENT PERMITTED BY APPLICABLE LAW, IN NO EVENT SHALL MICROSOFT OR ITS SUPPLIERS BE LIABLE FOR ANY SPECIAL, INCIDENTAL, INDIRECT, OR CONSEQUENTIAL DAMAGES WHATSOEVER (INCLUDING, WITHOUT LIMITATION, DAMAGES FOR LOSS OF BUSINESS PROFITS, BUSINESS INTERRUPTION, LOSS OF BUSINESS INFORMATION, OR ANY OTHER PECUNIARY LOSS) ARISING OUT OF THE USE OF OR INABILITY TO USE THE SOFTWARE PRODUCT OR THE PROVISION OF OR FAILURE TO PROVIDE SUPPORT SERVICES, EVEN IF MICROSOFT HAS BEEN ADVISED OF THE POSSIBILITY OF SUCH DAMAGES. IN ANY CASE, MICROSOFT'S ENTIRE LIABILITY UNDER ANY PROVISION OF THIS EULA SHALL BE LIMITED TO THE GREATER OF THE AMOUNT ACTUALLY PAID BY YOU FOR THE SOFTWARE PRODUCT OR US$5.00; PROVIDED, HOWEVER, IF YOU HAVE ENTERED INTO A MICROSOFT SUPPORT SERVICES AGREEMENT, MICROSOFT'S ENTIRE LIABILITY REGARDING SUPPORT SERVICES SHALL BE GOVERNED BY THE TERMS OF THAT AGREE-MENT. BECAUSE SOME STATES AND JURISDICTIONS DO NOT ALLOW THE EXCLUSION OR LIMITATION OF LIABILITY, THE ABOVE LIMITATION MAY NOT APPLY TO YOU.

MISCELLANEOUS

This EULA is governed by the laws of the State of Washington USA, except and only to the extent that applicable law mandates governing law of a different jurisdiction.

Should you have any questions concerning this EULA, or if you desire to contact Microsoft for any reason, please contact the Microsoft subsidiary serving your country, or write: Microsoft Sales Information Center/One Microsoft Way/Redmond, WA 98052-6399.

OWNER REGISTRATION CARD   *Register Today!*   0-7356-0721-4

Return the bottom portion of this card to register today.

Microsoft® Word 2000 Step by Step Courseware Expert Skills Student Guide

FIRST NAME   MIDDLE INITIAL   LAST NAME

INSTITUTION OR COMPANY NAME

ADDRESS

CITY   STATE   ZIP

(   )

E-MAIL ADDRESS   PHONE NUMBER

U.S. and Canada addresses only. Fill in information above and mail postage-free.
Please mail only the bottom half of this page.

For information about Microsoft Press® products, visit our Web site at

mspress.microsoft.com

Microsoft®